THE DISPUTED PRESIDENTIAL ELECTION OF 1876

THE HAYES-TILDEN DISPUTED PRESIDENTIAL ELECTION OF 1876

BY

PAUL LELAND HAWORTH

NEW YORK / RUSSELL & RUSSELL

1966

FIRST PUBLISHED IN 1906

REISSUED, 1966, BY RUSSELL & RUSSELL

A DIVISION OF ATHENEUM HOUSE, INC.

L.C. CATALOG CARD NO: 66—24702

PRINTED IN THE UNITED STATES OF AMERICA

To My Sister R. H.

Whose Self-sacrifice is not Forgotten

CONTENTS

PREFACE

Thirty years have now elapsed since the beginning of the presidential campaign which culminated in the most remarkable electoral controversy in the history of popular government. As yet, however, no adequate account of that controversy has been published. It has seemed to me that there is some need for such an account, and this book is the result of my effort, successful or otherwise, to supply it.

The book is based in large measure upon a collection of more than twenty thousand pages of congressional material, consisting of debates in Congress, of evidence gathered by various investigating committees, and of the proceedings before the electoral commission. This collection constitutes perhaps the most extensive and exhaustive one upon any subject of equal importance in American history, and the labor involved in examining and sifting it has been rendered all the greater by the fact that so much of the evidence contained in it is untrustworthy. As the reference notes will show, I have, in addition, drawn material from a great variety of other sources. I have, in fact, spared no pains to make my investigation as complete as possible. Upon most of the matters which are really vital I have, I believe, succeeded in obtaining the essential facts; but

I feel constrained to admit that I have not succeeded in penetrating the veil which surrounds some others. These last are matters which will, in all probability, always remain secrets, for the simple reason that those actors who could tell the truth concerning them will never do so. I may remark in passing that I have brought to light much that has never before been published, and that I have also learned many other interesting, though usually not very important things, which cannot be published because told to me under pledge of secrecy. In all cases, however, I have been able to make use of such facts in drawing conclusions.

It may be worth while for me to add that in interpreting the evidence regarding the situation in the contested states of Louisiana, Florida, and South Carolina I have been greatly aided by experience gained some years ago while making an extended investigation in certain southern states of the workings of negro suffrage under present day conditions. In fact, I may say that without the insight thus gained my task would have been well-nigh a hopeless one.

There remains only the pleasant duty of acknowledging my obligations to the many persons who have assisted me in the work. To Hon. Carl Schurz, Hon. John Bigelow, Col. A. K. McClure, Hon. John Goode, Hon. William Dudley Foulke, Dr. Charles R. Williams, and Mr. Yates Snowden of the Charleston *News and Courier;* to Col. Webb C. Hayes, who allowed me to see his father's papers and who read the entire manuscript; to Mr. Edward Cary of the New York

Times, who furnished me with information and read a portion of the manuscript; to Professor John R. Ficklen and Mr. Benjamin Rice Foreman, who read the chapter on Louisiana; to Hon. W. E. Chandler, who furnished me with much material and who read several of the chapters; to Mr. Joseph M. Rogers, who had himself intended to write a book on the subject but retired in my favor and with rare generosity gave me the results of his investigations and read the more important chapters — to these gentlemen and to many others I owe a debt which I fear I shall never be able to repay. Nor must I forget to mention the many kindnesses shown me by my publisher, Mr. Charles W. Burrows, and the assistance rendered me by my father and by my wife in correcting the manuscript. Above all, I am indebted to Professor William A. Dunning, leading authority in this period of our history, for reading both the manuscript and the proof and thereby helping me to avoid many errors.

In justice to some of the persons named it should, however, be added that I alone am responsible for statements of fact and for conclusions. In many cases, perhaps unwisely, I have disregarded their suggestions.

PAUL LELAND HAWORTH.

Columbia University.

THE DISPUTED PRESIDENTIAL
ELECTION

CHAPTER I

THE REPUBLICAN DYNASTY IN DANGER

The year 1876 was the most notable of the period in American history between the close of the war of Secession and the beginning of the war with Spain. It was the year in which occurred the last of our important Indian outbreaks — a conflict made sadly memorable by the massacre of Custer and his troopers on the Little Big Horn. It was the year which marked the one hundredth anniversary of our independence — an occasion fitly celebrated by the great Centennial Exposition at Philadelphia. It was also the year of an election which resulted in a strange controversy that put our institutions to one of the severest tests they have ever been called upon to endure.

The political outlook prior to that election was in some respects an unusual one. For the first time since

it had come into power there was real likelihood that
the Republican party would be unable to elect its
candidate for the Presidency.   Successful in 1860 by
grace of the lack of unity among its opponents,
it had in 1864 merged itself in that Union party
which gave Lincoln his second term, and four
years later, having resumed its independent status,
it had been led to another overwhelming victory by the military hero who had ended the
war.   In the new President's first administration had
occurred a division in the party fold.   The Liberal
Republicans, dissatisfied with the conduct of affairs
and despairing of getting their views adopted by the
party leaders, had in 1872 held a separate convention at
Cincinnati and had nominated Horace Greeley of New
York and B. Gratz Brown of Missouri.   Thereupon
the Democrats, seeing no hope of success with candidates chosen from among themselves, had, despite the
fact that Greeley had been one of the highest of the
high priests of Abolitionism, indorsed the Liberal
Republican candidates and platform.   But this unnatural alliance had wholly failed to avert a complete
triumph of Radicalism; out of the 349 electoral votes
counted by Congress for President, General Grant had
received 286, while the 63 remaining had been divided
(Greeley having died before the electoral colleges met)
among B. Gratz Brown, Thomas A. Hendricks, Charles
J. Jenkins of Georgia, and David Davis of Illinois. [1]

[1] *Cong. Globe*, 42d Cong. 3d Sess., p. 1305.   Three Georgia
votes which had been cast for Greeley were not counted, and all
the votes of Louisiana and Arkansas were excluded.

Rendered reckless by the seeming finality of their victory, the Radical leaders had fallen into the pleasant belief that the question of dispensing the loaves and fishes of political patronage was settled forever and that it was wholly unnecessary to carry through measures of reform which the Liberal Republicans had demanded and which many far-sighted men who had remained within the party desired. But there had soon been a rude awakening. The panic of 1873, the dissatisfaction due to the unsettled state of the monetary system, the bad condition of affairs in the South, the Credit Mobilier exposures, the so-called Salary Grab, the Sanborn Contract, and other scandals — all these things had worked mightily to the disadvantage of the party in power.[1] The result had been the great "Tidal Wave" of 1874. Out of thirty-five states in which elections were held twenty-three had gone Democratic; even such Republican states as Wisconsin, Ohio, Pennsylvania, and Massachusetts had arrayed themselves in the Democratic column; and only a comparative handful of Republicans had been returned to the House.[2]

In the new Congress, it is true, the Democratic members had not greatly distinguished themselves for wisdom or for political sagacity;[3] but the party had

---

1 These conclusions are based upon the files of *The Nation, Harper's Weekly,* and of the New York *World, Times,* and *Tribune.* See also Stanwood, History of Presidential Elections, 4th ed., p. 302; Foulke, Life of Morton, II, pp. 344-352; Hoar, Autobiography of Seventy Years. I, pp. 305-369.

2 McPherson, Handbook of Politics for 1876, p. 255.

3. See *Harper's Weekly,* XX, p. 112.

been favored by the almost clock-like regularity with which scandals continued to reveal themselves, so that, although financial conditions were becoming better and the "Tidal Wave" was now running much less strong, the Democratic leaders were able to look forward to the approaching election with at least as much confidence as the Republicans.

The chief count that could be brought against the party in power was maladministration.   That the government was in a deplorable condition no dispassionate student of history will venture to deny.   Nor are the chief causes difficult to find.   The nation had but recently emerged from the trying ordeal of the greatest civil war known to history.   That war had left many troublesome problems, some of which time alone could fully solve.   It had also necessitated a tremendous increase in the revenues and expenditures of the national government.   From March 4, 1789, to June 30, 1861, the entire net "ordinary expenditures" had amounted in round numbers to but $1,580,000,000, as against the enormous sum of $5,200,000,000 in the fourteen years from June 30, 1861, to June 30, 1875. Furthermore, the number of civil employees of the government had increased from about 44,000 under Buchanan to more than 100,000 under Grant. [1]   In the morally unhealthy atmosphere which inevitably follows

---

[1] These comparisons were made in the Democratic Campaign Text Book, pp. 747-748. The figures are from the Report of the Secretary of the Treasury for 1875 and from reports of the various departments. The "gross expenditures" were, of course, far larger.

a resort to arms, and amidst such favorable conditions as those just described, it was but natural that the Spoils System should produce its most noxious growth, and that political morality should reach perhaps the lowest ebb in our entire history. [1]

The administrative demoralization of the country was, it must be conceded, due in part also to the personality of President Grant. Like many a successful soldier before him, Grant was by no means a finished statesman. Prior to his inauguration he had never held a civil office, and he did not clearly understand the workings of our political system. Starting out with the assumption that the Presidency was a sort of personal possession given him by the people to manage as he thought proper, he had, with the best intentions in the world, entirely ignored the party leaders in choosing his first cabinet. This independent policy had soon proved a failure, and he had been brought to the necessity of securing some support. In the contest to gain control of him which followed, the Radicals — Butler in Massachusetts, Conkling in New York, Cameron in Pennsylvania, Patterson in South Carolina, Morton in Indiana, and so on — had triumphed over the Liberals and had become the Pres-

---

1 For a different view see Hoar, I, pp. 309-311, and Foulke, II, p. 410. The Republicans were able to show that the rate of defalcation per $1,000 under Grant was considerably lower than under any previous President. This argument failed to take into account the fact that most of the corruption at this time was not in the form of direct stealing from the government. Furthermore, there were under Grant many officials each of whom handled in the course of a year more money than was spent in that length of time by the entire government under Washington.

idential advisers and the dispensers of patronage. Thus
the man who had begun by ignoring the politicians
had in the end allowed himself to fall entirely into
their hands. The outcome was rendered all the more
disastrous because the President, although a keen
judge of military capacity, had no skill in choosing
political subordinates and advisers. A thoroughly
honest man himself, he was unable to detect dishonesty
in others. His confidence was frequently abused by
pretended friends, who brought him into disrepute, but
whom, with misguided fidelity, he was unwilling "to
desert under fire." In many ways, to be sure, his two
administrations were by no means failures. Under
him our disputes with England were peaceably and
honorably settled, the national debt was greatly
reduced, the Resumption Act was passed, and the
South was kept as tranquil perhaps as a section which
had so recently undergone such a complete social and
political upheaval could be kept. Probably no other
man then living could have filled the Presidential
chair as well as he; yet the fact remained that the
administration was pervaded with a lamentable demoralization which increased rather than diminished.
Disclosures of wrong-doing followed each other with
such astounding rapidity that inefficiency and fraud
were suspected even where they did not exist. [1]

1 For estimates of Grant which agree in the main with this
see Garland, Life of Grant, pp. 385-449; Cox, Three Decades
of Federal Legislation, pp. 672-673; McCulloch, Men and Measures of Half a Century, pp. 355-357; Andrews, The United States
in Our Own Times, pp. 23 *et seq.*; and John Sherman's Recollections, I, pp. 446-449, 474-475. Some excellent estimates of him

As the time for the campaign of 1876 drew near it was generally recognized that in Republican misgovernment the Democrats would find their best opportunity for attack. The wisest policy for them would be to drop the Southern issue and fight the battle on that of "Grant's maladministration," Said the New York *Herald* on April 1, 1876:

"Let the party trace every stream of corruption which now pollutes the country to its source, and call upon the country to rise and cleanse the source. Let the leaders begin the campaign on the violation of the Constitution involved in the appointment of staff officers and not statesmen to the Cabinet. Let them show how the moral sense of the nation was degraded by the selection of worthless relations and whiskey-drinking cronies to high offices here and abroad. Let them show how the Senate degraded itself by becoming a sharer in the plunder and patronage of the Executive. Let them show how the country was parcelled out like the provinces of the Roman Empire, every state with a Senatorial proconsul — Conkling in New York, Cameron in Pennsylvania, Patterson in South Carolina, and so on until the country, so far as the patronage is concerned, is under the dominion of an oligarchy which only opposes the President when he names men for office like Hoar and Dana, supporting him in his selection of a Billings or a Delano. Let them show how investigations in the House were made impossible so long as the brothers of members were allowed to hold trade posts and rob Indians and soldiers. Let

were given in the newspapers published at the time of his death. For his apology for his administrations see his last message to Congress.

them show how scandal after scandal supervened until we had a Secretary of War at the bar of the Senate as a confessed robber and a Secretary of the Navy rapidly on his way thither for having used a million of dollars to sustain a sinking banking house in London." [1]

The indictment that could be drawn was certainly a strong one. The Republican party, rendered reckless by the possession of too much power, had been weighed in the balance and had been found wanting. In the minds of many a sincere patriot, proud of the record of a hundred years but humiliated by the fact that the centennial of the nation's birth must witness so much corruption in high places, there inevitably arose a desire for a political change.

Yet there was one consideration among other less influential ones which might perhaps save the party in power from merited rebuke. Bad as that party had shown itself of late, there nevertheless existed a grave doubt whether its opponent, in the light of the record of the past, was any more worthy of confidence. [2] Rightly or wrongly, men had not yet forgotten that not more than eleven years before a large section of the Democratic party had stood beneath the Stars and Bars in battle array against the Union; that another section of that party had been worse than lukewarm in support of the government which they now sought to control. With more truth than poetry it was still said that "not every Democrat was a Rebel, but every Rebel

---

1 This, of course, is overdrawn.
2 See, for example, *Harper's Weekly,* XIX, pp. 90, 170, 210.

was a Democrat." Would it be safe to trust the nation's affairs with men many of whom had once raised their hands against her life? Would it not, after all, be better to keep in power a party which, whatever its faults, had always stood unflinchingly for the preservation of the Union? Upon the answers given to these questions seemed to depend the result of the forthcoming election.

CHAPTER II

With such a political outlook it was almost inevitable that there should be a readjustment in the Republican party. The Radicals, discredited and somewhat chastened by defeat, began to show themselves much more amenable to advice; it was apparent that the moderate element, whose watchword was "reform within the party," [1] would play a much more important part than hitherto. This state of affairs made it easier for many Liberals who were alarmed at the inflationist tendencies displayed by the Democrats and who approved the Republican stand on the Resumption Act to drift back into their former party.

For the first time since 1860 there was real uncertainty as to who would be chosen to lead the Republican hosts. There was, of course, much talk about a third term. The newspapers, and especially the New York *Herald,* took up the subject; and during 1875 a great deal was said about "dynasties," "dictatorships," "Cæsarism," and so on. In the spring of 1875 the Pennsylvania Republican state convention, moved by

[1] For an article on this subject see *Harper's Weekly*, XIX, p. 274.

this outcry, passed a resolution against a third term. Thereupon President Grant wrote to General Harry White, chairman of the convention, as follows: "Now for the third term. I do not want it any more than I did the first . . . I am not, nor have I ever been a candidate for a renomination. I would not accept a nomination if it were tendered, unless it should come under such circumstances as to make it an imperative duty — circumstances not likely to arise." The letter was regarded by many as a "declination with a string to it;" people remarked that in the past, at Ft. Donelson and elsewhere, Grant had never shown any inability to make his meaning unmistakable. [1] In consequence, the discussion of his availability was kept up until the following December, when an effectual quietus was put to it by the passage in the House of Representatives, by a vote of 233 to 18, of a resolution declaring that any attempt to depart from the precedent established by Washington and other Presidents "would be unwise, unpatriotic, and fraught with peril to our free institutions." [2]

With General Grant out of the way, the field was open for other candidates. Of these the most talked about were James G. Blaine of Maine, Roscoe Conkling of New York, Benjamin H. Bristow of Kentucky, and Oliver P. Morton of Indiana. In addition there were some "favorite sons," among whom were John F.

---

1 For an account of this matter and a copy of the letter see Garland's *Grant*, pp. 430-432; also *Harper's Weekly*, XIX, pp. 474, 494, 496, and 499.

2 *Record*, p. 228.

Hartranft of Pennsylvania, Marshall Jewell of Connecticut, and Rutherford B. Hayes of Ohio.

To outward appearances, Mr. Blaine seemed to have the best chance of securing the coveted nomination. He possessed a magnetic personality, and had attracted much attention as Representative and Speaker. In the Congress then in session he had kept himself in the public eye by systematically baiting the Southern members and drawing from them disloyal utterances which could be used by their opponents as party capital. [1] Mr. Blaine's friends were, in general, those men who were dissatisfied with the Administration yet were not reformers. [2] He was, of course, bitterly opposed by Senator Conkling, whom on a memorable occasion he had forever alienated by comparing him to a turkey gobbler. [3] Mr. Blaine was also regarded with but little favor by the reformers; and his availability in their eyes was vastly lessened by the disclosure not long before the convention met of the celebrated "Mulligan letters" which purported to make some uncomfortable revelations regarding his alleged improper relations with the affairs of the Little Rock and Ft. Smith Railroad. [4] Nevertheless he was sure of the support of Maine and of enough votes in other states to give him a decided lead over any of the other candidates.

---

1 *The Nation*, XXIII, p. 173; also Johnson, An American Statesman, ch. 6.
2 Hoar's Autobiography, I, p. 378.
3 See reference to this in *The Nation*, XXV, p. 373; also Stanwood's *Blaine*, pp 66-72.
4 Hoar, I, 379.

Senator Conkling would naturally have the support of practically all the delegates from his own state of New York, [1] and was generally believed to be the candidate favored by the Administration. This latter fact was, however, a source of weakness rather than of strength; for the influence of the Administration was at a very low ebb indeed, and one of the leading Republican weeklies declared that "the only man whom the Republicans can elect is some man whom the Administration coterie would strongly oppose, because his career and character would be the guarantee of a total change in the tone of the Administration." [2]

Senator Morton was still another candidate who was not favorably looked upon by the reformers. While a man of great ability as a leader, he was a Radical of the most intense type, and was credited with having defended the civil service as "the best upon the planet." [3] His nomination was opposed in the East because he was suspected of being a "soft money man;" this suspicion was borne out by the fact that his organ, the Indianapolis *Journal,* was demanding the repeal of the Resumption Act. In addition, his chances were greatly lessened by the fact that he was so infirm physically that he was obliged to use crutches. He was, however, loyally supported by Indiana, and was so popular with the negroes of the South that a national convention of that race at Nashville on April 7th showed itself almost unanimous in

1 See his Life by A. R. Conkling, p. 504.
2 *Harper's Weekly,* XIX, p. 1028.   3 *Ibid,* XX, p. 443.

his favor. An ungrounded attack begun about the same time by the New York *World* upon his personal honesty reacted strongly in his favor, for it gave him an opportunity in a speech in the Senate to bring once more before the country his splendid services as "War Governor" of Indiana. [1]

Of all the candidates, Mr. Bristow was apparently the man best fitted to lead a campaign whose watch-word should be "Reform within the Party." As secretary of the treasury he had conducted a ruthless warfare against the Whiskey Ring; had not hesitated to secure the conviction of personal friends of the President; and had even ventured to bring about the indictment and trial of Orville E. Babcock, the President's private secretary. [2] By his activity he had, however, gained the ill-will of the President and of the Radical official coterie and had been blackballed by the New York Union League Club. [3] His chances were also weakened by the fact that he had not long been known to the country at large. On the other hand, he was regarded with favor by the reformers and was supported by a large part of the more reputable Republican press. [4]

Of the two other candidates most frequently men-

1 For a good account of Morton's candidacy see Foulke, II, pp. 387-396. The attack was made in the *World* of April 29th; Morton replied in the Senate on May 5th.

2 For an account of Bristow's fight against the Whiskey Ring see an article by H. V. Boynton in the *North American Review* for October, 1876, p. 280.

3 *Harper's Weekly*, XX, p. 418; New York *Times*, May 12th.

4 For his candidacy see *Harper's Weekly*, XX, pp. 182, 202, 382, 418. *The Nation*, XXII, p. 344, and Stanwood, Blaine, p. 178.

tioned, Hartranft had the support of the great state of
Pennsylvania; but his name appears to have been put
forward less in hope of his securing the nomination
than of keeping the Pennsylvania delegation in hand
until it could be profitably thrown to some other man. [1]
Hayes, the other candidate, had been indorsed by Ohio.
He was then serving a third term as governor of that
state, and in his various contests for that office had
defeated three prominent Democrats — William Allen,
George H. Pendleton, and Allen G. Thurman. He
was sound on the money question, had a good war
record, was without any important enemies, but was
not much known outside his own state. Few persons
considered it likely that he would be nominated. [2]

A month before the time for the convention at which
the hopes of all but one of these candidates must be
blasted there occurred in New York City an event of
considerable political significance. In response to a
call issued by Carl Schurz, Theodore Woolsey, Horace
White, William Cullen Bryant, and Alexander H. Bullock, about two hundred gentlemen met in the Fifth
Avenue Hotel to confer upon the political situation.
Among those present, in addition to the persons who
had issued the call, were David A. Wells, Charles
Francis Adams, Mark Hopkins, Dorman B. Eaton,

---

1 Blaine, Twenty Years of Congress, II, p. 568. The attend-
ant circumstances bear out the theory.
2 McClure, in his Recollections of Half a Century, p. 99, says
that if there had been a belief that the nomination would go to
Ohio, Sherman would have been put forward. For Hayes's candidacy see *Harper's Weekly*, XX, pp. 122 and 162; *Times of*
April 9th; and *Herald* of April 21st. For an account of his
career see the campaign Life by William Dean Howells.

Thomas Wentworth Higginson, Parke Godwin. H. C. Lodge, and Professor Seelye.

This Fifth Avenue Conference, as it was called, continued in session during the 15th and 16th of May, and, in addition to adopting a resolution in favor of civil service reform, issued an elaborate *Address to the American People*. This paper, which was from the able pen of Mr. Schurz, was in the nature of a warning to both parties. After deploring the unprecedented "prevalence of corrupt practices in our national life," the address continued: "We therefore declare . . . that at the coming Presidential election we shall support no candidate who in public position ever countenanced corrupt practices or combinations or impeded their exposure and punishment"; no candidate "who has failed to use his opportunities in exposing abuses coming within the reach of his observation, but for personal reasons and party ends has permitted them to fester on; . . . no candidate, however conspicuous his position or brilliant his ability, in whom the impulses of the party manager have shown themselves predominant over those of the reformer;" no candidate about whom there could be room for question as to his being "really the man to carry through a thorough-going reform in the government."

Although the Radical Republicans and also many Democrats endeavored to belittle the importance of the conference by calling those in attendance "soreheads" and "sentimentalists," its action was generally felt to

be very significant.[1] The *Address* showed, for one
thing, that the independents would not accept a
candidate like Blaine, Conkling, or Morton, and would
support only a genuine reformer. The general sentiment of the conference had, in fact, been favorable
to Mr. Bristow; and one of the most distinguished
members, Mr. Charles Francis Adams, had openly
stated that in case Mr. Bristow was not named, he
would use his influence in behalf of the expected
Democratic nominee, Mr. Tilden.[2]

On June 14th, a month after the conference was
held, the Republican convention met at Cincinnati.
The meeting place was regarded as especially favorable to Bristow, for the people were more enthusiastic
for him than they were for Hayes, and the city was
also easy of access to·Kentuckians. Numerous as were
Bristow's supporters, however, they were, in the estimation of *The Nation's* correspondent, decidedly un-
practical. "Looking at them, and seeing the thoroughly 'visionary' way in which they tried to push
the fortunes of their candidate by appeals to the desire
of the convention for honest government, and to the
detestation of the delegates for all trickery and under-
hand proceedings, it was impossible for the most
genuine reformer not to regret that they were too

---

1 *Harper's Weekly* for June 3d.

2 In preparing this account of the conference I have consulted the files of the New York *Times, Herald, World* and *Sun;*
of *The Nation* and *Harper's Weekly;* and of the Indianapolis
News, Journal and *Sentinel.* Information has also been supplied me by Mr. Schurz.

moral to use other arguments."[1]   Mr. Bristow's
friends were not the only ones in evidence: Hoosier
supporters of Morton came "in trains and steamboats
chartered for the purpose 'as thick as mosquitoes in
blackberry time,' "[2] and "shouters" for most of the
other candidates were present in goodly numbers. Almost every candidate had some colored supporters, but
Morton was especially favored in this respect. Black
orators descanting upon the merits of their candidate
were numerous and voluble; their "speeches on the
whole were very nearly as good as the white speeches,
and infinitely more amusing, partly from internal
causes and partly because they were so universally
recognized as a piece of buncombe."[3]

One of the most talked of subjects at the convention
was the physical condition of one of the candidates.
On Sunday, the 11th, three days before the convention
was called to order, Mr. Blaine, while on his way to
one of the Washington churches, had been so badly
overcome by the heat that he had fallen at the church
door, and even after being removed to his home had
been in such a state that for many hours it was doubtful whether he would survive. His opponents naturally made the most possible out of his illness, and "had
no hesitation in predicting that he would be dead within
a week, or, if not dead, utterly incapable of using his
mind or bearing any strain."[4]

---

1 *The Nation,* XXII, p. 393.
2 Foulke, p. 397.
3 *The Nation,* XXII, p. 393.
4 *The Nation,* XXII, p. 392.

Although the effect of this reasoning was considerably diminished by the reception of a reassuring telegram from Mr. Blaine, an episode growing out of his
illness did have an important effect upon the ultimate
action of the convention. With a friend, Mr. Bristow
called upon his sick rival to extend his sympathy;
but as Mr. Blaine had come to believe that some of
the attacks made upon him were instigated by Bristow, the visit had unfortunate results. While Bristow
and his friend were at the house "an occurrence took
place which satisfied them both that the feeling against
Bristow on the part of Mr. Blaine and his near friends
was exceedingly strong and implacable. The story
was at once telegraphed in cipher to Mr. Bristow's
chief manager at Cincinnati," and later had, in the
opinion of the late Senator Hoar, a decisive influence
upon the course of events. [1]

On Wednesday, the 14th, the convention was called
to order, and was organized with Edward McPherson
of Pennsylvania as permanent chairman. [2] After certain other preliminary business [3] on this and the following day, the report of the Committee on Platform

---

1 Hoar's Autobiography, I, pp. 380-381.

2 The Blaine forces controlled the organization of the convention. From Alabama the Spencer delegation, favorable to
Morton, were excluded, and the Haralson delegation, some of
whom supported Blaine, were admitted.—Foulke, p. 400; McPherson, p. 210; *The Nation*, XXII, p. 390; *Times* and *Herald* for
June 15th and 16th.

3 A feature of the first session was the reading by Mr. G. W.
Curtis of an address issued some time before by the New York
Reform Club in favor of resumption and civil service reform
and criticising the Administration severely. The address was
regarded as a hard blow at Mr. Conkling.—*The Nation*, XXII, p.
392; *Times* of 15th.

and Resolutions was heard. When the report had
been read, Edward L. Pierce of Massachusetts moved
to strike out the eleventh resolution which called for
a congressional investigation into the effect of the. im-
migration and importation of Mongolians; but after
debate the proposal was rejected, 215 to 532.[1]

Edmund J. Davis of Texas then moved to strike
out the fourth resolution, which was to the effect that
the promise made in the first act signed by President
Grant pledging the nation "to make provision at the
earliest practicable period for the redemption of the
United States notes in coin" ought to be "fulfilled by
a continuous and steady progress to specie payment."
Mr. Davis proposed in its stead a declaration "that it
is the duty of Congress to provide for carrying out
the act known as the Resumption Act of Congress,
to the end that the resumption of specie payments
may not be longer delayed." But the Resumption Act
was not popular in the West, and the party leaders
deemed it better politics not to go on record as either
favoring or opposing it. Consequently the amendment, after a brief debate, was rejected.[2]

In other respects, also, the platform was a temporiz-
ing and rather weak document. It 'contained, of
course, the usual not undeserved eulogy upon the Republican party for its work in purging the land of
slavery. It asserted that the United States is a "nation, not a league;" contained a mild and half-hearted

1 *Times*, June 16th.
2 McPherson, p. 211; *Times, Herald*, and *World* for June 16th.

resolution against the spoils system; declared in favor
of protection, and against polygamy and public aid to
parochial schools; denounced the Democratic party as
"being the same in character and spirit as when it
sympathized with treason;" and asserted that "the
National Administration merits commendation for its
honorable work in the management of domestic and
foreign affairs, and President Grant deserves the continued hearty gratitude of the American people for
his patriotism and his eminent services, in war and
in peace." It also promised that all public officers
should be held "to a rigid responsibility" and "that
the prosecution and punishment of all who betray
official trusts shall be swift, thorough, and unsparing;"
but it nowhere contained a frank recognition of the
shameful condition of the public service or any promise of its thorough reform. [1]

The work of platform-building having been completed, the convention was ready for the more exciting work of selecting the nominee. Marshall Jewell
of Connecticut was named by Stephen W. Kellogg;
Morton, by Richard W. Thompson. Bristow was
nominated by General John M. Harlan of Kentucky,
and the nomination was seconded by George William
Curtis of New York, and by Richard H. Dana of Massachusetts. Conkling's name was presented by Stewart L. Woodford; that of Hayes, by E. F. Noyes; and
that of Hartranft, by Linn Bartholomew. The most

---

1 The platform is given in McPherson, p. 210, and in Stanwood, *History of Presidential Elections*, p. 315.

striking speech was that made by Col. Robert G. Inger-
soll in nominating Blaine; in the course of it he made
the famous comparison of his candidate to a "plumed
knight" — an appellation which continued to be used
by Mr. Blaine's many devoted followers down to the
time of his death. [1]   At the conclusion of the speech-
making the tide in favor of Mr. Blaine was running
so high that his opponents deemed it wise to move
an adjournment.   In all probability the motion would
have been voted down had not the discovery been
made that the lighting equipment of the building was
out of order.   It has since been charged that the
gas supply had been clandestinely cut off for the express purpose of forcing an adjournment.   The man
who planned and carried into execution this manoeuver
was Robert W. Mackay.   Mr. Mackay's roommate
was Matthew Stanley Quay. [2]

When the convention reassembled at ten next morning, the voting was at last begun.   On the first four
ballots the total number of votes cast varied from
754 to 755; 378 thus were necessary for a choice.   Mr.
Blaine received votes varying from 285 on the first
to 292 on the fourth.   On the first two ballots Morton
stood second, with 125 and 120 votes, but was then
passed by Bristow, who, on the fourth ballot, received

---

1 The effect of this speech was partly destroyed by one of
the seconders, a Georgia negro, who caused much laughter by
referring to Curtis as "the poet from New York," and to R. H.
Dana as "our minister to England," and by making himself
otherwise ridiculous.

2 McClure, Our Presidents and How We Make Them, p. 248;
personal statement by the same author.

126. Conkling started with 99 and dropped to 84; Hartranft rose from 58 to 71; and Hayes from 61 to 68. The strenuous support given to Mr. Blaine had now thoroughly convinced the supporters of the other candidates that he was the real enemy; and many of the party leaders, knowing that a bolt would take place should he be the nominee, began to cast about for some candidate in whose favor a combination could be made. "The reformers had convinced Conkling's followers that he could not be nominated, and Morton was out of the question as well as Hartranft. This left Bristow and Hayes as the only possible anti-Blaine nominees." [1]

On the fifth ballot began a decided movement toward Hayes. When Michigan was called, a veteran Republican, William A. Howard, who had been present at the birth of the party "Under the Oaks" thirty-two years before, hobbled out into the aisle, and in a voice tremulous with emotion said that there was one candidate before the convention who had already defeated three Democratic aspirants for the Presidency, — Allen G. Thurman, George H. Pendleton, and William Allen, — and that as he seemed to have a habit of defeating distinguished Democrats, it would be the part of wisdom to give him an opportunity to defeat yet another one. The speaker then announced that Michigan cast all of her 22 votes for Rutherford B. Hayes. This announcement was received with tremendous applause; and when the re-

1 *The Nation*, XXIII, p. 392.

sult of the ballot was announced, it was found that the vote for Hayes had increased from 68 to 104.[1]

On the sixth ballot, however, a Blaine stampede began. North Carolina, which on the previous ballot had voted for Hayes, now came over to Blaine; the Pennsylvania delegation, in which hitherto the unit rule had been enforced, gave him several votes; South Carolina swung into line for him; and in all he received 308 votes, or within 70 of the nomination. On the same ballot Hayes had gained only 9; Morton had received 85; Bristow 111; Conkling 81; and Hartranft 50.

It was now clear that the seventh ballot would be the decisive one. Mr. Blaine's followers were confident and even jubilant. The vote was taken amid great excitement and confusion. From the first few states Mr. Blaine gained many votes; and it was apparent that if he continued to gain at the same rate he would be nominated. When Indiana was called, Mr. Will Cumback, the chairman of the delegation, withdrew the name of Morton and cast 25 votes for Hayes and 5 for Bristow. The crucial moment came when Kentucky was reached. It was now evident that Bristow could not be nominated, and his name was withdrawn. Then, moved by the knowledge of Blaine's hostility to Bristow, the Kentucky delegates voted unanimously for Hayes.[2] They were followed by most of the remaining delegates who had opposed

---

[1] New York *Times*, June 17th; Johnson, An American Statesman, p. 275.
[2] Hoar, I, p. 382.

Blaine, with the result that Hayes received 384 votes and the nomination.[1]

The convention then proceeded to the less exciting work of choosing a Vice-Presidential nominee. As usual in such cases, this work was quickly accomplished. Messrs. William A. Wheeler of New York, Stewart L. Woodford of New York, Marshall Jewell of Connecticut, Frederick T. Frelinghuysen of New Jersey, and Joseph R. Hawley of Connecticut, were put in nomination; but before the first ballot had been completed it was apparent that Mr. Wheeler had received a majority; the other candidates were withdrawn, and he was declared the unanimous choice of the convention.[2]

After transacting some further business the convention, having done all that lay within its power to insure Republican success in the coming election, adjourned *sine die*.[3]

---

[1] The following table (see McPherson, p. 212) gives the vote in detail:

	1st	2d	3d	4th	5th	6th	7th
Hayes	61	64	67	68	104	113	384
Blaine	285	296	293	292	286	308	351
Morton	125	120	113	108	95	85	0
Bristow	113	114	121	126	114	111	21
Conkling	99	93	90	84	82	81	0
Hartranft	58	63	68	71	69	50	0
Jewell	11	(withdrawn)					
Wm. A. Wheeler	3	3	2	2	2	2	0
Elihu B. Washburne	0	1	1	3	3	5	0
Whole No. of votes	755	754	755	754	755	755	756
Necessary to choice	378	378	378	378	378	378	379

[2] McPherson, p. 212.

[3] Except where otherwise stated my account of the convention is based upon files of the New York *Times, World, Herald, Tribune,* and of the Indianapolis *Journal* and *Sentinel.*

CHAPTER III

The Democrats approached the campaign of 1876 in a more sanguine mood than did their opponents. Flushed by their triumph in the congressional elections of '74, encouraged by the fact that all but three of the Southern states had at last been "redeemed" from carpet-bag rule, and reassured by the continuous damaging exposures which threw discredit upon the Administration, the opposition, for the first time in twenty years, felt fairly confident that the next President would be a Democrat.

The question as to who should be the Democratic standard bearer in the expected triumph was not such an open one as in the camp of their opponents. The signs of the times pointed to Samuel J. Tilden, governor of New York, as the probable leader. Nevertheless, there were several other aspirants for the honor. The most talked of were Senator Thomas F. Bayard of Delaware, Senator Allen G. Thurman of Ohio, General Winfield Scott Hancock of Pennsylvania, and Governor Thomas A. Hendricks of Indiana. Senator Bayard had distinguished himself as one of the ablest Democrats in the Senate, and was acceptable to the South because he had opposed the coercion of that section, but his chances as an "available" candidate were greatly impaired by the smallness of the state from which he came.[1]   Senator Thurman had proved himself one of the ablest constitutional lawyers of the day, and had led the Democratic lawyers in many a hard fought parliamentary battle.   Being a "hard money" man, he was regarded with favor in the East, but the "soft money" tide was running high among the Ohio Democrats just then, and ultimately the candidate put forward by the party in that state was a "soft money" man, ex-Governor Allen.[2]   General Hancock, four years later to be the party's candidate against Garfield, had been a strong competitor for the nomination in the convention of 1868.   He was popular with the war veterans, and was looked upon as a possible "dark horse," though he would go into the convention with but little support outside his own state of Pennsylvania.[3]   A candidate whose fortunes were pushed with greater vigor than those of any other yet discussed was Governor Hendricks.   As congressman, senator, and governor, that gentleman had been prominent in state and national politics for many years, had been one of the leading candidates in the convention which nominated Seymour, and had received most of the votes of the Democratic electors in 1872 after the

---

1 *World*, April 29th, June 18th and 25th.   See also *Times* of April 1st, June 23d and 26th.

2 *Harper's Weekly* for June 3; *Times* and *World* for May 18th; *The Nation*, XXII, p. 327.

3 See Life by Goodrich, pp. 303-306; *Times* of June 23d.

death of Greeley.   He had an enthusiastic following in
Indiana and some other states of the Middle West, but
was regarded in the East as a "trimmer" and as unsafe
on the money question. [1]

Of all the men mentioned for the nomination, however, Governor Samuel J Tilden of New York appeared to be the logical candidate to lead in a "reform"
campaign.   Mr. Tilden's rise to national prominence
had been rapid, but his experience in local politics
had been long and varied.   At an early age he
had shown great precocity in political matters, and had
become intimately associated with that prince of politicians, Martin Van Buren.   He had followed his
leader in the Barnburners' revolt of 1848, in 1855
had been the candidate of the "soft shell' Democrats
for attorney-general, but in time had once more found
himself within the regular party fold.   Mr. Tilden
had won great distinction as a lawyer, and through
his success as a railroad "reorganizer" had managed
to amass a fortune of several millions.   Although his
stand during the Rebellion had not been exactly what
lovers of the Union could have wished, this had not
prevented him from receiving in 1866 the chairmanship
of the Democratic State Committee in New York.
In this capacity he had been more or less associated
with unscrupulous leaders of the party in New York

---

1 My information upon Hendricks's candidacy has been
largely obtained from files of the Indianapolis *Sentinel*.   See also
New York *Times* of Feb. 20th, 21st and May 15th.   For a sketch
of his career up to this time see Cook, Lives of Tilden and
Hendricks, pp. 363-375.   Bigelow says Hendricks was "more or
less infected with all the political heresies of the period and of
the section in which he resided."—Life of Tilden, I, p. 305.

City; but after the exposure of the Tweed Ring by *The Times* in 1871, he had at the eleventh hour thrown himself into a desperate struggle against the Ring, and it had been partly through his efforts that the organization had been broken up. Despite the opposition of Tammany, he had in 1874 become the party's candidate for governor, and had been triumphantly elected over John A. Dix by a plurality of about 50,000. As governor he had waged a relentless and successful war upon the so-called "Canal Ring," and had also succeeded in reducing the rate of taxation. Cold, calculating, and secretive, he did not possess the qualities which arouse great public enthusiasm; but by the activities just described he had gained a great reputation as a reformer, and, though he had incurred some bitter enmities in his own party, had succeeded in making himself in a certain sense the man of the hour. [1]

The Tilden "boom" was formally "launched" upon the country by the New York Democratic convention at Utica on April 27th, 1876. Despite the bitter opposition of Tammany under the leadership of John Kelly, the convention commended the work of Governor Tilden and adopted a resolution to the effect that

---

[1] The best Life of Tilden, although uncritical, is that by Bigelow. Blaine says of Tilden: "His hour had come; he promptly grasped the leadership thus left open. Starting out for the Presidential nomination, his plan embraced three features: his stepping stone was the governorship, his shibboleth was administrative reform, his method was organization to a degree which has never been surpassed."—Twenty Years in Congress, II, p.. 574. "Not a statesman in the highest sense of the word, nor a demagogue in the lowest sense of that word—a genuine American politician of the first order."—Burgess, Reconstruction and the Constitution, p. 282.

the Democratic party of New York "suggest, with respectful deference to their brethren in other States, and with a cordial appreciation of other renowned Democratic statesmen, faithful, like him, to their political principles and public trusts, that the nomination of Samuel J. Tilden to the office of President would insure the vote of New York and would be approved throughout the Union." [1]

When the Democratic hosts gathered at St. Louis in the latter part of June, it was already apparent that Tilden, whose campaign had been managed with consummate skill, was in the lead and would probably be nominated. Nevertheless, his opponents did not give up hope. They urged with some force that the Democratic standard bearer in each of the last three campaigns had been a New Yorker, and each time had gone down to disastrous defeat. The Westerners pointed out that Tilden was a "hard money" man and would not be acceptable in their section. Most of all, his opponents emphasized the fact that he had numerous party enemies in his own state. Of this last there was present concrete proof in the shape of a large contingent of Tammany "braves," led by John Kelly, who did all in their power to persuade wavering delegations that Tilden would, if nominated, be overwhelmingly defeated in New York. The Tilden forces were, however, admirably organized, and, under the leadership of such men as William L. Scott, Avery Smith, Senator Kernan, John Morrisey, ex-Senator Gwin,

---

1 New York *Herald*, *World* and *Times* for April 28th.

Lieutenant-Governor Dorsheimer, Montgomery Blair, and Henry Watterson, were able to convince many delegates that the proper candidate to lead a "reform" campaign was the "reform" governor of New York.

The convention assembled on June 27th in the Merchants' Exchange, and was called to order by Augustus Schell, chairman of the national committee. Henry Watterson of Kentucky was chosen temporary chairman; he, in turn, gave way in the afternoon to the permanent chairman, General John A. McClernand of Illinois. On the following day after listening to a number of speeches, among them the usual one by a representative of the woman suffragists, the convention received, through Mr. Dorsheimer of New York, the report of the Committee on Resolutions.

The platform thus submitted can be roughly summarized in the one word *reform*. "Reform," it proclaimed, "is necessary" to secure the country "from a corrupt centralism which, after inflicting upon ten states the rapacity of carpet-bag tyrannies, has honeycombed the offices of the Federal Government itself with incapacity, waste, and fraud, infected states and municipalities with the contagion of misrule, and locked fast the prosperity of an industrious people in the paralysis of 'hard times.' Reform is necessary," it contineed, "to establish a sound currency;" and it denounced the resumption clause of the act of 1875 as being a hindrance to a speedy return to specie payments, and demanded that the act should be repealed.

"Reform is necessary," it asserted, "in the sum and modes of federal taxation;" and it denounced the "tariff, levied upon nearly 4,000 articles, as a masterpiece of injustice, inequality, and false pretense." "Reform," it further declared, "is necessary in the scale oi public expense, — Federal, state, and municipal;" in the system of land granting, in order "to put a stop to the profligate waste of the public lands;" in the civil service; and even more in "the higher grades of the public service."

"When the annals of this Republic," it specified, "show the disgrace and censure of a Vice-President; a late Speaker of the House of Representatives marketing his rulings as a presiding officer; three Senators profiting secretly by their votes as law-makers; five chairmen of the leading committees of the late House of Representatives exposed in jobbery; a late Secretary of the Treasury forcing balances in the public accounts; a late Attorney-General misappropriating public funds; a Secretary of the Navy enriched or enriching friends by percentages levied off the profits of contracts with his departments; an Ambassador to England censured in a dishonorable speculation; the President's private secretary barely escaping conviction upon trial for guilty complicity in frauds upon the revenue; a Secretary of War impeached for high crimes and misdemeanors — the demonstration is complete, that the first step in reform must be the people's choice of honest men from another party, lest the disease of one political organization infect the body politic, and lest by making no change of men or parties we get no change of measures and no real reform." [1]

---

[1] The platform is given in McPherson, p. 215, and in Stanwood, p. 322.

With the greater part of the platform the entire convention was in hearty accord; but the financial plank, while ambiguous, was not satisfactory to the "soft money" element, and a hard fight was waged to substitute a minority report. This report, signed by Ewing of Ohio, Voorhees of Indiana, and others, provided for striking out the clause, "As such hindrance we denounce the resumption clause of the Act of 1875, and we here demand its repeal," and putting in its place the following, "The law for the resumption of specie payments on the 1st of January, 1879, having been enacted by the Republican party without deliberation in Congress or discussion before the people, and being both ineffective to secure its objects and highly injurious to the business of the country, ought forthwith to be repealed." Voorhees and other speakers, voicing the "West, the great and boundless West," spoke ardently in favor of the change; but the minority report was voted down by 550 to 219. The platform, as reported, was then adopted by 651 to 83. [1]

Nominations for the Presidency were then declared in order, whereupon Whitely of Delaware presented the name of Bayard; "Blue Jeans" Williams of Indiana that of Hendricks; Abbott of New Jersey that of Governor Joel Parker; Senator Kernan of New York that of Tilden; Ewing of Ohio that of ex-Governor Allen; and Clymer of Pennsylvania that of Hancock. Much excitement was caused by a speech made

---

[1] McPherson, p. 217; New York *Herald, World* and *Times* of June 29th.

by John Kelly in opposition to Tilden. He was interrupted and hissed, and was able to get a hearing only
after some of Tilden's own supporters had called upon
the audience for fair play. He then solemnly asserted
that the nomination of Tilden would result in disaster
to the party, and declared himself in favor of Hendricks.

When the balloting began, it soon became apparent, however, that the majority of the delegates were
of the same opinion as one of the speakers — that a
"reform campaign without Tilden would be like the
play of *Hamlet* with Hamlet left out." Of the votes
cast Tilden received 417 out of a total of 739. The
balloting in detail was as follows:

> Tilden 417
> Hendricks 140
> Hancock 75
> Allen 56
> Bayard 33
> Parker 18
>
> Total............739

But though Tilden had a majority of the votes, he
had not yet received the requisite two-thirds, so a second ballot was ordered. Before the result of the ballot was announced the anxiety of many delegates to
be on the winning side resulted in Missouri and other
states announcing changes in their votes, with the
result that Tilden received 535 votes and the nomi-

nation.[1]   The nomination was thereupon made unanimous, and the convention adjourned till the following day.

In the interval the delegates devoted much time to canvassing the possibilities for the Vice-Presidency. Among those mentioned for the honor were Hendricks of Indiana, Payne of Ohio, and M. R. Morrison, ex-Governor J. M. Palmer, and Cyrus McCormick of Illinois.   When the convention reassembled, however, sentiment had so crystallized in favor of Hendricks that, despite the fact that it was not known whether he would accept, he was nominated by acclamation.

After the transaction of some further business the convention, having done all that lay within its power to insure Democratic success in the forthcoming election, adjourned *sine die*.[2]

---

[1] The second ballot in detail was as follows:

Tilden	535
Hendricks	60
Hancock	59
Allen	54
Bayard	11
Parker	18
Thurman	7
Total	744

[2] My account of the Democratic convention is based in large measure upon files of the newspapers mentioned at the end of the preceding chapter.

CHAPTER IV

THE CENTENNIAL CAMPAIGN

The work of the two parties in their respective conventions was fairly well received by the rank and file of each. To be sure, the Republican nominees, while thoroughly respectable, did not arouse a great deal of enthusiasm; but it was felt to be something of a victory to have put in the field a ticket upon which all factions of the party could unite; and when the first shock of surprise caused by the nomination of Hayes had passed and a knowledge of his stubborn stand for sound money and of his war record — four honorable wounds and a brevet major-generalcy — had been more widely disseminated, not a few members of the party came to believe with reason that the choice for the head of the ticket at least had been the wisest possible. [1] As for the reception accorded the Democratic nominees, Tilden was for a little while looked upon with disfavor by some elements of the party in the "soft money" West; while a somewhat

[1] *Harper's Weekly*, XX, pp. 526 and 546; Burgess, Reconstruction and the Constitution, p. 281; Blaine, II, p. 572. Blaine naturally does not speak quite so strongly. The Conkling forces remained apathetic during the campaign; for a partial explanation see the Life of Conkling by A. R. Conkling, pp. 511-512 and 521. Conkling promised to make four speeches, but on account of illness made only one.

similar feeling towards his running mate was entertained by some Democrats in the "hard money" East; but in both sections the dissentients soon fell into line and supported the ticket. [1]

As regards the platforms, that put forth by the Democrats, though vague on certain important issues, particularly those of resumption and civil service reform, was looked upon by somt independents as the stronger.[2] *The Nation,* the most ably edited of the independent periodicals of the day, was of the opinion that the utterance of the Republican platform on the question of civil service reform was a "barren proposition," that the platform evaded the currency issue, and that, as a whole, it afforded "an excellent specimen of the sort of mild imposture which the politician of our day tries to practice on the people after his party ceases to have substantial and unmistakable work to do." [3]

The letters of acceptance received more attention from the public than did the platforms. [4] That of Mr. Hayes put him in higher favor with the reformers, for in it he denounced the spoils system as tending to "extravagance and official incapacity," and declared

---

1 The Cincinnati *Enquirer* called Tilden's nomination a blow at the West; the Evansville *Courier* temporarily bolted the ticket; and other western Democratic newspapers, notably the Indianapolis *Sentinel,* were for a day or two not at all enthusiastic for Tilden. Bigelow thinks that the nomination of Hendricks prevented many independents from supporting the ticket. —Life of Tilden, I, p. 306.

2 *The Nation,* XXIII, p. 4.

3 *Ibid,* XXII, p. 390.

4 *Ibid,* XXIII, p. 144. The letters are given in McPherson, pp. 212 and 217; also in the *Annual Cyclopaedia,* 1876, pp. 783 and 787.

himself unreservedly for civil service reform. [1] Mr.
Tilden devoted the greater portion of his long letter to
financial questions. His arguments, in general, were
able ones; but his plan for resumption, in view of the
past attitude of his party on that subject, was "cloudy
in the extreme." [2]

In the weeks immediately following the conventions
much curiosity existed as to what would be the action
of the Independents. In the main the members of the
Fifth Avenue Conference, though they had leaned towards Bristow, and were not entirely satisfied with the
Cincinnati platform, came out for Hayes; notable ex-
ceptions were Mr. Parke Godwin and Mr. Charles
Francis Adams, both of whom supported Tilden. [3]
The leaders of what remained of the Liberal Republican organization declared for Hayes and declined to
hold a convention. [4]

But though the Liberal Republican party thus disappeared from history, three other minor parties remained. One of these, the Prohibition Reform Party,
had in May nominated at Cleveland a ticket composed
of Green Clay Smith of Kentucky, and G. T. Stewart of Ohio. The Independent Nationals, or "Green-

---

1 *The Nation*, XXIII, pp. 17 and 84. Mr. Hayes also stated an
"inflexible purpose, if elected, not to be a candidate for a second term."

2 *Ibid*, p. 84.

3 See an article on "Independents in the Canvass" in the
North American Review for October, 1876; also *The Nation*,
XXIII, p. 222. A letter written by Godwin appeared in the
Tribune for July 22d; one by Adams in the *Sun* for August 5th.
Adams was nominated for governor by the Massachusetts Dem-
ocrats. Much was said by Republicans about "Adams's fall."

4 *The Nation*, XXIII, p. 49.

backers," in a convention held at Indianapolis in the
same month had nominated the philanthropist, Peter
Cooper, of New York, and Newton Booth of California; but Booth had subsequently declined the honor,
and Samuel F. Cary of Ohio had been substituted. A
third organization, the American Nationals, had in
June met in mass convention at Pittsburg and had
nominated James B. Walker of Illinois, and Donald
Kirkpatrick of New York. [1] The race made by these
three parties served to give a humorous side to
the canvass, but all serious interest was concentrated
upon the doings of the Republicans and the Democrats.

The Democrats, under the direct but secret management of Mr. Tilden himself, fought the campaign on
lines laid down in the platform. Their speakers denounced the extravagance of the Republican rule, and
contrasted the cost of Democratic government under
such Presidents as Buchanan with the enormous cost
under Grant. They pointed to the "Salary Grab;" to
the whiskey frauds, by which, they asserted, the treasury had lost not less than $15,000,000 annually; to
the Clews Banking Company scandal; to the Emma
Mine scandal, with which the minister to England had
been connected; to the Credit Mobilier scandal; to the
Venezuela scandal; to the Post Trader frauds; and
to all the other malodorous transactions in which in-
cautious congressmen, cabinet officers, and other per-

---

[1] Accounts of all these conventions, with the platforms, are
given by McClure, pp. 257-260; of the first two by McPherson,
pp. 224-225, and by Stanwood, pp. 310-313.

sons high up in the Republican party had been involved.[1] And having brought their indictment, they
tried to convince the people that the only way to secure an efficient, honest, and economical administration would be to turn the Republicans out and put
the Democrats in.

The Republican leaders were quite aware that their
party's recent record was not one with which it would
be safe to go before the people. Practically their only
hope of securing a new lease of power lay in creating
a still greater distrust of Democrats than was entertained for Republicans. They set about doing this
by reviving the sectional issue, by denouncing the
Democracy and all its works, and by attacking with
great virulence the personal record of Mr. Tilden.
As already related, the way for the revival of the sectional issue had already been prepared by Mr. Blaine.
The party orators "waved the bloody shirt" with great
vehemence, dwelt upon the horrors of Andersonville,
harped upon the intimidation of negroes, and sought
to identify the Democratic party with the party which
brought on the war. Another argument was that if
the Democrats should come into power, they would
pay about two billion dollars' worth of Southern war
claims, and would also ruin our credit abroad.[2] Much

1 A good summary of the Democratic case is given by Bigelow, II, pp. 1-4. See also the Democratic Campaign Text Book
for 1876. Some unimportant attacks were made upon the integrity of the Republican candidates. Much also was said about
Republican misgovernment in the South.

2 *The Nation*, XXIII, pp. 247, 263, 277. Tilden issued a statement denying that he would allow the payment of the claims.

was made of the conflicting opinions of the Democratic candidates on the currency question. One of
the cartoons of the day represented the party as a
double-headed tiger, one head being that of Tilden,
the other that of Hendricks; the collars round their
necks were labelled respectively "Contraction" and
"Inflation;" below was an inscription, part of which
read, "This double-headed, double-faced Tiger can
be turned any way to gull the American people." [1]
As an offset to Republican frauds, the orators said a
great deal about Tweed and Tammany Hall. And,
when all other resources were exhausted, they fell back
upon "the general cussedness of all Democrats, their
moral degradation, liking for liquor, antipathy to 'good
men,' and fondness for brawling, fighting, and general deviltry." [2]

The attack upon Mr. Tilden was led by the New
York *Times*. The chief charges brought against him
were that he had been a railroad "wrecker," that he
had extorted excessive fees for legal services, that he
had been a Rebel sympathizer, that he had failed to
make full and fair returns of his income to the tax
assessor, and that he was a mere sham eleventh-hour
reformer, who had gone into the fight against the
Tweed Ring and the Canal Ring merely to pave his

1 Nast in *Harper's Weekly*, July 22d; see also number for
August 26th.

2 *The Nation*, XXIII, pp. 115-116. For a humorous view of
the campaign see *Ibid*, p. 308. Many independents had hoped
that the campaign would be one of reason not of feeling. Not
much was said about civil service reform except at the very
last. A good deal was said in some quarters about state aid to
parochial schools.

way to the Presidency. Most of these charges were wholly without foundation; some of them were even absurd; but there was a modicum of truth in some of them; they were seized upon with great avidity by the Republican press and orators; and Mr. Tilden was kept busy "explaining." [1]

Despite all their efforts, however, the Republicans, even under the able management of the astute Zachariah Chandler of Michigan, were not immediately able to turn back the tide which had been running against them so strongly during the past three years. The results of the elections in the "October States" were slightly unfavorable to them. West Virginia went Democratic by more than 12,000, and Indiana by more than 5,000, while in Ohio the Republican majority was less than 9,000. [2]

Throughout the campaign the Republican newspapers were full of stories of Democratic outrages upon the negroes in the South. With the idea of weakening the Republican charges a Northern Dem-

---

1. Upon the subject of his work as a railroad "reorganizer" see *Harper's Weekly*, XX, p. 751, and *The Nation*, XXIII, pp. 111, 115, 219. "Sly Sam, the Railroad thief," was one of the pleasant appellations bestowed upon him in one of the campaign songs. For his attitude during the war see *Harper's Weekly*, XX, pp. 590, 730, 750, 826; *The Nation*, XXIII, p. 111; and speeches of J. A. Kasson and A. S. Hewitt in House of Representatives on August 14th. The income tax charge was pressed with great vigor. See Bigelow, II, pp. 5-7, 225-260; *The Nation*, XXIII, pp. 125, 141, 157, 174, 187, 190, 206, 263. On all these matters I have made use of files of the *Times, Herald* and *World*.

2 *Annual Cyclopaedia*, 1876, pp. 411, 648, 805. In Indiana the Republicans were handicapped by the discovery that their candidate for governor, G. S. Orth, had been implicated in the Venezuela scandal. He was forced to withdraw, and Benjamin Harrison was substituted, but the scandal did the party great harm.—Foulke, II, p. 415.

ocrat, Scott Lord of New York, in August introduced into the House of Representatives a resolution to the effect that "all attempts by force, fraud, terror, intimidation, or otherwise to prevent the free exercise of the rights of suffrage in any state, should meet certain, condign, and effectual punishment." The resolution was put forward rather unexpectedly without a party conference on the subject, and for various reasons it proved rather embarrassing for some Democrats. However, after attempts had unsuccessfully been made to dodge it, it was passed by a large majority, although many Democrats refrained from voting either for or against it. [1]

Much more effective steps to prevent disorder in the South were taken by other branches of the Federal government. On the 15th of August the secretary of war, in an order which quoted the above mentioned resolution, directed General Sherman, the commander-in-chief, to hold all available troops in readiness for use, upon call or requisition of the proper legal authorities, in assisting to secure the political rights of all citizens, irrespective of color or condition. On September 4th the attorney general issued a circular of instructions for the guidance of the United States marshals, whose duty it was, under the Federal election laws, to exercise an oversight over the conduct of elections for congressmen and electors. Three days

---

[1] *Congressional Record,* 44th Congress, 1st session, p. 5414; *The Nation,* XXIII, p. 97.

later a general order was issued for the guidance of the army. [1]

But despite all these resolutions and instructions, there came up from time to time from the Southland rumors of intimidation, of "massacres," and of other manifestations of a bitter determination on the part of the Southern Democrats, particularly in the "unredeemed" states of Florida, Louisiana, and South Carolina, to win their way to political power at any cost. In South Carolina the activity of "rifle-clubs," riding "up and down by day and night in arms, murdering some peaceable citizens and intimidating others," became so great that in October the governor appealed to the President for military aid, and more than thirty companies of troops were sent thither. But the exact truth concerning the situation in these states is so intimately connected with conclusions which must later be drawn that the subject will be taken up in detail in future chapters.

---

1 All these papers are given in House Ex. Doc. No. 30, 44th Cong., 2d Sess., pp. 5-10. The order issued by the secretary of war aroused much "Democratic fury" and denunciation.—*Harper's Weekly*, XX, p. 806.

CHAPTER V

The returns which came in on the night of Tuesday, November 7th, were such as to indicate the election of Tilden and Hendricks. The Democratic morning papers were almost unanimous in claiming victory;[1] jubilant headlines on the pages of journals which had taken no satisfaction in chronicling the results of a Presidential election for twenty long years announced the news.[2] The Republican newspapers were scarcely less unanimous in either directly or indirectly admitting defeat. A fair sample of what appeared in many such papers that morning is the following, taken from the Indianapolis *Journal,* one of the most intensely partisan in the country:

---

1 It has erroneously been claimed that all the newspapers in the country, with the exception of the New York *Times,* announced a Democratic victory. The New York *Herald,* for example, did not; in its 2:30 edition on the morning of the 8th it stated that the "Result is undecided." On the 9th its summary was: 181 for Hayes, 184 for Tilden, with Florida in doubt. "Is Tilden's election," it queried, "a Snark or a Boojum?"

2 "The new era begins," said the New York *World.* "Peace on Earth and to men of good will is the glorious message of this glorious day."

"THE RESULT

"Tilden and Hendricks Undoubtedly Elected.
Connecticut, New York, New Jersey, and
Indiana Join the South. Which Gives Them
123 Votes and Swells the Aggregate to 188."

An editorial in the same paper read as follows:

"With the result before us at this writing we see no
escape from the conclusion that Tilden and Hendricks
are elected. The Democrats have doubtless carried
every Southern state, together with the states of New
York, New Jersey, Connecticut, and Indiana, with possibly Wisconsin. No returns have been received from
the Pacific coast, but none that may be received can
materially alter the present aspect of the case. Tilden
is elected. The announcement will carry pain to every
loyal heart in the nation, but the inevitable truth may
as well be stated."

But there was one Republican newspaper office,
namely that of the New York *Times,* in which a different view of the result prevailed. Many erroneous
statements have been made regarding what took place
in *The Times* office that night. [1] One story which has
gained wide currency is to the effect that as Mr. John
C. Reid, the news editor, sat in his sanctum deploring
the defeat of Hayes, he received from the chairman of
the Democratic national committe, a note inquiring
about the result in Louisiana, South Carolina, Florida,

---

1 See, for example, Bigelow, II, p. 9.

and Oregon;[1] that Mr. Reid thereupon, without any
information on which to base his belief other than this
hint of Democratic uncertainty, proceeded to claim
these states for the Republicans; and that at that moment was born a "conspiracy" which ultimately resulted
in the seating of Hayes. As a matter of history,
"neither 'conspiracy' within the office nor 'inspiration'
from without had anything to do with the verdict."
In the editorial council, composed of Mr. John Foord,
Mr. George Shepard, Mr. Edward Cary, and Mr. Reid,
there was, to be sure, a difference of opinion as to
what attitude to assume, for the dispatches received,
especially in the earlier part of the evening, had been
unfavorable; but "the clear and composed intellect of
Mr. Edward Cary [not of Mr. Reid] exercised a pre-
ponderating weight" against conceding Democratic
victory.[2]   Accordingly the following non-committal
editorial, prepared by Mr. Cary, appeared in the first
edition of *The Times:*

"A DOUBTFUL ELECTION.

"At the time of going to press with our first edition

1 At 3:45 A. M. the following dispatch was sent to *The Times*:
"Please give your estimate of electoral votes secured for Til-
den. Answer at once." But the dispatch was signed by D. A.
Magone, not by Senator Barnum, as some writers have stated.—
H. R. Mis. Doc. No. 31, 45th Cong., 3d Sess., I, p. 527.

2 My authority for this account is in part the Jubilee Supplement of *The Times*, September 18, 1901, pp. 17-18. "The dili-
gence of the gentleman last named [Mr. Reid]," says this account, "in awakening the Republican managers to a perception of
the duty which awaited them in the South may account for the
prevalent impression that the stand of *The Times* in regard to
the election of Hayes and Wheeler was especially his work."
As a matter of fact, Mr. Reid favored admitting defeat. For
some of the facts not contained in the Jubilee Supplement I am
indebted to one of the gentlemen who was present at the "editorial council."

the result of the presidential election is still in doubt. Enough has been learned to show that the vote has been unprecedentedly heavy; that both parties have exhausted their full legitimate strength; that the peculiar Democratic policy for which such extensive preparations were made in the large registry in this city, and in Brooklyn, has had its effect, and that in some of the states where the shotgun and rifle club were relied upon to secure a Democratic victory, there is only too much reason to fear that it has been successful."

Then came a paragraph conceding New York and after that figures showing that Tilden had received 175 votes for certain and Hayes 178 votes for certain. The editorial closed thus:

"This leaves New Jersey, Oregon and Florida still in doubt. If the Republicans have carried New Jersey, they have 187 votes, or a majority of five. If they have carried Florida and Oregon, they have 185 votes, or a majority of one. The Democrats, in order to gain the election (New York being conceded), must have carried New Jersey, and in addition either Oregon or Florida. The returns from New Jersey leave the state in doubt. Oregon is not heard from. Florida is claimed by the Democrats."

Later returns proved more favorable, and in a subsequent edition published at 6:30 A. M. a slightly more confident editorial displaced the one just quoted. The pessimistic sentence about the shotgun and rifle clubs was struck out of the first paragraph, but the paragraph to the effect that New York had probably gone Democratic was retained. Then came the following:

"Conceding New York to Mr. Tilden, he will receive the electoral votes of the following states:

Alabama,	10	Mississippi,	8
Arkansas,	6	Missouri,	15
Connecticut,	6	New Jersey,	9
Delaware,	3	New York,	35
Georgia,	11	North Carolina,	10
Indiana,	15	Tennessee,	12
Kentucky,	12	Texas,	8
Maryland,	8	Virginia,	11
		West Virginia,	5
		Total,	184

"General Hayes will receive the votes of the following states:

California,	6	Nevada,	3
Colorado,	3	New Hampshire,	5
Illinois,	21	Ohio,	22
Iowa,	11	Oregon,	3
Kansas,	5	Pennsylvania,	29
Louisiana,	8	Rhode Island,	4
Maine,	7	South Carolina,	7
Massachusetts,	13	Vermont,	5
Michigan,	11	Wisconsin,	10
Minnesota,	5		
Nebraska,	3	Total,	181

"This leaves Florida alone still in doubt. If the Republicans have carried that state, as they claim, they will have 185 votes—a majority of one."

Believing that the situation was not correctly understood by the party leaders, Mr. Reid, the news editor, hurried to the Republican headquarters in the Fifth Avenue Hotel. Arrived there, he found the

committee rooms deserted save by some employees of
the hotel; for, a couple of hours before, the committeemen and their friends had given up all as lost, and
had either gone home or gone to bed in the hotel. Mr.
Reid at once decided to hunt up Zachariah Chandler,
the national chairman, and started for the hotel office
in order to ascertain the number of Mr. Chandler's
room.

On his way thither he met a small man wearing a
greatcoat with a heavy military cloak, with his hat
drawn down over his eyes, and carrying a gripsack
and a copy of the New York *Tribune*. The newcomer
was Mr. W. E. Chandler, a member of the Republican
committee, who had just returned to New York after
a short trip to New Hampshire. Mr. Chandler believed that the Republicans were defeated, but Mr.
Reid told him that this was a mistake, that the Democrats themselves were still uncertain as to the outcome. In support of this statement he showed Mr.
Chandler a dispatch from Democratic headquarters
asking for what information *The Times* had upon the
situation.[1] Mr. Reid urged that the Republicans ought
to keep up their heads and claim the election of
Hayes. The two then repaired to Mr. W. E. Chandler's room, "where they went over the ground carefully, state by state, from Maine to Oregon, counting
the electoral vote in each state, and showing the vote
as it was finally counted for Hayes and Tilden."

As the situation seemed to contain possibilities, the

---

1 See note 1, p. 47.

two then went in search of Mr. Zachariah Chandler, the
chairman of the committee. After one or two rather
ludicrous mistakes they found his room, and after
considerable knocking the door "was opened, and Mr.
Zachariah Chandler was discovered standing in his
night dress." He was, however, so utterly worn out
that he was with difficulty made to understand the situation, and merely authorized Mr. W. E. Chandler
to do what he thought necessary.

Mr. W. E. Chandler and Mr. Reid then hurried to
the hotel telegraph office in order to dispatch some
messages to the states which were in doubt. Finding
the office locked, they decided to take the messages to
the main office of the Western Union, and therefore
ordered a carriage. In the interval before it arrived,
messages were prepared to Governor Chamberlain of
South Carolina, to S. B. Conover, Tallahassee, Florida,
to S. B. Packard, Republican candidate for governor
of Louisiana, and to persons in Oregon and California.
The import of all these telegrams can be inferred from
that sent to South Carolina, for it was typical. It
was as follows:

"Hayes is elected if we have carried South Carolina,
Florida, and Louisiana. Can you hold your state?
Answer immediately."

Mr. Reid then took the telegrams to the Western
Union office and dispatched them.[1]

---

1 This account is based upon an article by Mr. Reid in *The
Times* for June 15, 1887; on Mr. W. E. Chandler's testimony be-
fore the Potter Committee, in H. R. Mis. Doc. No. 31, 45th
Cong., 3d Sess., I, pp. 525, *et seq.;* and upon information supplied

Later in the day Mr. Zach. Chandler, who had now become fully alive to the possibilities of the situation, sent out the following famous telegram:

"Hayes has 185 electoral votes and is elected."

To this claim the Republican leaders consistently and stubbornly adhered until the end. And thus began what was in some respects the most remarkable contest which any country has ever witnessed.

The changed face of affairs quickly became known throughout the country, and the Republican newspapers definitely claimed the election of Hayes. The Indianapolis *Journal,* for example, had this headline on the morning of the 9th:

"A CHANGE

"The Republicans Take Their Turn at Rejoicing. The Conclusion of Yesterday Reversed. Latest Returns Give Hayes 185 Votes. A Majority of One. All the Pacific States, Louisiana, South Carolina, and Florida, Are Claimed by the National Committee as Certainly Republican."

An editorial in the same issue ran as follows:

"During the last twenty-four hours the political situ-

by Mr. Chandler, who has read this and other chapters. Mr. Chandler denies using language attributed to him by Reid, and also denies that Reid dictated the telegrams. For a humorous commentary on Reid's article see New York *Sun* for June 19, 1887.

ation has undergone a remarkable change, and one entirely favorable to the Republicans. At the time of
going to press yesterday morning the returns indicated
very clearly the election of Tilden and Hendricks, and
the *Journal,* in common with all the leading papers of
the country, conceded the fact. At this writing, apparently trustworthy advices indicate almost unmistakably that Hayes and Wheeler are elected. . . . .

"You could have told a Republican five hundred
yards by the length of his visage yesterday morning,
and when groups of them gathered on the street cor-
ners pedestrians instinctively looked around for the
corpse. There was every outward indication of a fun-
eral, and it only needed the presence of a well filled coffin to make the delusion complete. They had given up
the ship the night before, and the news in the morning
confirmed their fears. . . . .

"Democrats could be recognized, too, at long range,
and their rubicund faces told plainly that they 'liked
it pretty well, thank you.' The experience of a national victory was a novel one, and the taste was sweet
indeed. It was intoxicating in its effects, and operated
on the Democratic system like a dose of hashish on a
cultivated Hindoo stomach. They were wild with joy,
and wanted to bet their substance on Tilden and Hendricks. They swapped stories with each other until
Tilden was elected unanimously. Then they got together and yelled, and gaining confidence with each
yawp, yawped again. . . . . This sort of thing
was kept up until 11 o'clock, when a reaction set in.
. . . . Our boys began to brace up at this cheer-
ful intelligence. During the afternoon public opinion
underwent an almost complete revolution, and the Republicans emerged from the valley and shadow of dark
despair into the sunshine of hope, and the world looked
less wicked to them. Telegrams continued quite fa-

vorable all the afternoon, and it looked very much as though the name of the babe would be Rutherford."

Many of "Rutherford's" friends continued for a day or two to believe that he had been defeated,[1] but meanwhile the Republican managers were doing yeoman work for him. They were fully aware of the desperate necessity of securing every doubtful vote, and left no stone unturned to obtain that result. Agents, among them W. E. Chandler, were immediately dispatched southward to the three states of Florida, Louisiana, and South Carolina. Ample funds were provided for their use.

As it was not improbable that disorders might occur in the disputed states, the Republican leaders deemed it wise to secure troops for the protection of the canvassing officers. The task of getting them was not a difficult one;[2] for the President was a Republican, his secretary of the interior was the head of the Republican organization, and, furthermore, in the nick of time Governor Stearns of Florida telegraphed that a special train sent out to get returns had been "ku-

---

1 Several writers have represented Hayes as admitting defeat. An alleged interview in which he was reported to have said that he regretted his defeat most because of the effect it would have on "the poor colored men" was published in many newspapers at the time (e. g., in the New York *Sun* of November 9th). This interview was later denied.—H. R. Mis. Doc. No. 31, 45th Cong., 3d Sess., I, p. 880. Col. Webb C. Hayes, who was his father's secretary, says that Governor Hayes never admitted defeat.

2 It appears that the "conspirators," as the Republican leaders have been called by the Democrats, talked with Grant, who was then in Philadelphia, over Jay Gould's private wire. This of itself would seem to be no great crime. See Gibson, A Political Crime, p. 55. Gibson's book, it may be remarked here, was prepared under the eye of Mr. Tilden.

kluxed" and thrown from the track, and he urgently asked for aid.[1] On the night of the 9th, therefore, several companies were ordered to Tallahassee; and further dispositions of troops in the disputed states were subsequently made.[2] The President's action in the matter aroused a storm of protest at the time and has been much condemned by Democratic writers since; but, whatever the motives which actuated him, there can be little doubt that the presence of the troops went far towards preserving the peace not only in the states in which they were stationed but also in the entire country.

On the 10th the President issued an order which was copied into probably every newspaper in the United States. It was as follows:

"To Gen. W. T. Sherman, Washington, D. C.:

"Instruct General Augur, in Louisiana, and General Ruger, in Florida, to be vigilant with the force at their command to preserve peace and good order, and to see that the proper and legal Boards of Canvassers are unmolested in the performance of their duties. Should there be any grounds of suspicion of fraudulent counting on either side, it should be reported and denounced at once. No man worthy of the office of President would be willing to hold the office if counted in, placed there by fraud; either party can afford to be disappointed in the result, but the country cannot afford to have the result tainted by the suspicion of illegal or false returns.   U. S. GRANT."

The President was anxious to secure an honest set-

---

1 H. R. Mis. Doc. No. 42, 44th Cong. 2d Sess., pp. 435-436.
2 H. R. Ex. Doc. No. 30, 44th Cong. 2d Sess., pp. 22 *et seq.*

tlement of the contest in the disputed states, and with this purpose in mind requested a number of prominent Northern men to go down and witness the canvass. Unfortunately, he seems to have had no confidence in the fairness of Democrats, for he confined his requests to Republicans. The Democrats, on their side, had a corresponding distrust of Republican fairness; leading members of the party therefore packed their grips and journeyed southward. Within a few days after the election each disputed state had within its borders delegations of "visiting statesmen," each of whom was eager to safeguard the interests of the nation by securing the vote of the state for his particular candidate.

Now followed a period of the most intense suspense and excitement, marked also by ever-increasing bitterness of feeling. During the first part of this period the attention of the country was fixed upon the states in which the result was being contested. To give an account of the situation in these states will be the province of the next four chapters.

CHAPTER VI

THE CONTEST IN FLORIDA

Just how much the election of 1876 lacked of being "fair and free" in the state of Florida[1] no historian will ever be able to determine. That it did fall short of this ideal, is as certain as the fact that Hayes was inaugurated, or that the supporters of Tilden believed he was cheated out of a four years' residence in the White House. Both parties were about equally guilty, though their methods in the main were different; intimidation was the chief weapon used by the Democrats, and frauds in the conduct of the election and in the count were those used by the Republicans.

The task of determining the extent of the intimidation is a difficult, in fact, a hopeless one. It is all the more difficult because some of the evidence was

---

[1] The Republican state convention renominated Marcellus L. Stearns for governor and adopted a platform indorsing the state government as wise, just, and economical. The Democratic convention nominated George F. Drew for governor, and adopted a platform arraigning both state and national governments for corruption, extravagance, and oppression. Senator S. B. Conover, who had been accused of peculation by the Stearns Republicans, ran for a time as an independent Republican candidate, but in September withdrew. As the state debt was but $1,329,757.68, the state tax levy but seven mills on the dollar, and the expenditures but $190,000 while the receipts were about $220,000, the Democratic cry of extravagance was not particularly effective.—*Annual Cyclopaedia*, 1876, pp. 294-295; files of the Jacksonville *Daily Florida Union*.

probably manufactured out of whole cloth; for, both before and after the election, it was to the advantage of the Republicans to make it appear that intimidation was resorted to by their opponents. Nevertheless, when all due allowance has been made for the work of the "political outrage mills," the fact remains that there were many genuine outrages. The acceptance by Southern Democrats of the Fifteenth Amendment had never been anything save mere lip service; among them there was a pretty definitely conceived determination to eliminate as much of the negro vote as possible. To one who understands the full significance of this fact, even though he may be ignorant of the details of the particular case, the conclusion that intimidation was resorted to in Florida is the most natural in the world. But the conclusion is not a mere theory; it rests upon an overwhelming mass of evidence.

The methods employed were various. The "Mississippi plan," in a somewhat milder form than the original, was tried in some districts.[1] Armed men presented themselves at Republican meetings, demanded half of the time for their own speakers, and frequently subjected the Republican speakers to interruption and abuse.[2] In some instances negroes were

[1] S. R. No. 611 Part 2, 44th Cong. 2d Sess., p. 45.
[2] Some cases had an amusing side. At one public debate a negro speaker was continually interrupted by a white man, the burden of whose remarks was, "How many chickens have you stole?" When the negro attempted to turn the matter aside by saying he would like to have some chicken and would be glad, if given any, to return the favor, the white man took the badinage as an assertion of social equality and assaulted the negro, who did not dare to defend himself for fear of the other whites.— *Ibid*, p. 347. For other instances see pp. 173, 201.

threatened with death if they affiliated with Republicans, and were forced to join Democratic clubs.[1] There is evidence to show that in at least one instance an attempt was made to assassinate a prominent Republican candidate, State Senator Meacham of Jefferson county.[2] In a few districts the negroes were reduced to such a state of fear that hardly a Republican vote was cast.[3] In two of the wilder counties conditions were such that, at least after the election, Republicans did not dare travel there except under the protection of a pass from the Democratic state committee.[4]

In general, however, intimidation took a rather milder form. From the point of view of politics it was not to the interest of the Democratic party that much real violence should occur, for that might arouse the North. The work was to be done quietly; instances like those given above were therefore exceptional. Conditions were such that the work could be done quietly. The negroes, Republicans practically to a man, were almost as numerous as the white Democrats;[5] but they were still timid as a result of slavery and were quite incapable of holding their own in a physical contest with their opponents. Most of the white Republicans, the leaders of the blacks, lived in the towns and villages, and hence were frequently unable to afford much assistance to their sable allies,

---

1 S. R. No. 611, Part 2, 44th Cong. 2d Sess., pp. 241-253.

2 *Ibid*, pp. 335 *et seq.; Daily Florida Union,* Oct. 28.

3 L. c., S. R. No. 611, Part 2, 44th Cong. 2d Sess., p. 352.

4 *Ibid*, pp. 16, 364-368, 420.

5 The number of negroes according to the census of 1870 was 91,689, of whites 96,057.

the majority of whom resided in the sparsely settled country. [1] The number of political outrages in. Florida had not been so large as in some other states, but it had been large enough to instill a deep-seated dread into the minds of the freedmen. [2] In many cases, therefore, it was natural that a threat alone should prove sufficient to cool a negro's political ardor. Furthermore, the vast majority of the blacks were wholly dependent economically upon the white Democrats; and this fact afforded an opportunity of which full advantage was taken. Negro renters were given to understand that if they made themselves obnoxious politically, they would be ousted. Field hands were told that if they affiliated with the Republicans they would not be employed. [3] The following from the Monticello *Weekly Constitution* of November 9th is significant:

"The election is now over, and the contest is decided, but there remains a very important duty for the citizens of Jefferson [county] to perform. That they will discharge it impartially, even though it may conflict with their individual interests, we have not a doubt. *It is embraced in the following resolutions adopted and frequently reiterated by the reformers during the campaign;* and we call upon every man to enforce them to the very letter, to wit:
"1. That we pledge ourselves, each to the other,

[1] See H. R. R. No. 140, 45th Cong. 3d Sess., pp. 77-78, for a somewhat partisan discussion of these points.

[2] For accounts of some of these outrages see the Ku Klux Conspiracy reports, Vol. XIII, pp. 82-310.

[3] See, for instance, S. R. No. 611 Part 2, 44th Cong. 2d Sess., pp. 336, 343.

by our sacred honor, to give the first preference in all things to those who vote for reform; and that we give the second preference in all things to those who do not vote at all.

"2. That we affirm the principle that they who vote for high taxes should pay them, and that in employing or hiring or renting land to any such persons as vote for high taxes, in all such cases a distinction of 25 per cent, or one-fourth, be made against such persons. That merchants, lawyers, and doctors, in extending credit to such persons, make the same distinction.

"3. That in all such cases we extend as little credit or use of our means as possible, leaving them to their chosen friends.

"4. That in the ensuing year we positively refuse to re-employ one out of every three who may then be upon our places and who voted against reform and low taxes; and that a list of all such persons be published in the *Constitution,* in order that we may know our friends from our enemies.

"5. That we consider it dishonorable and unneighborly for any farmer, planter, merchant, lawyer, doctor, or any other person to violate any of the foregoing resolutions." [1]

In many cases no doubt the intimidators were content with keeping the blacks away from the polls, but in others the negroes were required to vote the Democratic ticket. The device of numbered ballots was used

---

1 S. R. No. 611 Part 2, 44th Cong. 2d Sess., p. 46. The use of the device indicated by these resolutions seems to have been tolerably common, though, for obvious reasons, not many such resolutions were published. This was published when caution was deemed unnecessary. Probably it would not have appeared a day or two later. There were instances during the campaign of such notices being posted in public places.

to a considerable extent to insure that an intimidated or purchased freedman voted as instructed; individuals given such ballots were told that if the ballots were not found in the boxes a reckoning would be exacted later. Thirty such ballots were voted at one poll, seventeen at another, and smaller numbers at others. All were counted, although their use was contrary to the law providing for a secret ballot.[1]

There was, of course, another side to the matter of intimidation. Occasionally pressure appears to have been brought to bear by Republican negroes upon negroes who showed Democratic leanings. At a place in Jefferson county, for example, a white Democrat named Bellamy and a contingent of negroes under his influence were attacked on their way to a polling-place by a mob of negro women and boys, who pelted them with sticks, bricks, and other missiles.[2] Probably there were more serious cases than this, but the number cannot have been large, for the number of Democratic negroes was small; campaign assertions of Southern Democratic politicians notwithstanding, there has never been, either in Florida or elsewhere, any considerable tendency of negroes, when left to themselves, to vote the Democratic ticket.

On the whole, the election proper passed off without any considerable disorder. A threatened invasion by

---

1 S. R. No. 611 Part 2, 44th Cong. 2d Sess., pp. 283-303; Doc. Evidence, pp. 141-144, 429-442. It was admitted by Democratic counsel before the canvassing board that marked ballots were used, and the right of employers to do so was defended!—*Ibid*, p. 143.

2 H. R. Mis. Doc. No. 35, Part 2, 44th Cong. 2d Sess., pp. 172 *et seq.* See also pp. 355, 373, 377.

Georgia Democrats, against which the Republican
state committee had warned the people and against
which Governor Stearns had fulminated in a proclamation, [1] did not take place. In some places arms were
displayed with too much freedom, and Republican challengers appear to have been intimidated at a few polls, [2]
but there was little or no bloodshed.

The election was conducted in accordance with a
law passed in 1868 and amended in 1872. The law
provided for a registration prior to the election by the
clerk of the circuit court in each county and for a subsequent revision of the list by the county commissioners. Each polling-place was ,in charge of three
inspectors appointed by the county commissioners and
of a clerk chosen by the inspectors. The law required
these inspectors to canvass the vote before adjourn-
·ment. Certificates of the vote must be sent to the
clerk of the circuit court and to the county judge. On
or before the sixth day after the election, the clerk,
the county judge, and a justice of the peace must
meet in the office of the clerk and canvass the returns
of the county. Should the clerk or the judge be
absent or unable to attend, the sheriff was empowered to act in his place. The result of the canvass
was then to be recorded by the clerk in a book kept
by him for that purpose, and duplicate certificates
were to be made out and forwarded to the secretary
of state and to the governor. The final canvass of

---

1 *Annual Cyclopædia,* 1876, pp. 296-297.
2 See, for example, S. R. No. 611, Part 2, 44th Cong.
2d Sess., p. 258 ; and Documentary Evidence, pp. 412, 413, 420.

the returns was to be made on or before the thirty-fifth day after election by the board of state canvassers, composed of the secretary of state, the attorney-general, and the comptroller of public accounts, or of "any two of them, together with any other member of the cabinet who may be designated by them." [1]

The members of this board were Samuel B. McLin, the secretary of state; Dr. Clayton A. Cowgill, the comptroller; and William Archer Cocke, the attorney-general. McLin, a native of Tennessee, was the editor of the Tallahassee *Sentinel,* had formerly been a Whig, had served in the Confederate army, but had deserted from it, and was now a Republican and hence what was termed a "scalawag." Dr. Cowgill, a native of Delaware, had been a surgeon in the Union army, and was likewise a Republican. Cocke, a native of Virginia, was a Democrat. [2]

The board did its work under the eyes, encouragement, and advice of a number of distinguished politicians from outside the state. On November 12th Mr. W. E. Chandler had arrived in Tallahassee, and had soon been joined by ex-Governor Noyes of Ohio, John A. Kasson of Iowa, General Lew Wallace, later famous as the author of *Ben Hur,* Francis C. Barlow of New York, and other Republicans, some of them salaried government employees. A number of prominent Democrats, including ex-Governor Brown of

---

1 The law is given in S. R. No. 611, Part 2, 44th Cong. 2d Sess., pp. 21-28.

2 *Annual Cyclopaedia,* 1876, p. 298; Jacksonville *Florida Union,* Nov. 28th.

Georgia, C. W. Woolley of Ohio, and John F. Coyle and Mr. Manton Marble of New York, had likewise gathered in the Florida capital to look after Democratic interests. Both contingents were well equipped with the "sinews of war," and both were active in advancing the interests of their respective candidates by collecting affidavits and testimony and by acting as counsel before the canvassing board.

Some of "the visiting statesmen" did not confine themselves to such legitimate work as that just described. On the part of the Democrats, negotiations were conducted looking to the purchase of one or more members of the canvassing board and perhaps of the governor; two propositions were transmitted to New York; a reply was received directing one of them to be accepted; but in the end the attempt at bribery failed. On the other side, the Republicans are accused of having stiffened the faltering by assurances that in case Hayes were counted in, he would "take care of" his Southern friends.[1]

The canvassing board met and began its work on the 27th of November. Six visiting statesmen from each party were admitted to the proceedings, and this number was subsequently increased to ten. The same courtesy was also extended to Governor Stearns, who was a candidate for re-election, to his opponent, George F. Drew, and to General Brannan, commander of the Federal troops in Florida.[2]

---

1 See chapter XIII.
2 Proceedings of the board, S. R. No. 611, Part 2, 44th Cong. 2d Sess., pp. 414-416.

Despite the assertions of partisan writers, there was at first little question as to the nature of the board's powers. In 1871 in the case of Bloxham *vs.* Board of State Canvassers it had been held that the board's powers were "mainly ministerial;"[1] but this decision had been rendered before the amendment of 1872, which provided that "If any such returns shall be shown or shall appear to be so irregular, false, or fraudulent that the board shall be unable to determine the true vote for any such officer or member, they shall so certify, and shall not include such return in their determination and declaration; and the secretary of state shall preserve and file in his office all such returns, together with such other documents and papers as may have been received by him or said board of canvassers." In 1874, in fact, the Democratic member of the board, Attorney-General Cocke, had written a formal opinion to the effect that this amendment conferred discretionary powers, and the board in canvassing the vote that year had acted in accordance with his view of the matter.[2] The board adopted the same view now; received written protests, arguments, affidavits, and documentary proofs; heard witnesses; and

---

1 13 Florida, p. 73. The court held, however, that the board possessed the "quasi-judicial" power of determining whether papers purporting to be returns were genuine and properly authenticated.

2 Testimony of Attorney-General Cocke, S. R. No. 611, Part 2, 44th Cong. 2d Sess., pp. 27-29. The opinion is given on page 27. Gibson in A Political Crime, pp. 27-28, and Bigelow in his Life of Tilden, II, pp. 23-24, charge that the exercise of discretionary powers was a bare-faced usurpation, that it was generally recognized that the board's powers were purely ministerial. Gibson quotes the decision of 1871, but fails to state that it was rendered before the amendment.

ultimately exercised their discretionary powers by rejecting returns. [1]

Seven public sessions were held, and then on Tuesday, December 5th, at a private session, the returns were finally canvassed. The board did its work in an unpardonably partisan manner, though in so doing, as was remarked at the time, it merely followed examples recently set by the Democratic majority in the national House of Representatives. In the case of Platt *vs.* Goode, the Democratic representatives, against the earnest protest of the Democratic chairman of the committee which investigated the case, had thrown out an entire Virginia county, which had given the Republican contestant an overwhelming majority, for the sole reason that a few words of attestation upon the return were omitted, although a copy correctly certified and attested was offered in evidence. [2] In the opinion of General Barlow, who was perhaps the fairest witness of the Florida count, this precedent, "far more flagrantly wrong" than any decision "made in the Florida case," greatly affected the judgment of the Republican members of the canvassing board. [3]

---

1 See the written arguments submitted to the board, *Ibid,* Documentary Evidence, pp. 1-18. The Democratic counsel took a middle view on the question.—See pp. 16-17.

2 See Congressional Record, 44th Cong. 1st Sess., pp. 4882 *et seq.*; and Digest of Election Cases, 1871 to 1876, H. R. Mis. Doc. No. 52 45th Cong. 2d Sess., pp. 650 *et seq.* For another almost equally flagrant case see Abbott *vs.* Frost, *Ibid,* pp. 594 *et seq.* Abbott was seated, and was later one of the Democratic members of the electoral commission. As such he drew up the scathing protest of the "Seven." This House, it should be said, was not the only one in which contests have been decided in a partisan way; the practice is a common one.

3 Letter of Barlow to President Grant, S. R. No. 611, Part 4, 44th Cong. 2d Sess., p. 12.

On the face of the returns, as the Republican members of the board conceived the returns, the vote for the Hayes electors was 24,337; for the Tilden electors 24,292.[1] However, only 26 counties were canvassed according to the face of the returns; in all the others the board exercised discretionary powers, rejected certain precincts and one whole county, and thereby raised the majority for the lowest Hayes elector over the highest Tilden elector to 924.[2]

To set forth in detail how this result was reached would require several hundred pages of print. A few instances will serve to show the spirit in which the work was done.

Baker county was one of the chief bones of contention. From that county there were three returns, only one of which was made out in seeming legal form. As already explained, the law provided that "on the sixth day after an election, or sooner if the returns shall have been received, it shall be the duty of the county judge and the clerk of the circuit court to meet at the office of the said clerk, and take to their assistance a justice of the peace of the said county (and in case of the absence, sickness, or other disability of the county judge or clerk, the sheriff shall act in his place) and shall publicly proceed to canvass the votes given for the several offices and persons as shown by the returns." It appears that the county judge, Elisha W. Driggers, notified the clerk, M. J.

---

1 S. R. No. 611, Part 2, 44th Cong. 2d Sess., p. 17.
2 *Ibid*, pp. 12 and 18-19.

Cox, to meet with him on Monday, November 13th, the sixth day after the election; but Cox, who was a Democrat, associated with himself a justice named Dorman, and on the 10th, while the judge was out of the county, the two, the sheriff refusing to act with them, made up a return. This return was not regular, for it had not been made by all the officers required by law. On the 13th the clerk, having meanwhile grown uneasy because of the irregularity of his proceeding, requested the judge to join with him in making another canvass. This the judge refused to do on the ground that the clerk's action in making the previous canvass constituted a refusal to act with the judge. The clerk and the justice thereupon proceeded to make a second canvass, which, however, was no more regular than the first. Now came the turn of the judge and the sheriff. These two worthies, in accordance with a plan already formed, met that evening, together with a justice especially commissioned for the purpose by the governor, in the clerk's office, to which the deputy clerk had given the judge the key, and proceeded to make a new canvass of the votes. In so doing they threw out, on the plea of fraud, two precincts which had given Democratic majorities; this they had no legal right to do, although it appears that such a practice had occasionally been followed in the past. The three then made out certificates, regular on their face, and forwarded them as required by law. It was by counting this return that the Republicans made it appear that on the face of the returns the state had gone for Hayes.[1]

The state canvassing board did not, however, accept the Driggers return. Instead they exercised discretionary power, canvassed the county by precincts, and counted the vote of the whole county as it had actually been cast, 143 votes for the Hayes electors and 238 votes for the Tilden electors. In this proceeding the Democratic member, Judge Cocke, concurred.[2]

Had the board stopped here, the state would have been given to Tilden, but they did not do so. They proceeded to go behind the returns in other counties. In Hamilton county 83 Democratic and 58 Republican votes were thrown out, because they had been illegally added to the return after it had been completed and signed. In the same county Jasper Precinct No. 2, which gave 323 votes for the Democratic electors and 185 votes for the Republican electors, was rejected on the ground that the inspectors had not completed the canvass until after an adjournment, had allowed unauthorized persons to handle the ballots and assist in the count, and had next day signed a return which they had neither made nor verified.[3] The attorney-general concurred in this action, but later, after

---

1 The evidence bearing on Baker County is very voluminous. See index to Baker County on p. 470 of S. R. No. 611, Part 2, 44th Cong. 2d Sess.; Documentary Evidence, pp. 76-82; H. R. Mis. Doc. No. 35, Part 1, 44th Cong. 2d Sess., pp. 284-300; and index to testimony regarding Baker County on p. 12 of H. R. Mis. Doc. No. 31, Part 5, 45th Cong. 3d Sess.

2 See minutes of board in Senate report above cited, p. 9.

3 *Ibid,.*

consultation with his party associates, protested against it in a written protest. [1]

In the town of Key West, Precinct No. 3, which gave 401 Democratic votes and 59 Republican votes, was thrown out on the plea that the inspectors had adjourned before the completion of the canvass, and had completed it the next day at a different place, without public notice. In addition, there was proof that there had been threats of violence and that the Republican challengers had been intimidated. The board did not, however, take this proof into account, holding that this was a matter over which the law defining their powers did not give them jurisdiction. [2] Judge Cocke at first concurred in throwing out the poll, but later wished to change his vote, and did denounce the board's action in his written protest. [3]

In Jackson county, Campbellton Precinct and Friendship Church Precinct, both of which gave considerable Democratic majorities, were thrown out. The first was rejected "on account of the violation of the election laws by the inspectors in removing the ballot-box from the election room at the adjournment for dinner into an adjoining store, and leaving it unsealed and concealed from the public during said adjournment; in not counting the ballots at the close of the polls and comparing them with the number of names on the poll-lists, and because only seventy-six Republican votes were counted out of the ballot-box,

---

1 S. R. No. 611, Part 2, 44th Cong. 2d Sess., pp. 33 and 41.
2 *Ibid*, pp. 9-10.
3 *Ibid*, pp. 6, 14, 30, 31, 33.

whereas 133 persons swear that they voted the full Republican ticket." The other precinct was thrown out because the inspectors placed the ballot-box in such a position as to be out of sight of the voter and of the public; because they did not complete the canvass at the polling place but in a bed-room two miles away; and because they did not count the ballots and compare them with the names on the polling-list. The attorney-general opposed the rejection of either of these precincts.[1]

The vote of Manatee county was thrown out on the plea that there had been an "entire absence of any and all legal steps in preparation for the election and in holding the same." In the main this was true. In the preceding September the clerk of the circuit court had resigned, and the person appointed by the governor to succeed him was either unable to give bond or purposely refrained from doing so. In consequence no registration was made, and the election was an informal one at which 262 votes had been cast for the Tilden electors and only 26 for the Hayes electors. By the Democrats it was claimed that the situation was a result of a Republican conspiracy, but whether or not such was the case the evidence does not conclusively show; it is possible that it was in part due to the fact that the county was a remote one on the edge of the Everglades and communication with it was slow and difficult. The exclusion of the county was objected to by the attorney-general.[2]

1 S. R. No. 611, Part 2, 44th Cong. 2d Sess., pp. 7, 10, 42.
2 *Ibid*, pp. 32-33.

Numerous changes of less importance were made, in most of which all three members concurred. Some of these changes were favorable to the Democrats, but did not affect the general result. That result, as finally promulgated, showed a substantial majority for Hayes, the election of the Republican state ticket, which had run some three hundred votes behind the national ticket, and also that of both of the Republican candidates for Congress. [1]

As has already been stated, the canvass was conducted in a highly partisan manner. In every important instance in which votes were thrown out the advantage inured to the Republicans. Furthermore, the majority of the board refused to eliminate other returns, the validity of which was questioned, when by so doing they would have seriously diminished the Republican vote. There were many such cases, but a few of the most conspicuous will suffice. Proof was brought to show that at Archer Precinct No. 2, Alachua county, 219 names had been fraudulently put upon the polling-list and the same number of votes added to the Republican majority. [2] Proof was also adduced to show that at Richardson's School House Precinct, Leon county, 73 "little joker" Republican bal-

---

1 S. R. No. 611, Part 2, 44th Cong. 2d Sess., pp. 9-10, 18-19, 32-33.

2 *Ibid*, see index pp. 469-470; Documentary Evidence, pp. 24 *et seq.*; H. R. Mis. Doc. No. 35, Part 1, 44th Cong. 2d Sess., see index pp. 304-305; contested election case of Finley *vs.* Bisbee, H. R. R. No. 95, 45th Cong. 3d Sess.; and H. R. Mis. Doc. No. 31, 45th Cong. 3d Sess., especially testimony of L. G. Dennis, I. pp. 477, 483, 554, 853. Dennis was one of the Republican election officers, and two years later, out of revenge for having been removed from office by the Administration, made a "confession" to the Potter Committee.

lots had been smuggled into the ballot-box, while to cover up the trick the poll-list had been correspondingly increased. [1]   There were irregularities of form in the return from Duval county, which gave a large Republican majority; [2] there was proof that there had been irregularities in the conduct of the election in certain Republican precincts in Jefferson county and elsewhere. [3]   Yet in all these cases, as well as in several others, the majority of the board voted to canvass the returns without change. [4]

What the result would have been if the returns had been canvassed by an unpartisan board it is impossible to say with certainty.   At the same time it is clear that if none of the returns had been rejected and if in Baker county the return containing all the precincts had been substituted for the Driggers return, the result would have been a majority for the lowest Tilden elector over the highest Hayes elector of 93 votes. [5]   How nearly these returns corresponded to the votes in the ballot-boxes can never be ascertained. Frauds in the count and return of votes were unquestionably committed by both sides.   In this kind of work the Republicans had the advantage of having a small majority of the election officers, but this was probably counterbalanced by the ease with which shrewd Democrats could hoodwink the illiterate ne-

1 H. R. Mis. Doc. No. 35, Part 1, 44th Cong. 2d Sess., pp. 1-80;
H. R. Mis. Doc. No. 31, 45th Cong. 3d Sess., II., pp. 94-96.
2 Documentary Evidence, pp. 113 *et seq.*
3 *Ibid,* p. 261 *et seq.*
4 Senate report above cited, pp. 1-43.
5 *Ibid,* pp. 402-409.

groes who acted as election officers in many places.[1]
On the whole, it is not improbable that an unpartisan
board, acting on the same theory of its powers as did
the actual board, would have held that the returns
did not in all cases correspond to the votes in the ballot-boxes, would have thrown out some returns contrary to the interests of each party, but would in the
end have found a small majority for Tilden. The
least partisan man who witnessed the count, namely
General Barlow, took that view of the case. He had
gone to Florida at the request of Grant, he was a
Republican, but he came to the conclusion that on the
evidence the board should give Tilden a majority of
from 30 to 55. He even urged one of the Republican
members of the board to adopt such a course, but
without effect.[2] Whether General Barlow's opinion
in the case was in any measure due to a tendency
sometimes noticeable in high-minded persons to concede all doubtful points to an opponent, it is impossible to say; certain it is that his opinion, though admit-
tedly based on only part of the evidence, is entitled to
very great weight.

But there is another aspect of the case which must
not be lost sight of by the investigator who would
arrive at the true merits of the tangled election of
1876 — an aspect which the canvassing board deemed

---

1 For an expression on this point see H. R. R. No. 140, 45th
Cong. 3d Sess., p. 84.

2 See two letters written by Barlow after his return from
Florida, S. R. No. 611, Part 4, 44th Cong. 2d Sess., pp. 12-13;
also his testimony before the Potter Committee, H. R. Mis. Doc.
No. 31, 45th Cong. 3d Sess., I, pp. 1361, 1388, 1408.

lay without its powers and one not taken into account by General Barlow. While a *fair count* of the votes cast in the state of Florida might have resulted in a small majority for Tilden, a *free election* would with far greater certainty have resulted in a substantial majority for Hayes. The board did not throw out votes, not even "marked ballots," on the score of intimidation; yet no one familiar with the evidence and with the attitude of the Southern Democrats toward negro suffrage will for a moment doubt that there was sufficient intimidation to change the whole result. To be sure, there was no such sweeping suppression of the negro vote as there was in Louisiana, South Carolina, Mississippi, Alabama, and some other states; but when the result was so close, that was not necessary. When all due allowances are made, therefore, it is a not unfair conclusion that *in equity* the electoral votes of the state of Florida belonged to Hayes.

The labors of the canvassing board were completed on the night of December 5th. On the following day, the date set by Federal law, the Republican electors met and cast their votes for Hayes and Wheeler.[1] The result, properly certified, was then dispatched to the president of the Senate.

The Democratic electors, although declared elected by no properly constituted authority, likewise met on

---

[1] The subject of the alleged ineligibility of Humphreys, one of the Republican electors, will be discussed in the chapter on the work of the Electoral Commission. It was also claimed that Charles H. Pearce, another elector, was ineligible, but the contention was ultimately given up. See S. R. No. 611, Part 4, 44th Cong. 2d Sess., p. 14.

the same day and cast their votes for Tilden and
Hendricks. The result, irregularly certified by Judge
Cocke, the attorney-general, was also forwarded to
Washington. [1]

Seemingly the situation was now sufficiently complicated, but it was to become much more so. George
F. Drew, the Democratic candidate for governor, petitioned the state supreme court for a *mandamus* to compel the canvassing board to canvass the returns of the
votes for governor in a strictly ministerial way. The
court, a majority of whom were Democratic in sympathy, [2] granted the petition. In so doing the court
dissented from the view "that the board of state canvassers is a tribunal having power strictly judicial,
such as is involved in the determination of the legality
of a particular vote or election." "All the acts which
this board can do under the statute," the court held,
"must be based upon the returns; and while in some
cases the officers composing the board may, like all
ministerial officers of a similar character, exclude what
purports to be a return for irregularity, still everything
they are authorized to do is limited to what is sanc-
tioned by authentic and true returns before them.
. . . . They have no general power to issue sub-
pœnas, to summon parties, to compel the attendance
of witnesses, to grant a trial by jury, or to do any act
but determine and declare who has been elected as

1 Both these certificates of votes are given in Electoral Count,
pp. 11-13.
2 Testimony of Geo. P. Raney, Democratic attorney general
under Drew, H. R. Mis. Doc. No. 31, Part 2, 45th Cong. 3d Sess.,
p. 59.

shown by the returns." The board must confine itself
to ascertaining and certifying the votes "actually cast,"
and must not assume the power to go behind the returns in an effort to ascertain the "legal vote," this
being a matter upon which the courts alone were
competent to decide. On December 23d the *mandamus* was issued. [1]

Under protest of the Republican members the board
reconvened, and after a second canvass of the returns
announced that Drew had received 24,179 votes and
Stearns 23,984 votes. In so doing the majority members, against the wishes of the Democratic member,
counted the Driggers return from Baker county as
being the only one regular in form, and threw out the
vote of Clay county because the return was so irregular that they could not, from it alone, ascertain the
true vote. Then, although the writ had merely directed them to recanvass the vote for governor, the
board, or rather the two Republican members, re-ex-
amined the vote for electors, and reported "that a recanvass of them, according to the said decision," would
show that the Republican electors had received majorities averaging about 211 votes. [2] This result was
made possible by the fact that Stearns had run some
hundreds of votes behind the Republican national
ticket.

The matter by no means rested here. The Democratic electors had already petitioned the court of the

1 The proceedings in this suit are given in S. R. No. 611, Part
2, 44th Cong. 2d Sess., pp. 388-401.
2 *Ibid,* pp. 400-401.

second judicial circuit for a writ of information in the nature of a *quo warranto* against the Republican electors, and a summons had been served upon the respondents just before they voted. The suit was later prosecuted to a conclusion, and on January 25th the judge of the court, P. W. White, a Democratic partisan, issued an order to the effect that the Democratic electors had been rightfully chosen.[1] The case was then appealed, but was never again brought to trial.[2]

Meanwhile the Democrats had displayed zeal in yet another field of activity. On the 2d of January their candidate for governor was inaugurated at Tallahassee without opposition;[3] the newly elected legislature was convened; and "an act to procure a legal canvass of the electoral vote of the state of Florida as cast at the election held on the 7th day of November, A. D., 1876," was passed and approved. The act created a canvassing board composed in much the same manner as the previous one had been, and it ordered the members of this new board to convene and recanvass the vote. The board, all the members of which were Democrats, did as ordered, and on January 19th certified the election of the Democratic electors by majorities over the highest Hayes elector of from 87 to 90 votes.[4]

A few days later the legislature formally declared that the Democratic electors had been duly elected.

1 H. R. R. No. 143, Part 1, 44th Cong. 2d Sess., p. 8 ; Part 2, p. 11 ; H. R. Mis. Doc. No. 35, Part 3, pp. 81-82.
2 Proceedings of the Electoral Commission, p. 56.
3 *The Nation*, XXIV, p. 19 ; *Florida Union*, Jan. 3d and 4th.
4 H. R. R. No. 35, Part 3, 44th Cong. 2d Sess., pp. 70-79.

It also directed the governor to make and certify "three lists of the names of the said electors," together "with an authenticated copy of this act," and transmit the same to the president of the Senate. The electors themselves were directed to meet and make and sign three additional certificates of all the votes given by them on the 6th of December and transmit one of the same to the United States district judge and the other two, one by messenger and the other by mail, to the president of the Senate. [1] These things were done, [2] and the Florida farce was complete.

1 H. R. R. No. 35, Part 3, 44th Cong. 2d Sess., pp. 80-81.
2 *Ibid,* pp. 70-71.

CHAPTER VII

BULLDOZERS AND RETURNING OFFICERS IN LOUISIANA

In perhaps no other state in the Union has there ever been such a disorderly condition of affairs as existed in Louisiana during the years from 1866 to 1877. Wholesale corruption, intimidation of negro voters by thousands and tens of thousands, political assassinations, riots, revolutions — all these were the order of the day in Louisiana politics.

That this reign of lawlessness exceeded that in any other of the reconstructed states was in part due to the nature of the population. The white inhabitants were in large measure French and Spanish Creoles, who had both the virtues and the weaknesses of their ancestors. The ante-bellum society of Louisiana, and particularly of New Orleans, had been polite and even brilliant; yet the state had been one of the least law-abiding of any of the long-settled communities. The custom of the duello was firmly fixed, and in the metropolis frequent bloody encounters took place beneath the moss-hung "duelling oaks" in what is now the city park.[1] Occasionally this lack of respect for

---

[1] Thompson, The Story of Louisiana, p. 248; King, New Orleans, pp. 292-299.

law revealed itself in political matters, as in the notorious Plaquemine frauds of 1844 [1] and the New Orleans riot of 1855, when for a time the city was in the hands of two rival factions, who seized public buildings and erected barricades. [2]   The freedmen, despite the presence of a considerable number of educated blacks in New Orleans, were on the average less intelligent than in most of the former slave states. This was in part due to conditions which had existed during slavery days.   The number of slaves had been exceedingly large, and most of them had lived on great plantations where civilizing contact with the superior race had been unusually slight.   Furthermore, many of the slaves had been persons of desperate or criminal character who in punishment had been sold "down the river."

As elsewhere in the South, the whites of Louisiana did not take kindly to emancipation.   They took still less kindly to enfranchisement.   The idea that the negro was "divinely created to be servant to the white" had so long been instilled into the Southern mind that it was an article of faith.   The possibility of the black man's occupying any other position was a thing unthinkable.   So long as the negro remained in his "place" the Southern white man was in a sense his friend, but any attempt on the part of the freedman to assert equal privileges became as a red rag to a bull.   As the negro was now "the nation's ward," he was a convenient

---

1 Sargent's Life of Clay, p. 254.
2 Gayarré, History of Louisiana, IV, p. 679 ; Thompson, p. 255.

object on which the unthinking could vent their impotent hatred for the North. This tendency was vastly increased by the outrageous manner in which the negro—too often at the instigation of Northern bureau agents—abused his new-found liberty. As a result of these and other causes, there followed throughout the South a period replete with instances of brutal outrage and murder. In Louisiana, owing partly to reasons already described, the number of these crimes was particularly great. [1]

An argument frequently employed in justifying the outrages on the freedmen is that the whites were goaded into it by the evils of negro domination. The argument holds good in part, but only in part, for unhappily outrages were committed before the suffrage was conferred upon the blacks, before such a step was even favored by any considerable number of Northern people. Had such outrages never occurred, it may well be doubted whether sweeping negro suffrage would have been bestowed; for the argument that the negro needed a weapon with which to defend himself was unquestionably a deciding factor with thousands of persons to whom the partisan political motive did not appeal.

Louisiana was one of the states in which the whites

---

1 H. R. Ex. Doc. No. 30, 44th Cong. 2d Sess., pp. 458-540, contains a partial list (not wholly reliable) of the murders and outrages. See also S. Ex. Doc. No. 43, 39th Cong. 1st Sess.; H. R. R. No. 16, 39th Cong. 2d Sess.; H. R. R. No. 101, 43d Cong. 2d Sess., various other congressional documents, and the newspapers of the time. My own conclusions are in large measure based upon files of the New Orleans newspapers.

did not wait to see the fruits of negro rule before falling upon the hapless freedmen. The first important conflict took place in New Orleans in July, 1866, as a result of an attempt of the radicals, with the consent of the governor and a judge of the state supreme court, to reconvene the constitutional convention of 1864 in order to enfranchise the blacks. Mayor Monroe made preparations to suppress the convention; a riot occurred; and a most inhuman massacre resulted, in which about forty negroes and white radicals were killed and about 136 were wounded. [1]

The next important race conflicts occurred in the late summer and fall of 1868. In the spring of that year an election was held at which the new constitution was ratified and at which H. C. Warmoth, Republican candidate for governor, was elected by a majority of over 26,000. Later in the year the Knights of the White Camelia, an organization similar to the Ku Klux, entered upon a campaign of violence and intimidation, with the result that the Republican majority of the spring was transformed into a Democratic plurality of about 46,000 for Seymour. This astonishing reversal was later explained by Republican members of a congressional investigating committee in the following language:

<hr>

1 The convention appears to have had no legal right to reassemble, but, on the other hand, the mayor's action was unwarranted. For an account of the affair and an unqualified condemnation of the mayor see Cox, Three Decades of Federal Legislation, pp. 430-432. H. R. R. No. 16, 39th Cong. 2d Sess. contains a vast amount of testimony bearing upon the subject. The massacre was used with great effect by the Radical Republicans in the North. See also Rhodes, History of the United States from the Compromise of 1850, V, pp. 611-613.

"The testimony shows that over 2,000 persons were killed, wounded, and otherwise injured in Louisiana within a few weeks prior to the Presidential election in November, 1868; that half the state was overrun by violence; and that midnight raids, secret murders, and open riot kept the people in constant terror until the Republicans surrendered all claim. . . . . But the most remarkable case is that of St. Landry, a planting parish on the river Têche. Here the Republicans had a registered majority of 1,071 votes. In the spring of 1868 they carried the parish by 678. In the fall they gave Grant no vote, not one — while the Democrats cast 4,787, the full vote of the parish, for Seymour and Blair. Here occurred one of the bloodiest riots on record, in which the Ku Klux killed and wounded over 200 Republicans, hunting and chasing them for two days and nights through fields and swamps. Thirteen captives were taken from the jail and shot. A pile of twenty-five dead bodies was found half-buried in the woods. Having conquered the Republicans and killed and driven off the white leaders, the Ku Klux captured the masses, marked them with badges of red flannel, enrolled them in clubs, made them vote the Democratic ticket, and then gave them a certificate of the fact." [1]

A detailed account of the political history of Louisiana from 1868 to 1876 is in this connection unnecessary. In general the period was one in which the party in opposition, consisting of most of the white inhabitants, pursued a policy of intimidation, even to

---

[1] H. R. R. No. 261, 43d Cong. pp. 11-12. Quoted by Cox, pp. 551-552. Cox thinks the statement "a good deal exaggerated, especially as to the number killed," but "the failure of the negroes to vote can be explained only on the theory that a reign of terror existed." 28 parishes which in 1868 gave Grant but 5,360, gave 35,010 to the Republican candidate for auditor in 1870, when the election was a comparatively peaceful one.

the extent of assassination; while the party in power, consisting chiefly of negroes and white carpet-baggers, resorted to election frauds and to unblushing misappropriation of public funds. The value of property greatly decreased ;[1] the payment of taxes fell more than $2,000,000 in arrears; and the state debt was increased to enormous proportions.[2] In 1870 the Republicans quarreled among themselves; and Governor Warmoth went over to the Conservatives, as the Democrats were called. A period of great confusion followed. The election of 1872 was claimed by both parties; but the Republicans were able through the complaisance of United States District Judge Durell, who issued the famous "midnight restraining order," to obtain the all-important aid of the Federal troops, and to install William Pitt Kellogg as governor. McEnery, the Democratic claimant, was also inaugurated, but after a few weeks found himself obliged to abandon temporarily all efforts to assert his authority. On the 14th of September, 1874, however, the White League,

[1] This was due in part to the war, to the emancipation of hundreds of millions of dollars' worth of slaves, to the disorders incident to the change from one labor system to another, to the panic of the early '70s, but in large measure to misgovernment.

[2] The increase in the debt was not wholly the result of actual stealing from the state, although the amount stolen was large enough. Expenditures were increased as a result of the bad condition of the levees, of subsidies to companies (fraudulent in many cases but not always so) engaged in undertakings which it was hoped would help the development of the state, etc. Furthermore, tax receipts fell off as a result of the decrease in the value of property, while the state bonds were floated much below par. Financiers had little faith in Southern bonds, partly because of the unsettled conditions in that section, and partly because in the period before the war so many of the states in that section had repudiated their debts. What faith they had was mostly misplaced, for after the states were "redeemed" a large proportion of the bonds were repudiated.

an armed quasi-secret organization consisting of Conservatives, rose against the Kellogg government; a battle ensued in the streets of New Orleans; and Kellogg and his supporters were forced to take refuge in the custom-house. Once more the President interfered, and Kellogg was reinstated by Federal bayonets. During the ensuing two years little better than a state of anarchy existed in parts of Louisiana; in a few parishes the officials were either driven out or murdered, sometimes because they were of bad character or incompetent, but in some instances solely because they were negroes or white Republicans. [1]

Such was the condition of affairs when the campaign of 1876 opened. The Republicans were the first to put a ticket in the field. Their convention met at New Orleans on the 27th of June and after some stormy sessions nominated S. B. Packard for governor and renominated C. C. Antoine for lieutenant-governor. Packard, a native of Maine, had for some years been United States marshal of Louisiana, and had been closely associated with the custom-house coterie of Republicans who managed the state's affairs. Antoine was a negro, and is said to have been a native of San Domingo. The Democrats held their convention at Baton Rouge on the 24th of July, and selected as their candidates General F. T. Nicholls of Assumption Parish and Louis A. Wiltz of Orleans. Nicholls

<hr>

[1] This sketch is based chiefly upon the hundreds of pages of testimony contained in S. R. No. 457, 42d Cong. 3d Sess., and H. R. R. Nos. 261 and 101, 43d Cong. 2d Sess., and upon files of the New Orleans *Picayune* and New Orleans *Times*.

was a graduate of West Point, and had lost both an arm and a leg while fighting in the Confederate army in Virginia, but at this time was engaged in the practice of law. In their platform the Democrats denounced Republican rule, both state and national, affirmed their acceptance of the last three amendments to the Federal Constitution, pledged a free and fair election, and promised equal educational advantages to both races. [1]

The manner in which the campaign that followed was conducted by the two parties was affected to a considerable degree by the nature of the election laws. These laws had been framed with the end in view of enabling the party in power to neutralize the effect of violence and intimidation on the part of their Democratic opponents; for, as an observer has remarked, "What the Republicans lacked of the lion's skin they eked out with the fox's tail." [2] At the head of the electoral system created by these laws stood a state returning board, consisting of five members, chosen originally by the senate from all parties, but with the provision that the members themselves should fill vacancies. This tribunal had the discretionary power of inquiring under certain restrictions into the conduct of elections, and of rejecting the vote of any precinct or parish wherein force, or fraud, or fear so prevailed as materially to affect the result. The power just

---

1 *Annual Cyclopaedia*, 1876, pp. 481-483, and 493 ; files of New Orleans *Times* and *Republican*.

2 Benjamin F. Butler's report as a member of the Potter Committee, H. R. R. No. 140, 45th Cong. 3d Sess., p. 96.

described was an unusual one; yet, considered as a remedy, it was to a certain extent inadequate, for while it enabled the board to throw out votes, it did not enable them to add votes which would have been polled had there been no violence and intimidation. [1]

This fact furnished the Democrats an opportunity of which they appear to have cunningly taken advantage in this campaign. Their plan involved two features. [2] They purposed to carry on in most sections of the state a canvass that was entirely devoid of violence. They even took pains to propitiate the negroes; employed colored preachers and other leaders to speak for them; gave barbecues with music and other attractions; and in some districts in promises of equality "outstripped the Republicans." [3] This policy was especially pursued in those parishes which usually gave Democratic majorities; in such parishes the party managers strove hard to prevent the occurrence of any act of violence which would give the Republican returning board a pretext for rejecting the vote; and in the main they were successful in this effort, although outrages were occasionally committed by Democrats whose hot blood got the better of their discretion. On the other hand, in a few selected parishes, such as

1 Act 98 of 1872, given in Sen. Ex. Doc. No. 2, 44th Cong. 2d Sess., pp. 160-168. The author would not, of course, have the reader believe that he would for a moment advocate such a law.

2 This theory was set forth by the Republican "visiting statesmen" in their report to the President, *Ibid*, pp. 4-9. The Democrats vigorously attacked the theory, but it seems to me that it is a true one. Facts which appear to me to be conclusive are presented in succeeding pages.

3 Report of Democratic members of Potter Committee, H. R. R. No. 140, 45th Cong. 3d Sess., p. 29.

Ouachita, East and West Feliciana, East Baton Rouge, and Morehouse, the Democrats pursued entirely different tactics. These were parishes in which, since the great majority of voters were negroes, the Democrats had everything to gain and nothing to lose. If, by a process of "bulldozing" in any one of these parishes, they should succeed in destroying the Republican majority, they would, if the vote were allowed to stand, be gainers to the amount of the majority destroyed plus whatever majority they managed to secure. If, on the contrary, they succeeded, but the vote were rejected, then the Republicans were at least deprived of their normal majority. So it was with the other alternatives; in any case it was "heads I win, tails you lose" for the Democrats.[1]

Conditions in other respects were favorable for carrying out the Democratic plans. From numerous bitter experiences in the past the negroes had learned that when the whites entered upon a campaign of intimidation, it was safest to yield peacefully and gracefully to the inevitable. When, therefore, the white rifle-clubs began to ride about the country at night singing such ditties as,

"A charge to keep I have, a God to glorify;
If a nigger don't vote with us, he shall forever die."[2]

---

1 This was not a new scheme. In 1872, when the Warmoth election officers were in control, cases occurred where Democratic commissioners appear to have stuffed ballot-boxes at Republican polls in order to furnish a pretext on which the returning board might reject such polls.—S. R. No. 457, 42d Cong. 3d Sess., p. 77.

2 S. R. No. 701, 44th Cong. 2d Sess., p. 19.

many freedmen needed no further warning, but joined Democratic clubs, attended Democratic barbecues, and ate Democratic roast ox with the best of them. Others who were slightly more stubborn were induced to change their politics or at least to refrain from voting by being threatened with loss of employment. Yet others were whipped or otherwise maltreated, while a few, more unfortunate still, were roused from their beds at night and brutally murdered. Thanks to the work of past years, however, the amount of actual violence needed was comparatively small. In those parishes where there had been recent conflicts the task of intimidation was particularly easy. [1]

The success of the Democratic policy in the selected parishes was so great that the Republicans, seeing that a free election was impossible, decided in some cases to make merely nominal contests and to devote themselves to collecting evidence of the bulldozing in order that the returning board might have grounds for rejecting the parishes either in whole or in part. Thus, says a congressional investigator, there was "presented this singular spectacle: That in portions of the state an active and vigorous campaign was going on between the parties and in other portions of the state there was substantially no campaign at all." [2] The Democrats later claimed that the Republicans gave up the fight in these parishes because the negroes volun-

1 These conclusions rest upon practically the whole mass of testimony collected by the Congressional committees.

2 H. R. R. No. 140, 45th Cong. 3d Sess., p. 96.

tarily joined Democratic clubs, but the argument seems hardly a reasonable one. All the bulldozed parishes had two years before given large Republican majorities, and there is no real evidence to show that they would not have done so again had it not been for disorders and outrages during the campaign itself or during the year preceding it by which the negroes had been thoroughly cowed.

The Republicans did not, however, rest all their hopes of victory upon their success in collecting evidence of bulldozing. Another matter to which they devoted much attention in the course of the campaign was that of registration. The appointment of the supervisors of registration and their clerks was in the hands of Governor Kellogg, and he appointed Republicans almost exclusively.[1] Many of those chosen for the work already held state or Federal offices; some of them were men of low character, one, for example, having formerly been, it was said, the "roper-in" for a snake show.[2] The registration officers were regarded by the Republican campaign committee as under their direction; and detailed instructions were issued to the supervisors by D. J. M. A. Jewett, secretary of the committee on canvassing and registration. These instructions informed the supervisors that they were expected "to register and vote the full strength of the Republican party," and that results "once ob-

---

1 H. R. Mis. Doc. No. 34,, Part 2, 44th Cong. 2d Sess., pp. 713, *et seq.*

2 *Ibid*, pp. 443, 1049, etc.; H. R. Mis. Doc. No. 31, 45th Cong. 3d Sess., I, pp. 1105, 1109, 1129, 1464, 1467, etc.

tained," their "recognition" would "be ample and generous." [1]

Thus encouraged, the supervisors worked with great effectiveness. In fact, shortly before the election their lists showed a total of 115,268 colored voters or almost 8,000 more than the number of colored men of voting age according to the census taken in 1880. [2] Most of this excess appears to have been in the city of New Orleans, where, owing to the laxity of the registration officers in failing to prevent double registration and especially in failing to strike off the names of negroes who had died or who had removed from the ward, a negro population of 57,647 yielded the astonishing registration of 23,495. That these figures were subsequently decreased by 3,368, and that at the election the Republicans cast but 14,801 votes for their highest elector, or about their real strength, was due almost wholly to the vigilance of the Democrats, not to that of the registration or election officers.

On the other hand, the registration officers were active in helping to keep down the white registration to the lowest possible limit. In New Orleans, for example, they worked with the Republican managers in executing a very successful scheme for detecting illegal Democratic registration. About 29,000 "sewing machine circulars" were sent by the Republican campaign committee to the addresses of registered per-

---

1 H. R. Mis. Doc. No. 31, 45th Cong. 3d Sess., I, pp. 1074-1076, 1441.
2 The registration figures are given in H. R. Mis. Doc. No. 34, Part 2, 44th Cong. 2d Sess., p. 494.

sons not known to the Republican leaders; many thousands of these circulars were returned by the letter carriers as "not found;" canvassers were then sent out to make a second search; and when they reported that a given person did not live at the address given on the registration books, his name was stricken off. Many mistakes were made, and some of the names were later restored, but the white registration was decreased by about 4,500. The claim was later set up that many thousands of Democrats were thereby deprived of their right to vote, but the evidence does not bear out the claim.[1]

Some days passed after the election before the figures of the vote actually cast could be ascertained. At first the Republicans were inclined to believe that they had obtained a majority,[2] but after word had been received from the outlying parishes it was found that the Democratic plan had worked so beautifully that on the face of the returns the highest Tilden elector would receive about 84,000 votes and the lowest about 83,000 votes, while the highest Hayes elector would receive only about 76,000 votes and the lowest about 74,000 votes.[3] Upon the strength of this showing the Democratic press of the country with great positiveness claimed the state for Tilden. But the Republican

[1] For some of the testimony regarding registration see H. R. Mis. Doc. No. 31, 45th Cong. 3d Sess., I, pp. 1001, 1051-1056, 1064; H. R. Mis. Doc. No. 34, Part 2, 44th Cong. 2d Sess., pp. 311, 319, 329, 396, 471, 484, 500, 537, 539, 555, 599, 603, 635, 713, 754.

[2] Testimony of Jewett before Potter Committee, H. R. Mis. Doc. No. 31, 45th Cong. 3d Sess., I, p. 1441.

[3] H. R. R. No. 140, 45th Cong. 3d Sess., p. 97.

managers transmitted words of cheer to their brethren in other states. The returning board, said they, has not yet performed its work. Wait till it gets through with the parishes in which there has been wholesale intimidation, and then see if Tilden has a majority.[1]

As in the case of Florida, Louisiana at once became the goal for many prominent politicians of both parties. John Sherman, James A. Garfield, Eugene Hale, E. W. Stoughton, and other Republicans hurried to New Orleans by special request of the President, and were joined there by some who had not been so honored. Not to be outdone, a goodly number of Democrats, among whom were John M. Palmer, Lyman Trumbull, Samuel J. Randall, J. R. Doolittle, Henry Watterson, and Oswald Ottendorfer, obeyed telegrams received from Abram S. Hewitt, chairman of the Democratic national committee, and repaired to the Crescent City on a like mission.

On the day after the Democratic statesmen reached their destination they addressed to the Republican visitors a letter suggesting that, " in view of the unhappy controversies which have heretofore arisen from the action of the returning board of the state," the two contingents unite in exerting their influence "in behalf of such a canvass of the votes actually cast as by its fairness and impartiality shall command the respect and acquiescence of the American people."

---

1 E. g., telegram of A. Dumont, chairman Rep. State Com., in H. R. Mis. Doc. No. 42, 44th Cong. 2d Sess., p. 16. Also of Kellogg in *Annual Cyclopaedia,* 1876, p. 486.

In their reply the Republican visitors declined to hold such a conference and pointed out that they were present merely as witnesses, "without power or legal influence over the result, or over the means by which, under the laws of Louisiana, the result is to be determined." They further called attention to the fact that the canvassing board possessed power to exercise judicial as well as ministerial duties, and that to reduce the whole question to the merely clerical duty of counting "the votes actually cast," as distinguished from the votes "legally cast," would involve "a nullification of the provisions of the laws of Louisiana." They assured the Democratic statesmen, however, that "we join heartily with you in counsels of peace and in the expression of an earnest desire for a perfectly honest and just declaration of the results of the recent election in Louisiana by its lawfully constituted authorities, and we may add that we know of no reason to doubt that such declaration will be made." Next day the Democrats returned to the charge with a letter in which they explained that by the expression "votes actually cast" they had not meant to include "votes illegally cast." They disclaimed any intention to interfere with the legally constituted authorities, but supposed it was not improper "to remind the authorities of this state, by our mere presence at least, that there are certain rules of fairness and justice which underlie all constitutions and laws, and upon whose observance must depend the acquiescence of the people of all parties in the declared result of the

Louisiana election." They frankly confessed they had no such faith in the returning board as was evinced by the Republican visitors. "We deem it not improper," they said in this connection, "to remind you that the very presence in this city of so many citizens from all parts of the Union at this moment seems to be evidence of a widely-prevalent distrust of the action of this board, and that such distrust has this foundation, at least, that the constitution of the board has not been changed since its returns were set aside by a Congressional committee of which the Republican candidate for the Vice-Presidency was a member." The Republicans still declined, however, to enter into any combination for concerted action. [1]

Unquestionably the Democrats had good reason for distrusting the board, while the Republicans took entirely too hopeful a view when they announced that they knew no reason for doubting that a perfectly honest and just declaration of the result would be made. To begin with, the board as then constituted consisted entirely of Republicans; for though the law provided that all parties should be represented on it, the sole Democratic member had resigned, and the remaining four members had ignored the provision requiring them to fill the vacancy. [2] Then, too, the character of the four was by no means such as to inspire any great degree of confidence. J. Madison

1 This correspondence is all given in S. Ex. Doc. No. 2, 44th Cong. 2d Sess., pp. 31-35.
2 See *post* p. 100.

Wells, the president, was a native of Louisiana, had
to his honor remained a Union man when the state
seceded, had been chosen lieutenant-governor under
the Banks reconstruction plan, and had later become
governor, but in 1867 had been removed by General
Sheridan, who had characterized him as "a political
trickster and a dishonest man." [1]   Thomas C. Anderson, also a native Louisianian, was known to have used
his influence as a state senator in obtaining a subsidy
for a navigation company in which he had a large
pecuniary interest. [2]   The other members were both
mulattoes.   One of them, Louis M. Kenner, was a sa-
loon-keeper, and at one time had been indicted for
larceny, but upon confession had been allowed to escape punishment. [3]   The other, Gadane Casanave, was
an undertaker and the most respectable member of
the board; but even he was not a man of the highest
intelligence or the finest moral grain. [4]   The board as
a whole had been severely criticised for its conduct on
a previous occasion by a committee sent out by the national House of Representatives to investigate the election of 1874.   Two of the Republican members of the
committee united with the Democratic members in declaring the action of the board in that election "unjust,
illegal, and arbitrary." [5]   The remaining Republican

1 Cited by *The Nation*, XXIII, p. 309.   For other opinions of
Wells see *Harper's Weekly*, XX, p. 988; S. Ex. Doc. No. 2, 44th
Cong. 2d Sess., p. 6; H. R. Mis. Doc. No. 34, Part 2, 44th Cong. 2d
Sess., pp. 506, 508, 509; *Ibid*, No. 42, pp. 143-163, 178-183.
2 H. R. Mis. Doc. No. 34, Part 2, 44th Cong. 2d Sess., pp. 589-
594.
3 *Ibid*, p. 598; also Part 1, pp. 59 *et seq.*
4 *Ibid*, pp. 52 *et seq.*
5 H. R. Mis. Doc. No. 261, 43d Cong. 2d Sess., p. 3.

members G. F. Hoar, W. A. Wheeler, and W. P. Frye, reported that the board had reversed the result as indicated by the votes actually in the ballot-boxes; but in consideration of the board's good intentions, Messrs. Hoar, Wheeler, and Frye simply expressed "emphatic disapprobation of its proceedings" and "dissent from the view it took of its own powers and duties," and pronounced its conduct "illegal" in "attempting to cure one wrong by another." [1]

The law required that the board should meet within ten days after the date of the election. On Friday, the 17th of November, the members assembled and held a secret conference. On the next day they met again and adopted a resolution to the effect that an invitation should be extended to each delegation of "distinguished gentlemen from other states" to send five members to witness the proceedings. The invitation was accepted, and the visiting statesmen took turns in attending the meetings of the board. [2]

At the first public session on the following day the board announced the rules which were to govern their proceedings. The rules provided that the board should "first take up, canvass, and compile" the returns from those parishes to which no objections had been made, and should then proceed to consider the returns from the disputed parishes; that all protests and arguments from candidates or their attorneys should be made in writing; that, except by members

---

1 H. R. Mis. Doc. No. 261, 43d Cong. 2d Sess., p. 28.
2 S. Ex. Doc. No. 2, 44th Cong. 2d Sess., pp. 35-36.

of the board, all interrogatories to witnesses must be in writing and must previously have been submitted to opposing counsel for cross-interrogatories; that candidates, or attorneys representing candidates, could be present only when contested cases were being heard; that whenever the members of the board should deem it desirable, they might "go into secret session to consider any motion, argument, or proposition which may be presented to them;" that, finally, after all the evidence was in, the board should make the final determination in secret session. After the rules had been read Judge Spofford, counsel for one of the Democratic candidates, made an urgent plea for entire publicity, but this the board refused to grant.[1]

A like answer was given to five protests which had been filed by the Democratic counsel at the last session. These protests dealt with such matters as the judicial powers of the board, the vacancy in its membership, and its right under the law to canvass the returns for electors. All the answers were reasonable with the exception of the one dealing with the subject of filling the vacancy. The law provided that all parties should be represented and that "in case of any vacancy by death, resignation, or otherwise of either of the board, then the vacancy shall be filled by the residue of the board." The members of the board now held that the law provided for the original organization only, that all political parties at that time organized were represented, that there was then no party

---

[1] S. Ex. Doc. No. 2, 44th Cong. 2d Sess., p. 40.

known as the Democratic-Conservative party, that
"there was no provision in the law for a reorganization
of the board, so it could not have been contemplated
that the board should be changed to suit shifting political organizations that might subsequently be made." [1]
This absurd view was stubbornly held to the end. At
a subsequent discussion of the matter Wells declared
that through the resignation of their representative
the Democrats had lost their right to representation
on the board. He also alleged that the members of
the board were unable to agree upon any one to fill
the vacancy. [2]

Seven sessions were devoted to canvassing and compiling the vote of those parishes against which there
were no protests. [3] Had the board complied with the
strict letter of the law, there would not have been much
other work to do, for, save in a very few cases, the
protests had not been regularly made. The law regulating the making of protests provided that whenever,
during the time of registration or revision of registration or on the day of election, there should be any riot,
acts of violence, intimidation, bribery, or corrupt influence which tended to prevent a fair and free election, the supervisor of registration, if such acts occurred during the period of registration or revision of
registration, or the commissioners of election, if such
acts occurred on election day, should make affidavit of
the fact and of the effect produced thereby, and these

---

1 S. Ex. Doc. No. 2, 44th Cong. 2d Sess., pp. 40-43.
2 *Ibid*, pp. 75-76.
3 *Ibid*, pp. 45-105.

affidavits must be corroborated under oath by three qualified voters of the parish. The affidavits were to be made in duplicate, and if made by the commissioners of election were to be forwarded to the supervisor of registration for the parish. [1]   One copy of each protest the supervisor must annex to his "returns of election by paste, wax, or some adhesive substance" so that the same could be kept together; the other copy he must deliver to the clerk of the parish court. [2]   As another section of the law provided that commissioners of election must make their returns within twenty-four hours of the close of the polls and that the supervisors of registration must within twenty-four hours after the receipt of all returns consolidate such returns and forward them by mail to the returning board, it is clear that definite time limits were set to the making of protests by these various officers. [3]   If the law in this respect was mandatory and not merely directory, then almost all the protests upon which the board based their jurisdiction to go behind the returns were illegal; [4] for, according to one witness, there was but one protest which had been made and forwarded in strict accordance with the law. [5]

The reasons why no more protests were made in time were various. Some officials appear to have re-

---

1 But in New Orleans to the secretary of state.
2 Section 26 of Act 98, 1872, given *Ibid*, p. 164.
3 *Ibid*, p. 166.
4 It was provided, however, that candidates should be allowed a hearing before the board upon making application within the time allowed for the forwarding of the returns.—*Ibid*, p. 161.
5 Statement of Jewett in brief given to Benj. F. Butler, cited by Gibson, p. 364.

frained through fear, some through inattention or stu-
pidity, some because nothing had occurred in their
parishes on which a protest could be based, some because they meant to force the Republican managers to
pay them for protesting, and some because they believed there would be a Republican majority which
would obviate the necessity of throwing out any votes. [1]

This belief that there would be a majority on the
face of the returns had for a time been held by the
leaders at New Orleans.   When the reverse had been
found to be the case, the lack of protests had been seriously felt.   But this lack, while very inconvenient,
had not been allowed to prevent the consummation desired by the Republican managers.   Luckily most of
the supervisors had brought their returns to New Orleans in person, instead of forwarding them by mail
as the law required, and, arrived there, had in the majority of instances deposited the returns at the custom-house instead of delivering them at once to the
board; even of those returns sent through the mails
some at least had been held in the post-office.   An
opportunity was thus afforded of which the Republican
managers had taken full advantage.

"It is in testimony and uncontradicted, so far as I
know," says one of the later congressional investi-
gators, "that on or about the 23d of November these
sealed up returns of supervisors were, in the presence
of the secretary of the Republican campaign committee, opened and new and further protests inserted,

1 Gibson, pp. 365, 368-371.

upon the strength of which parishes or polls might be thrown out by the returning board. In one or more of these protests interpolations were made, over the jurat, seven or eight days after the same were sworn to, of new matter, by which votes might be thrown out by the returning board. New protests were inserted into other of the packages of vague and indecisive character, and then a most active, vigorous, and successful search for witnesses was made to sustain these new protests by evidence." [1]

Equally active efforts were made on the Democratic side to meet these protests. The result was that soon two affidavit "mills" were running overtime and were turning out the desired product with machine-like rapidity. [2] Owing to the fact that the Republicans controlled more of the officers before whom such affidavits could be made, they seem to have been able to produce a slightly larger quantity than their opponents. Which party surpassed the other in making the larger number of affidavits out of the smaller quantity of truth, none but a Solomon could determine.

In pursuance of the jurisdiction acquired through the irregular protests the board not only received these affidavits but also heard oral evidence. The first oral evidence taken bore upon conditions in Ouachita, a parish in the northern part of the state, not far from the Arkansas line.

The first of the witnesses introduced by the Republi-

---

1 H. R. R. No. 140, 45th Cong. 3d Sess., p. 99.

2 H. R. Mis. Doc. No. 31, 45th Cong. 3d Sess., I, pp. 414, 1072, 1076 ; III, pp. 102, 127, 535-540, 560-565, 580-587. The Republican "mill" was in the custom-house.

cans was Henry Burrell, a colored man. He pictured a very disorderly and lawless state of affairs as having existed in his parish prior to the election. According to his account the negro Republicans had been terrorized by five Democratic rifle-clubs which had ridden about the country at night, forcing negroes to join Democratic clubs, and whipping, maiming, and even murdering the leaders or those who were particularly stubborn. Burrell had himself been shot by a white man, though the motive for the shooting is not entirely clear. Just before the election he had also been captured by bulldozers, and had been forced by threats of death to destroy about 1400 Republican ballots which were in his possession. [1]

Eaton Logwood, another colored man, corroborated Burrell's testimony regarding the condition of affairs in Ouachita. He had suffered bodily harm on account, he alleged, of his political principles. Two white men, blackened to look like negroes, had ridden up to his cabin, had shot him, and had killed his brother-in-law, Primus Johnson, who at the time was holding a child in his arms. Logwood's own wounds had been frightful ones, and were not yet healed. [2]

But this evidence was as nothing to that given by the next witness, Eliza Pinkston. Attended by a woman with restoratives, Mrs. Pinkston was borne into the room on a chair by two stalwart negroes. In this proceeding and in what followed there was an evident

1 S. Ex. Doc. No. 2, 44th Cong. 2d Sess., pp. 105-110.
2 *Ibid*, pp. 110-113.

striving after effect — a striving which was altogether unnecessary, for the story needed no embellishment. What she had to tell caused a great sensation among the Northern visitors, [1] and was telegraphed to the remotest parts of the Union.

She testified that up to the Saturday night before the election she had lived with Henry Pinkston in a cabin on what was known as "The Island" of Ouachita parish. On that night a party of white men, some of whom she claimed to have recognized, and two negroes had ridden up to the cabin, and had called for Pinkston. Failing to entice him out, they had broken in the door, had seized him, and had sworn that if he voted the Republican ticket he would have "to vote it in hell." When the woman had attempted to interfere, she had been knocked down. The ruffians had then gagged the man; had gashed him with knives, making a sound "just like cutting in new leather;" had then dragged him outside; and had there shot him seven times. Some of them had then re-entered the cabin; had killed a baby which the woman held in her arms; had assaulted the woman several times; and had then shot her, cut her, gashed her with an axe, and left her for dead. In proof of her story she exhibited her wounds, which were still unhealed. They were a shocking sight, for she had unquestionably

---

1 S. Ex. Doc. No. 2, 44th Cong. 2d Sess., pp. 115-116. Ex-Governor Palmer, a Democrat from Illinois, was especially horrified by the recital. "If this woman's story is true," said he, "the people who could practice any such violence would have no right to complain of any sort of government that would be put over them."—S. Mis. Doc. No. 14, 44th Cong. 2d Sess., p. 102.

been brutally dealt with; on her thigh there was a frightful gash, there were wounds in her head and neck, and there was a deep wound in one of her breasts.

Every possible effort was made by the Democrats, both before the returning board and before later congressional investigating committees, to break down the story of this outrage. It was claimed that the murder had no political significance, that, as a matter of fact, Pinkston was a Democrat.[1] Charles Tidwell, the owner of the plantation on which the murder occurred, reluctantly admitted before a Senate committee, however, that while Pinkston had two years before voted with the Democrats, he was at the time of his death a Radical;[2] there was also evidence to the effect that by remaining away from a Democratic rally Pinkston had endangered his life.[3] Another theory propounded by the Democrats was that Pinkston was killed by a negro named Brooks, with whom he had had a fight some months before.[4] But there was no real evidence to support the theory; while there was evidence, both direct and circumstantial, that the killing was the work of several men.[5] Much evidence was brought in by the Democrats to show that because Eliza was of bad character no weight should be attached to her

---

[1] This claim was put forward by the Democratic members of the House Committee.—H. R. R. No. 156, Part 1, 44th Cong. 2d Sess., p. 46. It appears that he had so voted in 1874.

[2] S. R. No. 701, 44th Cong. 2d Sess., p. 735. See also pp. 90 and 596.

[3] *Ibid*, pp lxxxi, 502, 515.

[4] H. R. R. No. 156, Part 1, 44th Cong. 2d Sess., p. 46.

[5] S. R. No. 701, 44th Cong. 2d Sess., pp. 90, 91, 97, 623.

story of the outrage. [1]   As regards her character there
was no room for doubt.   Her own testimony [2] showed
her to be vulgar and indecent to a degree scarcely conceivable; and she was much given to embellishing her
account with details that were evidently fictitious.
Yet the essential portions of her story were not successfully impeached.   The anxiety of some partisan
writers, such as Gibson and Bigelow, to prove the outrage all a pretense has betrayed them into some rather
grim absurdities.   Gibson triumphantly points to the
fact that the child's throat was not cut, as she alleged,
and that Pinkston's body was not mutilated in the manner she described. [3]   He seems to lose sight of the fact
that the child was nevertheless killed, that its body
was thrown into a pond, where it was not found for
a week; of the fact that Pinkston was shot seven
times and that his dead body was so distorted that
it was not put into a coffin but was buried in a quilt.
So fiendish an outrage may appear incredible to some
people, yet it is a matter of history that outrages fully
as brutal were committed by the Ku Klux — are
still committed in some sections.   The explanation lies
in the barbarous character of a portion of the white
population and in the low value attached to a "nigger's" life. [1]

---

1 S. R. No. 701, 44th Cong. 2d Sess., pp. 517-536. Pinkston
himself was represented as a "good negro."

2 *Ibid,* pp. 909 *et seq.*

3 A Political Crime, p. 163.

4 For some of the other evidence see index to S. R. No. 701,
44th Cong. 2d Sess., p. clxxiv; H. R. R. No. 156, Part 1, 44th
Cong. 2d Sess., pp. 41-46, discusses the case from the Democratic

But whatever may have been the facts and motives attending the Pinkston murders, the evidence before the returning board — even the evidence introduced by the Democrats — revealed a most disorderly condition of affairs in the parish of Ouachita. Beginning in August with the murder of J. H. Dinkgrave, a prominent white Republican, by an unknown assassin, there had been a series of murders and assaults upon negro Republicans by persons who escaped the consequences of their crimes. White rifle-clubs were active; and, largely as a result of the fear which their activity inspired, about 700 negroes joined Democratic clubs. It appears, however, that there was fear among some of the Democratic leaders that all these recruits might not "stick," [1] so, as an object lesson, a demonstration was made on the Saturday night just prior to the election. On that night parties of men severely whipped Abram Williams and Willis Frazier, two colored Republicans; attempted to catch the son of Abram Williams, but not finding him at home, whipped his wife and outraged her; killed Merrimon Rhodes and threw his body into a bayou; whipped Randall Driver; and murdered Henry Pinkston and child in the manner already described.

Seeing the situation of affairs in the parish, the Republican managers had already decided not to at-

standpoint and gives references to important testimony. See also newspapers of Nov. 29th, 30th and Dec. 1st. No importance should be attached to the story circulated in 1878 that Eliza had made a counter-confession.—See *The Nation*, XXVII, pp. 1 and 62.

1 Letter of the chairman of the Democratic executive committee.—S. R. No. 701, 44th Cong. 2d Sess., p. xix.

tempt to have their followers vote at the outlying
polls, but to have them come into Monroe, the chief
town, where there was a small detachment of United
States troops. There was nothing unlawful in this
procedure, for the law allowed a man properly registered to cast his ballot at any poll in the parish; but
to prevent the movement, the rifle-clubs picketed the
approaches to the town; while the Democratic mayor
issued a proclamation directing the negroes to return
to their homes.[1]

The evidence before the returning board showed
that in a number of other parishes there had been a
condition of affairs somewhat similar to that just described in Ouachita. For example, in East Feliciana,
a parish in which the Republican vote for state officers
in 1874 had been 1,688, the negro Republicans had
been so demoralized as a result of a reign of violence
which had begun more than a year before that the
Republican managers appear to have given up all hope
of carrying the parish and to have issued instructions
to their followers not to attempt to vote. In consequence, only a single Republican ballot, and that a
defective one, was cast; and the Republican majority

1 For the Republican affidavits regarding the situation in
Ouachita see S. Ex. Doc. No. 2, 44th Cong. 2d Sess., pp. 330-420.
They are *ex parte* and little reliance can be placed upon most of
them.   The most valuable are those of Captain Hale and Lieutenant McCawley of the United States Army, pp. 330 and 336
respectively.   For the Democratic affidavits see S. Mis. Doc. No.
14, 44th Cong. 2d Sess., pp. 775-915.   The mayor's proclamation
mentioned above is given on page 823.   See also H. R. Mis. Doc.
No. 34, Part 6, 44th Cong. 2d Sess., pp. 1-195, and index of S.
R. No. 701, 44th Cong. 2d Sess., pp. clv *et seq.*

of 841 in 1874 was transformed into a Democratic majority of 1,741.[1]

After twelve public sessions the board on Monday, December 4th, met in private and began the really important portion of their work. What would be the outcome of their labors was a matter about which the general public was uncertain, for there were rumors and counter rumors of bribery. How much truth there was in these various rumors will probably never be exactly ascertained. There is evidence to show that Wells at least "was in the market." On November 21st he wrote to Senator West, who was then in Washington: "Millions have been sent here and will be used in the interest of Tilden, and unless some counter move [is made], it will be impossible for me or any individual to wrest its productive results."[2] This letter he committed to the care of Joseph H. Maddox, a special agent of the treasury, who journeyed to Washington, and after failing to secure any encouragement from Republican leaders, entered into an alliance with Col. John T. Pickett, a soldier of fortune who had some years before achieved notoriety and cash by selling the Confederate archives to the national government. In accordance with an agreement between the two, Col. Pickett proceeded to New York City, and there informed Abram S. Hewitt, chairman of the

1 For some of the evidence regarding East Feliciana see S. R. Ex. Doc. No. 2, 44th Cong. 2d Sess., pp. 223-258; for some of the evidence taken by the Senate investigating committee see S. R. No. 701, 44th Cong. 2d Sess., index under East Feliciana, pp. clx-cxciii. For the "confession" of Anderson, the Republican supervisor, see chapter xiii.

2 H. R. Mis. Doc. No. 42, 44th Cong. 2d Sess., p. 180.

Democratic national committee, that the Louisiana board would in consideration of the sum of $1,000,000 render a decision favorable to Tilden, but the proposition was not accepted.[1] It appears also that Wells personally offered for $200,000 to secure the counting in of the Democratic state ticket. Some steps were taken to raise the money, but the deal ultimately failed.[2] What negotiations if any he carried on with Republicans, is a matter of greater uncertainty. It has been said but not proved that he refused to promise a Republican decision until the state authorities had cashed at par some state warrants worth only about thirty cents on the dollar.[3] It has also been alleged that he arrived at an understanding with certain of the Republican "visiting statesmen,"[4] but upon this there exists no evidence whatever. It is only known that after the inauguration of Hayes he became surveyor of the port of New Orleans, that Anderson became the deputy collector, and that Kenner became the deputy naval officer.

But whether or not the members of the board were spurred on by the hope of a reward, they certainly worked zealously to evolve a Republican majority. The task proved a more complex one than had originally been anticipated. The first hypothesis, made before the returns had been opened, appears to have been that the board would be able to get rid of enough

---

1 H. R. Mis. Doc. No. 42, 44th Cong. 2d Sess., pp. 131, 135, 143, 156, 178.
2 Testimony of Duncan F. Kenner, *Ibid*, pp. 376, 383.
3 H. R. Mis. Doc. No. 31, 45th Cong. 3d Sess., I, pp. 1426-1431.
4 Gibson, p. 222.

votes in the five parishes of East Baton Rouge, Ouachita, Morehouse, and the two Felicianas;[1] but it
had soon been discovered that a number of other parishes would have to be purged of Democratic polls.[2]
The necessity arose in part out of the fact that in certain parishes the names of some Republican electors
had been omitted from the ballots, with the result that
a part of them had run more than 2,000 votes behind
the rest of the ticket.[3] The board were therefore
obliged to do some heroic work in accomplishing their
purpose. They rejected the entire vote of East Feliciana on the ground of intimidation, and that of Grant
parish on the plea that there had been no legal election
because the supervisor had fled from the parish more
than a month before the election. In addition, they
threw out 69 polls from 22 other parishes, and also
refused to receive the vote of certain polls which
the supervisors of Tangipahoa, East Baton Rouge,
Lafayette, La Fourche, and the assistant supervisors of
wards 2, 7, and 11 of New Orleans, had, without lawful authority, excluded from their returns. In this
way the board got rid of 13,213 Democratic votes, but
in the process were obliged to throw out the votes of
2,415 Republicans. The result was a substantial majority of 3,437 for the Republican elector lowest on

1 Sherman to Hayes, H. R. Mis. Doc. No. 31, 45th Cong. 2d
Sess., I, p. 771.

2 H. R. R. No. 140, 45th Cong. 3d Sess., p. 97.

3 Sen. Mis. Doc. No. 14, 44th Cong. 2d Sess., pp. 21, 45, 76,
165   The board also threw out many votes in order to secure
a Republican legislature, the election of as many Republican
congressmen as possible, etc.

the list, a majority for Packard of 3,426, and the choice of a Republican legislature. [1]

The announcement of this happy result was not officially made known to the general public until Wednesday morning, December 6th, the legal date for the meeting of the electoral college. But the Republican electors were present in New Orleans ready to do their work. At four o'clock in the afternoon the college convened, with all but two of the electors present. [2] These two, O. H. Brewster and A. B. Levissee, had been objected to as ineligible because they had held offices of trust and profit under the United States at the time they were elected. Having now resigned their offices, they remained away in order that the other electors might take advantage of the state law providing for the filling of vacancies caused by the death, sickness, or absence of electors. The other members, in accordance with a prearranged plan, chose Brewster and Levissee to fill their own vacancies. The two then appeared, [3] and the college thereupon proceeded to cast the eight votes of the state of Louisiana for Hayes and Wheeler. [4]

Now, however, began a peculiar complication. In accordance with the Constitution triplicate certificates

---

1 H. R. Mis. Doc. No. 34, Part 2, 44th Cong. 2d Sess., pp. 790-794; also S. R. No. 701, 44th Cong. 2d Sess., pp. 3110-3118.

2 For proceedings of the college see H. R. Mis. Doc. No. 31, 45th Cong. 3d Sess., I, pp. 80, 95, 128.

3 Levissee announced to the other electors that he had been offered $100,000 to cast his vote for Tilden.—*Ibid,* pp. 80 *et seq.*

4 It has been charged that the electors failed to vote for President and Vice-President by distinct ballots as the Constitution requires.—H. R. R. No. 140, 45th Cong. 3d Sess., p. 50. The certificates stated, however, that separate ballots were taken.—Proceedings of the Electoral Commission, p. 206.

of the vote were made out, and one of these was mailed to the president of the Senate, one was filed with the judge of the United States district court, and one was delivered to T. C. Anderson, who was chosen to carry it to Washington. When Anderson reached Washington and presented the package to Mr. Ferry, the president of the Senate, that officer called his attention to the fact that the envelope was not properly endorsed. Following the same course which he pursued with regard to irregular returns from North Carolina, Tennessee, and other states, [1] Mr. Ferry allowed Anderson to retain the certificate in order to have the defect rectified. Before leaving Washington Anderson began, somewhat unnecessarily, [2] to fear that the certificates themselves were not in regular form because the lists of votes for President and Vice-President were not on separate sheets of paper. When he reached New Orleans, therefore, he communicated his fears to some of the Republican leaders, and it was decided that new certificates must be made. But the time was short, and two of the electors were so far away that they could not possibly get to New Orleans before the work must be done. The Republican leaders were not men to be discouraged by such an

---

1 The returns from almost half the states were in some respect irregular.—Testimony of Ferry, H. R. Mis. Doc. No. 31, 45th Cong. 3d Sess., I, p. 139. The statement is taken from his memorandum.

2 In every essential the original certificates were in this respect as regular as the Democratic certificates from Louisiana, Florida, Oregon, and South Carolina. Compare certificates given on pp. 13, 206, 208, 662 of Proceedings of the Electoral Commission.

obstacle as this. The signatures of the six who could
be reached were secured, and then those of the other
two were forged. Just who committed the forgery
does not appear; but it is certain that Governor Kellogg, H. Conquest Clarke, the governor's private secretary, and perhaps others, were privy to the forgery. [1]

On the same day on which the Republican electors
originally met, the Democratic claimants, basing their
authority on an irregular canvass of certified copies of
the returns, likewise assembled and cast their ballots
for Tilden and Hendricks. Their certificates were
signed by John McEnery, who claimed to be *de jure*
governor of Louisiana. [2]

It is needless to say that the result announced by the
returning board had been attained by a series of
grossly partisan and illegal acts. The board had failed
to obey the statute requiring them to fill the vacancy
in their membership. They had entertained protests
which had been irregularly made. They had allowed
to stand the action of supervisors and assistant-super-
visors who had refused to compile certain polls. One
or more of them had, it appears, even altered and falsi-
fied the returns from Vernon and perhaps from other
parishes. For this offense they were all in the following year indicted; and one of them, Anderson, was
tried, convicted, and sentenced to the penitentiary for
two years, but was ultimately released by the supreme

---

1 See H. R. R. No. 140, 45th Cong. 3d Sess., pp. 50-63 and
89-91. References are there given to the important testimony.
2 New York *Times* and *World* of Dec. 7th.

court of the state on the ground that the offense was not covered by the statute.[1]

Nevertheless, the decision of the board was final; there was no redress against its actions however irregular. In the case of Moncure *vs.* Dubuclet, decided in May, 1876, the state supreme court had in effect decided that the actions of the returning board were beyond the reach of judicial inquiry because the legislature had omitted to enact a law under which proceedings in such cases could be conducted.[2]

An interesting question which remains to be considered is: Did the returning board in the exercise of their extraordinary powers override the real will of a majority of the legal voters in the state of Louisiana? Or, to speak brutally, did they by an illegal process which acquired the force of law, merely take back stolen property? To put it in yet other words, was the situation one of those rare situations in which two wrongs go to make a right?

This much may be said at the outset, namely, that, despite affidavits and frantic assertions to the contrary, there was not a full, fair, and free election. Some partisans perhaps persuaded themselves that there were no rifle-clubs, no threats, no whippings, no murders; but there were partisans on both sides quite equal to the task of persuading themselves, or at least of attempting to persuade others, that all the blacks

1 See Report of Trial of Thomas C. Anderson. A copy of this pamphlet is in the Lenox Library, New York City. See also Gibson, pp. 232-237.

2 See also the case of Bonner vs. Lynch, 28 La. Ann., p. 208.

were whites, had the result of the election hinged upon such a demonstration. Intimidation was, in truth, one of the central facts of the campaign. It was occasionally resorted to by Republicans, but it would roughly be correct to say that it was a weapon belonging to the Democrats. It was the chief means by which Republican negroes were induced to change their politics. Very few were convinced by talk about misgovernment or by appeals of that sort. All assertions to the contrary notwithstanding, the negro, when left to his own choice, was as naturally a Republican as his former master was naturally a Democrat.

That the methods employed by the whites were effective is shown with startling distinctness by the following table:

| | Election of 1874 | | Regis. of 1876 | | Elect. of 1876 | |
	Dem.	Rep.	White	Colored	Dem.	Rep.
East Baton Rouge	1,556	2,546	1,867	3,400	1,102	1,476
East Feliciana	847	1,688	1,004	2,127	1,736	....
West Feliciana	501	1,358	399	2,213	1,248	778
Morehouse	654	1,017	938	1,830	1,371	782
Ouachita	766	1,694	992	2,392	1,865	793
Total	4,324	8,303	5,200	11,962	7,322	3,829

These figures [1] taken alone are sufficient proof that extraordinary things must have occurred in these parishes. When we know, in addition, that Republican officials in certain of these parishes had, during the preceding year, been driven out or killed, that the white Democrats were organized into secret military organizations which rode up and down the country at night threatening, beating, and even murdering negroes, that

1 For figures see H. R. Mis. Doc. No. 34, Part 2, 44th Cong. 2d Sess., pp. 494 and 788.

Democratic employers, who owned practically all property, threatened to discharge every one who affiliated with the Republicans, that the Republican negroes were weak-spirited and poor, so poor that they were in absolute dependence from day to day upon their Democratic employers for their daily rations of bread and meat, we cannot avoid the conclusion that, whatever may be said in justification, electioneering methods were used in the "selected" or "bulldozed" parishes which are not usually regarded as legitimate. Efforts to explain the falling off of the Republican vote on other grounds are futile, for there is no real proof that the situation in these parishes differed from that in others in any material respect save that different methods were employed by the whites and the negroes were more thoroughly terrorized.

That in a full, fair, and free election the Republicans would have received a majority cannot, of course, be absolutely proven; and yet by processes of comparison it is possible to arrive at a pretty definite conclusion regarding the matter. If, for example, it be assumed that the number of voluntary negro Democrats was about equal to the number of white Republicans — and the assumption is a reasonable one — then the Republicans were in a clear majority in the state of several thousands. But the following comparison is much more convincing: In 41 parishes in which the amount of intimidation was relatively small, the colored registration amounted to 87,999, [1] and the white registration to 72,034, leaving a colored majority of 15,965. [2]   These parishes yielded in the election a Republican majority of 6,353.   In the remaining 17 •parishes, in which terrorism was alleged, the colored registration was 27,269; [3] the white registration, 20,-320, giving a colored majority of 6,949.   Yet these parishes returned a Democratic majority of 10,153. Had the proportion of negroes who voted Republican in these parishes been the same as in the other 41, there would have been a Republican majority in the 17 parishes of between 2,000 and 3,000.   Thus the majority in the state as a whole would have been from 8,000 to 10,000.   Or, to make a yet more convincing comparison: Had even the five bulldozed parishes of East Baton Rouge, East Feliciana, West Feliciana, Morehouse, and Ouachita, voted approximately as they did in 1874, the result would have been changed sufficiently to give the lowest Republican elector a small majority of about 800 of the vote as

1 According to the census of 1880 the negro population of the state exceeded the white population by 26,364.   The white males of voting age exceeded the colored males of voting age by 833, but many thousands of the whites were foreigners who were not voters.   The state census of 1875 showed 104,192 colored voters and 84,167 white voters, but this census is wholly unreliable. The same is true of the national census of 1870, at least for the negro population.—See Frederick Hoffman, Race Traits and Tendencies of the American Negro, p. 4.   For some Democratic statistics compiled by Prof. Chaillé of New Orleans, see H. R. Mis. Doc. No. 34, Part 2, 44th Cong. 2d Sess., pp. 470-478.   Some of his conclusions are well taken, but others are fully as absurd as the census of 1875.

2 These figures include the padded registration in New Orleans. As previously pointed out the Republicans derived little advantage from the excess.

3 Practically all this registration was *bona fide* and ought to have yielded a heavy vote.

actually cast, or of about 3,000 as the vote was sent in by the election officials to the returning board.[1] All things considered, it would be pretty safe to say that in an absolutely fair and free election the state would have gone Republican by from five to fifteen thousand.[2]

But whatever might have been the result under other conditions, there was in the actual Louisiana situation one fact which was in the end to prove decisive. The body to which, in accordance with the law of the state and the decisions of the courts, belonged the final determination of the result of the election had declared in favor of the Republican electors. These electors had met and had cast their ballots for Rutherford B. Hayes and William A. Wheeler; and the returns of their vote had been certified by the man who, rightly or wrongly, had been recognized by all branches of the Federal government as the chief executive of the commonwealth.

---

[1] For the figures used in making these comparisons see H. R. Mis. Doc. No. 34, Part 2, 44th Cong. 2d Sess., 2 folders between pp. 494-495; S. R. No. 701, 44th Cong. 2d Sess., pp. xli-xlii, liii-lviii; S. Ex. Doc. No. 2, 44th Cong. 2d Sess., pp. 178-185.

[2] But it should not for a moment be supposed that the returning board was moved by high ideals of its duty as a court of equity. Doubtless they would have proceeded in the same way had they known that the election had been absolutely free and fair.

CHAPTER VIII

Rarely have a proud people drunk deeper of the cup of humiliation than did the white inhabitants of South Carolina in the sixteen years following the suicidal ordinance of December, 1860. Forced during four years of mingled triumph and defeat to endure the vexation of a blockading fleet which winter or summer never relaxed its watch upon their coasts, they at last recognized the inevitable end when an invading army swept through the state consuming and destroying everything in its path and leaving the capital in ruins. At intervals for more than a decade thereafter troops wearing the hated blue were stationed here and there about the state, and from their camps at sunset had floated not infrequently through the quiet evening air the strains of a song relating to a certain Brown late of Osawatomie.[1] But no such gentle reminder was necessary to make apparent the fact that the old order had passed away. Other things brought that fact home in a far more tangible form.

---

1 Pike, The Prostrate State, p. 79.

The pyramid of society had been turned upside down. [1] Those who had been the slaves were become the rulers. In the government, in the places of the now impoverished aristocracy, stood black and brown freedmen, led by hated Yankees and equally hated "scalawags;" and from the panels over the doors of the stately capitol at Columbia the marble visages of George McDuffie and Robert Young Hayne looked down upon the incomings and outgoings of a strange legislature, three-fourths of whose members belonged to that despised race once the victims of the institution which had formed the "corner-stone" of the fallen Confederacy.

There may have been somewhat of poetic justice in the situation just described, but the *bouleversement* was unquestionably bad for the economic interests of the state of South Carolina. However good his intentions — and the intentions of some were of the best — an untutored black man, fresh from slavery in the Sea Island cotton fields, could not possibly be a thoroughly satisfactory legislator or even citizen. A reign of misgovernment therefore followed enfranchisement — a period which, while not quite so replete with pitched battles and revolutions, was in its economic aspects fully as deplorable as that in Louis-

---

1 "De bottom rail is on de top, an' we's gwine keep it dere," said the negroes.—*Scribner's Magazine*, VIII, p. 151. They argued that their labor had made the whites wealthy and that now the wealth should be taken away by taxation. Governor Moses in a message advocated taxing the land so heavily that the owners would be forced to sell to the negroes.—*Ibid*, p. 136.

iana.[1] The amount of money actually stolen has probably been exaggerated by some writers and by partisan investigating committees, and yet the bare truth was sufficient to make a chapter previously unparalleled in American history. During the six years from 1868 to 1874 the public debt was increased by about $14,000,000, while in the period from 1860 to 1874 the total valuation of property decreased from $490,000,000 to $141,624,952. Of this decline, amounting in round numbers to $348,000,000, from $170,000,-000 to $200,000,000 was due to the freeing of the slaves,[2] and many more millions to losses occasioned by the war, to the economic effects of that struggle and of the transformation of the labor system, and to the existence of a great business depression throughout the country; yet unquestionably a large part was the direct result of misgovernment.

(Despite the fact that they and their white leaders held the offices during this period and were the beneficiaries of this reign of extravagance and corruption, the state was not entirely an Elysium for the freedmen. As elsewhere in the South, the Ku Klux early became active,[3] and against them the negroes were powerless

---

1 For an extremely interesting account of South Carolina under negro government see Pike, The Prostrate State. Also Leland, A Voice from South Carolina; Reynolds, Reconstruction in South Carolina; *Atlantic Monthly*, XXXIX, pp 177-194, 467-475, 670-684. One of the most candid statements will be found in an article by Governor Chamberlain on Reconstruction in South Carolina, *Ibid*, LXXXVIII, pp. 473-484.

2 Pike, p. 252; message of Governor Chamberlain given in Allen, Governor Chamberlain's Administration in South Carolina, p. 49.

3 See vols. III, IV and V of the Ku Klux Reports and Reynolds, pp. 179-217.

to protect themselves. In some cases no doubt the
operations of the klans were to a certain extent justifiable, but in others the outrages committed not only
were wholly without extenuation, but were brutal and
fiendish beyond description. Says a Democratic writer
on the period:

"In reference to South Carolina, the report of the
joint select committee of the two houses of Congress
of 1872 contains such a mass of revolting details that
one cannot decide where to begin their citation or
where to stop. Murders, or attempts to murder, are
numerous. Whippings are without number   Probably the most cruel and cowardly of these last was the
whipping of Elias Hill. He was a colored man who
had, from infancy, been dwarfed in legs and arms.
He was unable to use either. But he possessed an
intelligent mind; had learned to read; and had acquired
an unusual amount of knowledge for one in his circumstances. He was a Baptist preacher. He was
highly respected for his upright character. He was
eminently religious, and was greatly revered by the
people of his own race. It was on this ground that
he was visited by the Ku-Klux, brutally beaten, and
dragged from his house into the yard, where he was
left in the cold at night, unable to walk or crawl.
After the fiends had left, his sister brought him into
the house. Although this man was a Republican, his
testimony gave evidence of the mildness and Christian
forbearance of his character, as well as his freedom
from ill-will toward the white race. In answer to a
question as to his feelings towards the whites, he replied that he had good-will, love, and affection toward
them; but that he feared them. He said that he had
never made the wrongs and cruelties inflicted by the

white people on his race the subject of his sermons;
but that he preached the gospel only — repentance
toward God, and faith in our Lord Jesus Christ." [1]

As a result of outrages such as this and also of an
ever-present fear that a Democratic victory would
result in a reaction towards slavery, the negroes,
despite flagrant misgovernment, remained Republican
almost to a man. A negro would come to his former
owner for advice upon every other subject, but let the
subject of politics be broached and he became "as silent
as a tombstone;" for this was "a subject with which
'Old Massa' had nothing to do." [2] As the negroes
outnumbered the whites in the ratio of about five to
three, the Republican candidates for state office, no
matter how dishonest or disreputable, were invariably
chosen. In 1868 R. K. Scott was elected governor,
in 1870 was re-elected, and in 1872 was succeeded by
the notorious F. J. Moses, Jr. [3]

In 1874, however, Daniel H. Chamberlain, a man of
entirely different character, was elected. Mr. Chamberlain was a native of Massachusetts, was a graduate of Yale, had studied law at Harvard, and
had served as a lieutenant in the colored regiment
commanded by Charles Francis Adams, Jr. After
the war he had settled in South Carolina and had
engaged in cotton planting. In the constitutional
convention of 1868 he had borne a leading part,

---

1 Cox, p. 456.
2 Leland, p. 40.
3 Reynolds, pp. 106-218.

and had soon afterward been elected to fill the attorney-generalship, an office he continued to fill for four years.[1] Whether during that time he managed to keep his hands entirely clean, is a matter concerning which there is decided difference of opinion; but certain it is that the fact that most of his colleagues were unscrupulous men created an impression which caused many people, when he was nominated for governor in 1874, to regard his protestations of zeal for reform as so much buncombe.[2]

But no sooner was Mr. Chamberlain inaugurated than it appeared that he was in dead earnest about reform — that whatever his course in the past he would strive to preserve "the civilization of the Puritan and the Cavalier, of the Roundhead and the Huguenot."[3] He set his face against the corrupt schemes of his party; he opposed and, with the help of reform Republican and Conservative members, defeated an attempt of an unscrupulous element in the legislature to secure the removal of F. L. Cardoza, the colored state treasurer, who obstructed the execution of nefarious designs; he vetoed no less than nineteen vicious bills passed during the first session of the legislature; he secured much greater economy; and,

---

1 Allen, pp. 524-526.
2 Chamberlain's position during his four years as attorney-general was not unlike that which Tilden long occupied when on friendly terms with Tweed. See Allen, pp. 8-9, 140-151. A Democratic newspaper, *The News and Courier*, said on May 14, 1875: "It is our fixed belief that Mr. Chamberlain has never, in great things or little, consented to, or aided in, any fraud upon this people." For a different view see Reynolds, pp. 465-470, 492-494.
3 Allen, p. 201.

boldest step of all, he refused to issue commissions to two infamous characters, W. J. Whipper and ex-Governor Moses, whom the legislature had chosen circuit judges. [1]

By these actions he gained the hearty commendation of the better class of citizens in the state and attracted much attention from the country at large. The Charleston *News and Courier,* the most influential Democratic newspaper in the state, declared that he "richly deserves the confidence of the people of this state," and on another occasion expressed the opinion that "Governor Chamberlain has done for the people of South Carolina what no other living man could have done." [2]   Other Democratic newspapers in South Carolina used similar language; while many periodicals outside the state, irrespective of party, commended his course in high terms. [3]

The element which he had opposed was very indignant at his courageous stand. A vigorous effort was made to read him out of the party as a traitor. The effort culminated in April, 1876, in the Republican state convention which met at Columbia to choose delegates to the Republican national convention. Governor Chamberlain announced his desire to go as a delegate, but there appeared to be little chance that he would be able to do so, for in the contest for the temporary chairmanship his friends

---

[1] For a very full account of these matters see Allen, pp. 10-258.

[2] Quoted by Allen, pp. 107, 199.

[3] *Ibid,* pp. 106-114, 236-243; *South Atlantic,* I, pp. 332-340; H. R. R. No. 175, Part 2, 44th Cong. 2d Sess., pp. 25-31.

were defeated by a vote of 80 to 45. The triumph of his enemies seemed a foregone conclusion; but at four o'clock on the morning of April 14th, after a tumultuous session which had lasted for many hours, the governor secured the floor, and by one of the most effective speeches on record so confounded his enemies and so swayed the convention that when he concluded he was chosen over United States Senator Patterson by an overwhelming majority.[1]

The activity of Governor Chamberlain in the cause of good government was such that for a long time the Democrats were undecided whether to nominate any one to oppose him. Those who favored the policy of abstaining from such a nomination were known as the "Co-operationists," while those who wished to name a full ticket received the name of "Straight-outers."[2] The Charleston *News and Courier* was especially active in endeavoring to prevent a separate nomination. It advocated concentrating all "our efforts on the other state officers and the members of the legislature. With Mr. Chamberlain as governor, and a Conservative Democratic majority, or thereabouts, in the lower house, the state, in every sense of the word, would be safe. In attempting to gain more we might lose

---

1 Allen, 258-271; New York *Times* and New York *Herald,* April 16th. The correspondent of the *Times* called Chamberlain's speech "one of the grandest orations ever listened to in America," while the correspondent of the Washington *Chronicle* described it in equally high terms. Patterson was working for the nomination of Governor Morton for the Presidency. At Cincinnati Chamberlain supported Bristow and then Hayes. The vote of the delegation was divided.

2 Allen, pp. 258-272; H. R. R. No. 175, Part 2, 44th Cong. 2d Sess., pp. 27-32.

everything." In arguing in support of this plan the paper declared — and the statement is most significant in the light of later events — that the Republican majority could be overcome in "only one way: *by armed force.*" [1]

In the end the "Straight-outers" were victorious. A number of causes contributed to this result. Chamberlain, while a reformer, was, after all, a Republican and a native of Massachusetts; these facts weighed heavily against him in the minds of most of the white inhabitants of South Carolina. In addition it was felt by many that to adopt the "Co-operationist" policy would lessen the chances of choosing Democratic Presidential electors, while it was recognized that an indorsement of Chamberlain would weaken the Democratic position in the country at large, because such an indorsement would be tantamount to an admission that here at last was an honest "carpet-bagger." All these motives, together with hunger for office and pressure from Democratic politicians from outside the state, weighed heavily with many Democratic leaders and impelled them to adopt a "rule or ruin" policy. [2] Nevertheless the "Straight-out" movement might have failed had it not been for an event which greatly intensified partisan feeling and forced Governor Chamber-

---

1 May 8th. Italics so printed in original. In July the paper published a series of elaborate articles defending his administration.

2 Allen, pp. 307-331, 336. See also pp. 181, 244-245, of Vol. XII of *Southern Historical Society Papers*; the reference is to a series of articles by F. A. Porcher on the Last Chapter of Reconstruction in South Carolina.

lain to take a stand which alienated many of the white inhabitants. [1]

This event was the so-called "Hamburg Massacre," which took place in Aiken county on the 8th of July. The massacre grew out of an incident which occurred on the 4th. On that day while the negro militia company of the town was marching on one of the public streets two young white men drove up in a buggy. According to one version of the affair the company purposely blocked up the entire street and refused to allow the whites to pass; according to the other the whites, disdaining to turn to one side, drove against the head of the column and ordered the company to break ranks and let them through. [2] At any rate a wordy altercation followed, which finally resulted in the negroes allowing the whites to pass. Complaint was later made by the father of one of the young men before Trial Justice Rivers, a colored man, against Dock Adams, the captain of the company, for obstructing the highway. After a stormy preliminary hearing on the 6th the case was postponed until the 8th. On that day about a hundred armed white men assembled in the town; and Adams, on the plea that he feared violence, failed to appear before the justice and took refuge with other negroes in the armory. A demand was then made by General M. C. Butler, who was acting as attorney for the prosecution, and who was later

---

1 *Southern Historical Society Papers*, Vol. XII, p. 245 ; *South Atlantic*, I, pp. 340, 412-415.

2 The negro companies were viewed with great dislike by the whites. The members were often insolent and lawless.

United States senator from South Carolina, that the militia should give up their arms to the whites. [1] The demand was refused, and firing began. One white was killed early in the conflict; but his fellows bombarded the armory with a cannon brought over from Augusta, Georgia; and after a time the negroes, having exhausted about all their ammunition, attempted to escape. Some succeeded, but James Cook, the colored town marshall, who lived in the armory, was killed; and about twenty-five others were captured. Of these, five were afterwards murdered in cold blood, and three were badly wounded. Not content with this violence, some of the mob then robbed and maltreated a number of other negroes, including Trial Justice Rivers. [2]

As soon as he received notice of the affair Governor Chamberlain sent the attorney-general to make an investigation, announced his intention to do all in his power to bring the offenders to justice, and asked the President whether the general government would assist him in maintaining order in case violence in the state should get beyond the control of the state authorities. [3] His attitude in the matter was indorsed by some of the more liberal whites, but was severely

---

1 The status of the negro company was somewhat irregular; the whites claimed that it had no right to the arms. For the official papers relating to the company's status see S. Mis. Doc. No. 48, 44th Cong. 2d Sess., pp. 582 *et seq.*

2 My account is based upon Allen, pp. 307-330; the *South Atlantic*, I, pp. 412-413; *Southern Historical Society Papers*, XII, pp. 245-252; Leland, pp. 156-157; and the great mass of testimony in S. Mis. Doc. No. 48, 44th Cong. 2d Sess., and H. R. Mis. Doc. No. 31, 44th Cong. 2d Sess.

3 Allen, pp. 313 *et seq.*

criticised by persons in whose estimation the killing of a few negroes was not a matter of very great importance.[1]

The passions and prejudices aroused at this time proved decisive in determining the action of the Democrats.[2] While the excitement was at its height the state executive committee issued a call for a convention to meet at Columbia on the 15th of August. When the convention assembled the "Co-operationists" did their best to secure the adoption of a "watch and wait" policy; but the "Straight-outers" carried through a resolution "to nominate candidates for governor and other state officers."[3]

Having decided upon the policy to pursue, the convention chose as its nominee General Wade Hampton. The choice was a wise one, perhaps the wisest that could have been made. General Hampton was a member of the old aristocracy, and had been one of the wealthiest men in the state. In the Rebellion he had commanded Lee's cavalry after the death of J. E. B. Stuart, had later unsuccessfully opposed Sherman's march through the Carolinas, and while he had won

1 *The News and Courier* said: "Governor Chamberlain appears to think that a company of United States soldiers will have a more sedative effect than rifle clubs or civil *posses.* This was the position taken a few weeks ago by the newspapers that berate Governor Chamberlain for calling for troops. These very journals, at the time of the Combahee troubles, were clamorous for troops, and were furious in their denunciations of Governor Chamberlain because he would not call for them."

2 *South Atlantic,* I, p. 414.

3 Allen, pp. 335-336; *South Atlantic,* I, pp. 416-427; *Annual Cyclopaedia,* 1876, p. 721; Reynolds, pp. 347-356; files of *News and Courier* and of the Columbia *Union Herald.*

no great successes had shown much military ability. He had early accepted the results of the war, and had been one of the first of the Southern leaders to advocate a liberal policy towards the freedmen. While not the possessor of oratorical nor even of intellectual gifts of the highest order, he yet had exactly the qualities of leadership indispensable for success in the present emergency. [1]

The platform on which he was nominated professed acceptance of the three war Amendments; stated that "we turn from the settled and final past to the great, living, and momentous issues of the present and the future;" and contained a bitter arraignment of the Republican party, for "arraying race against race," for "prostituting the elective franchise" and "tampering with the ballot-box," and for having brought about a condition of "venality and corruption" unparalleled in history. [2] In the opinion of *The Nation*, the platform contained "all the things that proper platforms have to contain in these days — acceptance of the Constitutional Amendments and other results of the war, devotion to equal rights, love of peace and order, immeasurable hatred of theft, fraud, and other forms of villainy. . . . The only thing the Republicans can say against it is that it is hypocritical." [3]

The Republicans did not hold their convention until

---

1 For Hampton's character see *South Atlantic*, I, pp. 416-419. and 424; *Sewanee Review*, X, pp. 364-373; McClure, Recollections of Half a Century, pp. 406-414.

2 *Annual Cyclopaedia*, 1876, p. 721.

3 Vol. XXIII, p. 111.

almost a month later. [1]   When it assembled on the 13th
of September, a strong effort was made by R. B. Elliott, the mulatto speaker of the House of Representatives, C. C. Bowen, B. F. Whittemore, and other
anti-reformers, to overthrow Chamberlain.   A bitter
contest followed in which the governor was only partially victorious.   He secured the adoption of a platform pledging a large number of specific reforms, and
also secured his own renomination as well as that of
State Treasurer Cardoza and others of his adherents;
but unfortunately he was unable to prevent the convention from putting R. B. Elliott, T. C. Dunn, and others
of the most corrupt element in the party on the ticket.
By this step a considerable number of honest men of
both races were alienated. [2]

The Democrats did not wait for the Republican convention to be over before beginning their campaign.
All sections of the party at once united and entered
upon a determined and wonderfully enthusiastic effort
to "redeem" the state.   The plan of procedure was to
attempt to conciliate the blacks by making glowing
promises [3] and by nominating negroes for the legislature in some of the counties in which the Republican
majorities were too large to overcome, [4] and at the

---

1 For accounts of the convention see Allen, pp. 352-354; Reynolds, pp. 362-372. *Southern Historical Society Papers*, 311-316;
Atlantic, XXXIX, p. 186; *Annual Cyclopaedia* for 1876, p. 722;
files of the New York *World, Herald*, and *Times*, and of the
Charleston *News and Courier*, and the Columbia *Union Herald*.

2 Allen, pp. 360, 504-505; Chamberlain in *Atlantic*, LXXXX-
VII, p. 480.

3 *South Atlantic*, I, pp. 45-50; H. R. Mis. Doc. No. 31, Part 1,
44th Cong. 2d Sess., pp. 306-310.

4 *Atlantic*, XXXIX, p. 184.

same time to bring forms of pressure to bear which would convince the recalcitrant that it would be safer to affiliate with the Democracy. The leaders of the party fully understood that only by drastic methods could they hope to overcome the large Republican majority. Resort was therefore had to the "Mississippi plan." "Rifle-clubs," "artillery companies," "sabre clubs," uniformed in red shirts and fully armed, were organized throughout the state. They at once began systematically to appear at Republican meetings and demand a division of time. As an example of how they behaved at these meetings may be taken the following description by Governor Chamberlain, who at the time the incidents occurred was making a tour of the state for the purpose of defending his administration and securing a renomination. Says Mr. Chamberlain:

"On the return of Judge Hoge and Mr. Jillson from Newberry on the 19th of August, they strongly advised the abandonment of the meeting at Abbeville in view of their experience at Newberry, and especially on account of a violent and threatening harangue made at the depot at Newberry on the morning of the 19th, to a band of his partisans, by Col. D. Wyatt Aiken. I replied that I should keep my engagement at Abbeville from a sense of imperative duty to my Republican friends there. Unwilling to allow me to go alone, these gentlemen gallantly consented to accompany me on the 21st to Abbeville Court House. On arriving at Abbeville, I found our Republican friends, as at Newberry, firmly convinced that if we held our meeting prudence would compel us to allow the Democrats to occupy half the time, and even then they were greatly apprehensive of trouble. An arrangement was accordingly entered into by which three speakers from each party were to take part in the meeting. At the hour appointed we proceeded to the place of meeting, where we found the Republicans assembled, after the manner of ordinary political meetings. As soon, however, as the Republicans were assembled, companies of mounted white men, marching in martial order, and under the command of officers or persons who gave orders which were obeyed, began to pour over the hill in front of the stand and to take their places at the meeting. At this time I sat beside General McGowan, and we agreed in our estimate that there were from 800 to 1,000 mounted white men present. They came, as I know, from Edgefield County, and, as I was informed, from Newberry, Anderson, and Laurens Counties, as well as from Abbeville County. When fully assembled, they covered more than one-half the space around the stand, besides entirely encircling the whole meeting with mounted men. I spoke first. In the course of my speech, in response to loud and repeated cries from the white men, 'How about Hamburg,' 'Tell us about Hamburg,' I replied, 'Yes, I will tell you about Hamburg,' whereupon I saw a sudden crowding towards the stand by the mounted white men on my right and heard distinctly the click of a considerable number of pistols.

"I was followed by Col. D. Wyatt Aiken, in a speech filled to overflowing with the spirit of intolerance and violence. With his thousand mounted and armed partisans cheering him on, he shouted to the five or six hundred colored Republicans, 'If you want war you can have it — yes, war to the knife, and the knife to the hilt.' With a thousand armed white men drinking in his words, he singled out one colored man in the crowd for special personal denunciation. . . . Later in the day Mr. Jillson while speaking was so greatly interrupted by the white men that he was unable to make a connected speech or to pursue his intended line of argument. After the meeting was closed and while the colored republicans were carrying a United States flag past the public square in the village, an effort was made by a party of mounted white men to snatch it from them, fifteen or twenty pistols were discharged in the air, and a general riot was thereby made imminent." [1]

The object of activity such as this was well set forth at the time by H. V. Redfield in a letter to the Cincinnati *Commercial.* "The outsider," wrote he, "is apt to be puzzled by accounts of affairs here. He may not understand the formation of rifle-clubs, rifle-teams, artillery companies, among the whites. What are they afraid of? They are not afraid of anything. Why, then, this arming? They intend to carry this election, if it is possible to do so. The programme is to have rifle-clubs all over the state, and, while avoiding actual bloodshed as much as possible, to so impress the blacks that they, or a number of them, will feel impelled to vote with the whites out of actual fear. The blacks are timid by nature, timid by habit, timid by education. A display of force unnerves them. The whites understand this, and an immense marching about at night,

---

[1] H. R. Mis. Doc. No. 31, Part 1, 44th Cong. 2d Sess, pp. 359-360. In pages both before and following there are accounts of similar meetings at other places. For yet other accounts see *Ibid,* pp. 187, 223, 228, 230, 231, 239, 243, 246,279, 359, 395, 459, 460; Part 2, pp. 153, 228, 237; and Part 3, pp. 117, 197, 224. Some of this evidence was given by officers of the United States army. See also *Southern Historical Society Papers,* XII, pp. 309-310. Chamberlain's accounts are by no means exaggerated. if one is to believe the stories told by South Carolinians today.

and appearance at any republican meeting 'to divide time' is with a view to impress the blacks with a sense of the danger of longer holding out against white rule." [1]

The Democrats, in fact, did everything in their power to produce a reign of terror among the freedmen. Threats of violence flew thick as birds in spring; the homes of colored men were fired into at night; and negroes were whipped, assaulted, and in some instances murdered. [2]

An equally effective weapon used against the blacks was industrial proscription. Democrats openly announced that they would not employ Republicans nor rent land to them, and the Democratic newspapers were filled with resolutions to that effect. Out of the many such resolutions which might be cited, this one, taken from the *News and Courier* for September 18th, will suffice:

"The following resolutions, adopted by the Easterlin's Mill Democratic Club, are commended to the attention of the different clubs throughout the state. Similar resolutions have been adopted by the Willow Township, Graham's, and Bamberg clubs, and no doubt by many other clubs in Orangeburgh and Barnwell Counties. It is intended that the names of the obnoxious leaders in each township be sent to the different clubs throughout the county:

"1. *Resolved,* That we will not rent land to any

---

1 H. R. Mis. Doc. No. 31, Part 1, 44th Cong. 2d Sess., p. 365.
2 For evidence on these points see index to *Ibid*, pp. 470-471. The use of violence is not now denied by candid persons.—See *Sewanee Review*, X, p. 367, and *Atlantic*, LXXXVIII, p. 480.

radical leader, or any member of his family, or furnish a home, or give employment to any such leader or any member of his family.

"2. That we will not furnish any such leader, or any member of his family, any supplies, such as provisions, farm-implements, stock, etc., except so far as contracts for the present year are concerned.

"3. That we will not purchase anything any radical leader or any member of his family may offer for sale, or sell any such leader or any member of his family anything whatever.

"4. That the names of such persons who may be considered leaders be furnished to this club at the earliest date, and that a list of the same be furnished each member of the club." [1]

The Republicans, on their part, worked unceasingly to counteract the Democratic efforts. Speakers played upon the freedman's ever-present fear of being once more reduced to slavery. [2] Democratic negroes were stripped naked and beaten with whips and clubs, or were cut with knives or razors. According to the Democratic members of an investigating committee later sent out by the Federal House of Representatives, "Women utterly refused to have any intercourse with men of their own race who voted against the Republicans. One instance was proven of the actual desertion of a

---

[1] H. R. R. No. 175, Part 2, 44th Cong. 2d Sess., p. 39. Other instances are given on the same page. See also *Ibid*, Mis. Doc. No. 31, Part 1, pp. 219, 221, 223, 224, 228, 237, 244, 260, 264, 271, 291. General M. C. Butler of Hamburg fame later testified that he had told his tenants that if they voted the Republican ticket they would have to leave his plantation.—First report just quoted, pp. 38-39.

[2] *Southern Historical Society Papers,* XII, p. 310.

wife with the children of a husband because he made campaign speeches for the Democrats." [1] But, com- pared with the intimidation practiced by their oppon- ents, the amount of which the Republicans were guilty appears to have been comparatively small; while the very abhorrence in which Democratic negroes were held by the people of their own color is pretty conclu- sive proof that when left alone the negroes were almost unanimously Republican.   The freedmen not only employed violence in preventing desertions, but, exas- perated by the Democratic invasions of their meetings, they also showed in some localities an unexpected determination to resist the whites.   They began to carry arms to their meetings, and to indulge in the most diabolical threats. [2]

In the month of September there were, in fact, two serious collisions between the races.   The first took place in Charleston on the 6th, and was due to an unjustifiable attempt on the part of colored Republicans to call two colored Democratic speakers to account for their utterances.   Before the riot was subdued by the Republican authorities several persons on both sides

---

1 H. R. R. No. 175, Part 1, 44th Cong. 2d Sess., pp. 11-12. For other evidence along this line see H. R. Mis. Doc. No. 31, Part 1, pp. 399, 417, 422, 436, 438, 446. One negro said that on a certain occasion when he hurrahed for Hampton, men and women of his race fell upon him "the same as ants," and tore off all his clothing except his trousers. The same negro stated that the reason he voted the Democratic ticket was that he was able to borrow money from a Democrat, who asked no questions about repayment. "I thought the Democratic party was good, and we'll give them our support."—*Ibid*, 402.

2 *Atlantic*, XXXIX, p. 185.

had been injured, and one white man had been fatally wounded. [1]

The other riot was a far more serious affair. It occurred at Ellenton, in the same county in which Hamburg was situated. As a result of race and political hatreds, conditions in that section had for some time been favorable for an outbreak. An occasion was offered by the attempt of two negroes to commit a robbery. The opportunity "to teach the negroes a lesson" was too favorable to be lost. Rifle-clubs from a radius of thirty miles collected; all the negroes of the locality became alarmed; conflicts took place; and before quiet was restored one or two whites and from fifteen to thirty negroes had lost their lives. Most and probably all of the negroes killed were wholly innocent of the original offense, and many were simply shot down. Particularly cold-blooded was the murder of Simon P. Coker, a member of the legislature. A far greater massacre was prevented only by the opportune arrival of a company of United States troops, who saved about one hundred colored men surrounded in a swamp. Even then the killing of colored men continued for several days. [2]

In view of the violence and disorder in the state, Governor Chamberlain on October 7th issued a proc-

---

1 *Southern Historical Society Papers*, XII, pp. 554-558; Allen, p. 351; H. R. Mis. Doc. No. 31, Part 2, 44th Cong. 2d Sess., pp. 7 *et seq.*

2 My account of the Ellenton affair is based chiefly on *Southern Historical Society Papers*, XIII, pp. 47-53; and on the enormous mass of evidence contained in H. R. Mis. Doc. No. 31, 44th Cong. 2d Sess., and in S. Mis. Doc. No. 48, 44th Cong. 2d Sess.

lamation ordering the rifle-clubs and other military organizations not a part of the militia to disband. As the disturbances continued and the order was not obeyed, he soon afterwards appealed to the President for troops. The President accordingly issued a proclamation against the rifle-clubs, and sent more than thirty companies of United States troops into the state. [1]

These actions on the part of the governor and the President evoked, of course, a storm of criticism. [2] It was denied by the Democrats that the call for troops was warranted by the facts. It was said that Chamberlain ought to have called upon the rifle-clubs to put down the disorders. It was urged that he ought to have convoked the legislature. On the whole, however, there can be little doubt that the use of troops was justifiable, even though it be granted that the governor and the President were actuated by partisan motives. The governor unquestionably showed wisdom in not attempting to make use of the negro militia, for that would have brought on yet more terrible consequences; while, as for making use of the rifle-clubs, that, as he remarked, would have been calling in the

---

[1] *Annual Cyclopaedia*, 1876, pp. 719-720, and Allen, pp. 365-422.

[2] H. R. Mis. Doc. No. 31, Part 1, 44th Cong. 2d Sess., pp. 338-340, *Southern Historical Society Papers*, XIII, pp. 53-55. Some of the judges denied Chamberlain's charges; some even represented South Carolina as a very elysium of peace and good order. A United States army officer later testified that the judges lied. Judge Wiggin, whose circuit embraced the counties of Aiken and Barnwell, stated that domestic violence certainly existed and expressed the opinion that the sending of troops had saved many lives.—H. R. Mis. Doc. No. 31, Part 4, 45th Cong. 3d Sess., p. 340.

wolves to guard the sheep. [1] The use of troops in an election is, to be sure, to be deplored as a usual thing; but conditions in South Carolina were such that the only pity was there were not more troops available. As for the absurd claim that the presence of the troops would scare the negroes into voting the Republican ticket, [2] the later admission by the Democratic members of a House investigating committee that the bearing of the troops "was both prudent and wise" [3] is sufficient refutation. The "true inwardness" of the outcry lay in the fact that the presence of the troops interfered with the Democratic plan of campaign. Had the troops not been sent, there can be little doubt that the Democrats would have carried the state by a large majority. But as General N. P. Banks later remarked: "The last card — one which had been played with so much success in adjoining states, upon which in fact every expectation of success depended, the revolver and rifle, which had been carefully dealt out, according to the rules of the game as practiced in the best political society, to each member of the club organized for intellectual and social pleasures only — was unexpectedly and scandalously trumped by a Federal bayonet." [4]

The presence of the troops did much to secure a more peaceful condition of affairs. After the issuance of the President's proclamation there was but one considerable riot. This occurred at a Republican meeting

---

1 Allen, p. 387. For Chamberlain's defence see New York *Tribune* for October 5th and November 2d .
2 E. g., New York *Herald* of Oct. 28th.
3 H. R. R. No. 175, Part I, 44th Cong. 2d Sess., p. 12.
4 *Ibid*, Part 2, p. 227.

held at Cainhoy near Charleston. As usual the Democrats had forced the Republicans to divide time, and
while the meeting was in progress some young white
men seized some guns belonging to the negroes. A
fight ensued in which the negroes for once stood their
ground, killed six of the whites, and put the rest to
flight, with the loss of but one of their own number. [1]
In all places where troops were stationed the negroes
were comparatively safe from physical violence, for so
thoroughly had South Carolinians learned to respect
the United States that the presence of a single blue uni-
form was sufficient to hold a whole company of "red-
shirts" in check. In the back country where there
were no troops, however, there continued to be something of a reign of terror among the freedmen.

The election proper was attended with terrible excitement, yet on the whole it was more peaceable than
might have been anticipated. In some respects, however, it was scarcely more than a farce. While there
were no great riots, there were minor disturbances at
many places, and there was much intimidation of individuals, buying of votes, and repeating. In Charleston, Beaufort, and other "black counties" bands of
negroes, armed with guns, clubs, swords, knives, bayonets, and other weapons, surrounded some of the
polls; swore they would "kill any —— Democratic
nigger" who offered to vote; and violently handled
some who disregarded the warning. In these counties

---

[1] For some of the evidence see H. R. Mis. Doc. No. 31, 44th
Cong. 2d Sess., pp. 160-260. See also *Southern Historical Society
Papers,* pp. 57-59, for a very partisan account.

the Republicans also appear to have done considerable repeating. [1] In other counties similar tactics were pursued to an even greater degree by the Democrats. Negroes and even white election officials were intimidated and in some cases assaulted, and parties of white men rôde about from poll to poll casting their votes at each. [2] In this sort of work the native whites were materially aided by Georgians and North Carolinians, who crossed the border to help their fellow Democrats.[3]

Since the state census of 1875 gives the number of males of voting age and since the election managers in all but four counties classified the voters according to color, it is possible to arrive at some conclusions by a process of comparison. [4] Such a study seems to show that by far the greater amount of illegal voting was done by the whites. In only two counties did the colored vote exceed the census figures, the excess being 928; in the other counties [5] the negro vote fell below the census figures by 6,727. In only four counties did the white vote fall below the census figures, the decrease in these being 328; in all the other counties, exclusive of those in which no classification was made, there was an excess amounting to 3,505, while in the non-classified counties there was an estimated excess

---

1 See *Atlantic*, XXXIX, p. 187; index to H. R. Mis: Doc. No. 31, Part 1, pp. 471-472; index to S. Mis. Doc. No. 48, p. xiii.
2 *Ibid*, pp. x-xiii; House report just cited, pp. 470-471; *Atlantic*, XXXIX, p. 187.
3 *Ibid*; House report, Part 1, pp. 235, 241; S. Mis. Doc. No. 48, 44th Cong. 2d Sess., pp. 328, 352, 410, 675, 861.
4 For figures see H. R. R. No. 175, Part 2, 44th Cong. 2d Sess., p. 62. The four counties were Charleston, Laurens, Edgefield, and Williamsburgh.
5 Disregarding the four mentioned.

of 3,026. In only one county, namely Barnwell, do
the figures show conclusively that there was Republican
repeating. Most of this repeating was done in Robbins Precinct. About noon of election day the regular
polling-place was fired on and was deserted, but the
Republican manager opened another one at an abandoned school-house. The voting at this new poll
proceeded so briskly that, when evening came, 1,317
ballots, all for the Republican candidates, were taken
out of the box. As this was about four times the
number of votes cast at the election of 1874, it is tolerably clear that some citizens must have deposited more
than their share.[1] It was also claimed by the Democrats that the Republicans did much repeating in
Charleston county; but the figures alone do not bear
out the claim, for the total vote of the county lacked
more than 1,000 of equalling the census figures. However, as it was notorious that great numbers of blacks
were induced by the whites to absent themselves from
the polls, it is quite conceivable that some who did go
cast extra ballots for those who remained away.[2]

But the Democrats certainly bore away the palm in
the matter of illegal voting. Edgefield county, which
in 1874 had given a Republican majority of 498

---

1 For index to part of the testimony regarding this precinct see
p. 469 of H. R. Mis. Doc. No. 31. Part 1, 44th Cong. 2d Sess. The
Democrats claimed that the Republicans themselves fired on the
polling places. The Republicans tried to explain the size of the
vote by pointing out that in a neighboring precinct no election was
held and that the voters from that precinct voted in the Robbins Precinct. The board of canvassers threw out all the votes.
Not all the cheating in this county was done by Republicans, for
the white vote exceeded the census figures by 416, whereas the
colored vote was less by 971.

2 *Atlantic*, XXXIX, p. 187.

out of a vote of 6,298, was this time made to
return a Democratic majority of 3,134 out of a
total of 9,374, which was 2,252 more votes than
the total number of adult males in the preceding year.[1]
In Laurens county likewise there was much crooked
work done. In that county the Democratic majority
was 1,112, as against a Republican majority of 1,077
in 1874. [2] In these two counties ballot-box stuffing,
intimidation, repeating, and similar practices were
everywhere rampant.

The ballots were counted much more fairly
than they were cast. With a liberality which did him
honor, Governor Chamberlain had appointed a Democrat as a member of the board of managers in each
election precinct and had composed the board of county
canvassers in like manner. [3]

The election was scarcely over before it was apparent
that the result would be very close. At once there
began a contest similar to those in Florida and Louisiana. Like those states South Carolina had a board of
state canvassers. This board was composed of the
secretary of state, the comptroller-general, the attorney-
general, auditor, treasurer, adjutant and inspector-gen-

---

[1] For testimony regarding Edgefield see p. xii of index to S.
Mis. Doc. No. 48, 44th Cong. 2d Sess. The Democrats had
claimed that the census figures were too large.—*Atlantic*, XXXIX,
p. 187.

[2] *Ibid*, pp. xii-xiii.

[3] Allen, p. 428. In compiling the vote the county canvassers
made some changes in the precinct returns. The names of some
of the candidates had not been correctly printed on some of the
tickets, and in several cases candidates running for one office had
by mistake received votes for other offices. Some of the boards
credited the candidates with votes clearly intended for them.—
Atlantic, XXXIX, p. 188.

eral, and the chairman of the committee on privileges
and elections of the House of Representatives.[1] All
these gentlemen were Republicans, three were colored
men, and three were candidates for re-election. Under
the act creating it, the board had the power to receive
and canvass the returns for all officers except governor
and lieutenant-governor, the returns for these two
being canvassed in joint session of the general assembly. In performing their work the board had the
further power, and it was "made their duty, to decide
all cases under protest or contest" that might arise.[2]
At previous canvasses this section of the statute had
been interpreted as giving the board discretionary
powers.[3] At this canvass, however, the Democrats resolved to make an effort to confine the board to merely
ministerial duties. In this work they found an instrument ready at hand in the state supreme court. That
body was composed of Chief Justice F. J. Moses,
father of the notorious ex-governor whose judicial am-
bitions had been thwarted by Chamberlain; of Associate Justice Willard; and of Associate Justice Wright,
who was a colored man.[4] All three had been chosen
by the Republicans, but the first two had opposed
Chamberlain and they now displayed a willingness to
lend themselves to actions almost if not quite as par-

---

1 The last mentioned and the auditor did not act.—P. 67 of
Appendix to H. R. Mis. Doc. No. 31, Part 3, 44th Cong., 2d
Sess.

2 Act approved March 1, 1870.

3 Allen, p. 429.

4 *Ibid.*

tisan as many of those already described in Louisiana. [1]

On the 14th of November, four days after the board began its proceedings, the Democrats applied to the court for a writ of prohibition to restrain the board from exercising judicial functions, and for a writ of *mandamus* to compel it to perform the merely ministerial functions of ascertaining from the returns which candidates had the highest number of votes and of then certifying the statements thereof to the secretary of state. On the 17th the court complied as far as to issue an order, auxiliary to its final judgment, directing the board forthwith to proceed to canvass the returns, and then make a report of the result to the court. [2]

Very much against their will the board on November 21st brought in such a report, but at the same time submitted a vigorous protest against the claim that the board was by law compelled to render account of its actions to the court. The board stated that many allegations and evidences of fraud and other irregularities had been filed regarding the election in Edgefield, Barnwell, Laurens, and other counties. They further reported that, taking the face of the returns but omitting Robbins Precinct, the result would be the election of two Democratic congressmen, two Democratic state

---

1 Maxwell in the *South Atlantic,* pp. 328-330, pays a tribute to the court's "judicial integrity."

2 For the documents in the case see Appendix to H. R. Mis. Doc. No. 31, 44th Cong. 2d Sess., pp. 78-91. Justice Wright dissented from that part of the order which required the board to certify its action to the court.

officers, [1] enough Democratic members of the general
assembly to give that party a majority of one on
joint ballot, three Republican state officers, four Republican congressmen, and all the Republican electors
by majorities averaging about 816. [2]

The Democrats now found themselves in an extremely puzzling dilemma. The face of the returns gave
them control of the legislature, and consequently
the governorship and lieutenant-governorship, into
their hands; but, notwithstanding the frauds in Edgefield, Barnwell, and Laurens, the vote for the electors
was favorable to Hayes. If the returns were allowed
to stand, then most of the state ticket would be saved,
but Tilden would be lost; if, on the other hand, the
court should decide to allow the board discretionary
power, then the state officers, about which the Democrats were by far the most anxious, would probably
be lost without there being much chance that a majority would be evolved for Tilden.

After consulting among themselves and probably
with New York the Democratic managers asked the
court to grant two orders, one for each horn of the
dilemma. The first order was to force the board to
"certify to be correct the statement of the whole number of votes for members of the general assembly
. . . . and determine and declare what persons have
been by the greatest number of votes elected to

---

1 But not if certain votes cast for John B. Tolbert were
counted for John R. Tolbert, and certain votes cast for F. C.
Dunn were counted for T. C. Dunn.

2 For this report see appendix to H. R. Mis. Doc. No. 31, 44th
Cong. 2d Sess., pp. 91-114.

such offices . . . . make certificate of this determination, and deliver it to the secretary of state
. . . . and do the same in reference to members of
Congress." By this means the Democrats would
secure beyond the chance of loss two members of
Congress, two minor state officers, and a majority of
the members of the legislature and the consequent
declaration by that body in favor of the claims of
the Democratic candidates for governor and lieutenant-governor. The request for the other order
recited that there were discrepancies between the
returns of the precinct managers and the returns of
the boards of county canvassers and asked that the
state board be compelled to correct such discrepancies,
and after doing so make a report to the court, and also
deliver to it "all official papers on which the same is in
any manner based, including the returns of the several
managers and the statements of the county canvassers."[1] This petition looked to the saving, if possible,
of one or all of the electors.

The court entertained both petitions, but delayed
action upon them. This delay probably had a hidden
motive.[2] The statute defining the powers and duties
of the board limited that body's sittings to ten days;
if, therefore, the board did not fulfill its duties within
that time, it would no longer have any legal authority
in the matter; the court, being in possession of the

---

1 Appendix to H. R. R. No. 31, Part 3, 44th Cong. 2d Sess., pp.
133-135. This request was first made on the 20th and was
again brought forward.
2 So charged by Allen, p. 434. See also New York *Times* of
Nov. 24th *et seq.*

records of election, could then have assumed the responsibility of declaring the result. It goes without
saying that that declaration would have been for Tilden.[1]

The plan was a shrewd one, but the first step, upon
which all the rest depended, was delayed a little too
long. The ten day limit expired shortly after noon of
the 22d. At 11 o'clock of that day the court met, and
issued a writ of peremptory *mandamus* granting the
first petition; then, after a short recess, ordered that
a "rule do issue" requiring the board of canvassers to
show cause why another writ of *mandamus* should not
issue requiring them to comply with the second petition.[2]

But before the second order was issued and before
the writ granted had been served, the board of state
canvassers had ceased to exist. That body met at 10
A. M.; "corrected certain errors" in the returns; threw
out the counties of Edgefield and Laurens (which certainly ought to have been thrown out); certified the
election of the Hayes electors, of all the Republican
candidates for state offices except the candidates for
governor and lieutenant-governor, and of other candidates, both Republicans and Democrats, for whom
they found majorities. The board then adjourned
sine die.[3]

1 See *Times* of Nov. 23d and 24th.
2 Appendix to report just cited, pp. 114-118; *Times* of Nov.
23d; *Herald* of Nov. 23d.
3 See appendix just cited, pp. 118-122. For the protests and
evidence before the board see *Ibid,* pp. 37-67. For the minutes
of the board see *Ibid,* pp. 67-78. The board did not return any
one as elected to the legislature from Edgefield and Laurens.

The rage of the Democrats when they discovered
that they had been outwitted was very great indeed.[1]
Hampton declared the action of the board "a high-
handed outrage;"[2] public excitement ran so high that
an armed conflict seemed not improbable; the court
endeavored to avenge itself by fining each member
of the board $1,500 for contempt and by committing
all of them to the Richland county jail until further
orders.[3]   From thence they were, however, almost immediately released on a writ of *habeas corpus* issued by
Judge Bond of the United States circuit court.[4]

The Democrats now resorted to a number of other
expedients to secure one or more electors for Tilden.
A proceeding in the nature of a *quo warranto* was instituted in the supreme court by the Democratic claimants against the Republican electors, but the case was
ultimately dismissed.[5]   An attempt was made to bribe
one of the electors; but, like a previous attempt to
bribe the canvassing board, it failed.   A scheme was
also formed to prevent the electors from voting by a
process which involved bribery, violence, and the lock-

---

1 *Southern Historical Society Papers*, XIII, p. 64.

2 *Annual Cyclopaedia*, 1876, p. 725.   Hampton behaved with
great prudence, however, throughout this exciting period, and
discouraged all resorts to violence.   He and the other leaders
saw, of course, that violence would bring them into conflict with
the United States.

3 Appendix to H. R. Mis. Doc. No. 31, 44th Cong. 2d Sess.,
pp. 127-133.

4 *Southern Historical Society Papers*, XIII, p. 64; *Herald* of
Nov. 28th.

5 Appendix cited above, pp. 190-220; H. R. R. No. 175, Part 1,
44th Cong. 2d Sess., p. 9.

ing up of the electors in separate cells until after the legal day for casting their ballots; but it, too, failed. [1]

On the 6th of December, therefore, the Republican electors met unhindered, and cast their ballots for Hayes and Wheeler. Returns of their vote, duly certified, were then forwarded both by mail and by messenger to Washington.

On the same day the Democratic claimants also met and voted; but it is rather difficult to see on what ground they based their right to do so, for the Democrats admitted among themselves that the national contest had gone against them. As early as the 14th of November Mr. Smith Mead Weed, who had come to the state in the interests of Tilden, had telegraphed in cipher to New York: "Best I can figure, Tilden will be 2,600 behind Hampton, and see little hope; shall keep up appearances." [2] At a later date, when the committee of the House of Representatives came to the state, the Democratic members were unable to make any coherent case for their candidate. In their report they felt constrained to admit that, after "ascertaining the votes cast at all the precincts and correcting the mistakes made by the managers in the returns," the lowest Hayes elector had received over the highest Tilden elector "a majority of 831." [3] To be sure, the Democratic members added that "no opinion is advanced upon the truth and accuracy of these returns;"

---

1 H. R. R. No. 31, Part 1, 44th Cong. 2d Sess., p. 456. For a full account of these matters see *post* Chap. XIII.
2 H. R. Mis. Doc. No. 31, Part 4, 45th Cong. 3d Sess., p. 133.
3 H. R. R. No. 175, Part 1, 44th Cong. 2d Sess., p. 3. This was exclusive of Robbins Precinct.

pointed to the use of the army and to the intimidation of Democratic negroes; and made certain other objections; but the case they presented was a perfunctory one.

There is, in fact, not the slightest doubt regarding the electoral result in South Carolina.[1] On the face of the returns the Republicans had a substantial majority.[2] By excluding Edgefield and Laurens, which certainly ought to have been excluded, the majority would have been increased by more than 4,000. And, finally, if the election had been free and fair, the majority would have been increased by many thousands more.

Nevertheless, the Democratic leaders and newspapers throughout the country continued to claim the state; and it therefore became a bone of contention in the forthcoming struggle at Washington.

---

1 As Governor Chamberlain has remarked: "The historian here is no longer compelled to spell out his verdict from a wide induction of facts; he need only accept the assertions, even the vaunts, of many of the leading figures in the canvass since the canvass was closed."—*Atlantic*, LXXXVII, p. 180.

2 Reynolds admits that "the Republicans got in their electoral ticket."—p. 391.

CHAPTER IX

In Oregon, the remaining state from which a double set of returns was forwarded to Washington, the election produced a situation different from those described in Florida, Louisiana, and South Carolina. In Oregon there was no dispute about the result of the election; for it was freely admitted by all that the three Republican candidates for electors had received majorities, the smallest of which was 1,049 votes.[1] But shortly after the result was known a fact which had attracted practically no attention during the campaign began to assume vast importance not only to the people of Oregon but also to those of the whole country. The fact in question was that John W. Watts, one of the Republican electors, was a postmaster. To be sure, his office was one of the fourth class in the little village of La Fayette in Yam Hill county, and the compensation he received was only about $268 per year;[2] nevertheless, the position was unquestionably one of "trust" and "profit," and by

---

1 S. R. No. 678, 44th Cong. 2d Sess., pp. 1-2. This will be cited as "Report of the Committee."

2 *Ibid*, pp. 2-3. The reference is to the committee's report, but the report accords with the evidence.

holding it he was thereby disqualified by section 1, article 2, of the Federal Constitution from being appointed an elector.

The Democrats were somewhat slow in recognizing the possibilities of the situation which thus presented itself; but after telegrams from the East had announced that a contest had arisen over the eligibility of a postmaster-elector in Vermont the state leaders at last awoke to the fact that perhaps here was an opportunity to secure the one more vote which Tilden must have to secure his election. They at once began to bestir themselves to see what could be done.[1]

In one respect the situation was favorable; in another not so much so. The governor, L. F. Grover, was a Democrat, and was partisan enough to lend himself to almost any plan which gave hope of success. The state law was not so promising. It nowhere said anything about the power of the governor to appoint an elector or the right of a minority candidate to take the place of a successful but ineligible opponent; on the contrary, section 2 expressly provided that "if there shall be any vacancy in the office of an elector, *occasioned by death, refusal to act, neglect to attend, or otherwise,* the electors present shall immediately proceed to fill, by *viva voce* and plurality of votes, such vacancy in the electoral college." The governor's power in the premises, in accordance with the state law, was confined to being present when the secretary of state, who was the returning officer, should can-

---

1 Report of the Committee, p. 3; files of Portland *Daily Oregonian.*

vass the votes, and to granting certificates of election to the persons "having the highest number of votes."

These certificates were to be prepared by the secretary, "signed by the governor and secretary, and by the latter delivered to the college of electors at the hour of their meeting." [1]

Notwithstanding the plain intent of the law, the Democratic leaders in the state resolved to claim that the ineligibility of Watts served to give the electorship for which he had been a contestant, to E. A. Cronin, who had received the highest number of votes among the minority candidates. This resolve was by no means the unaided conception of the Democrats of Oregon, but in part at least was due to a deluge of telegrams from W. T. Pelton, Tilden's nephew and acting secretary of the Democratic national committee, from Abram S. Hewitt, chairman of that committee, and from other prominent Eastern Democrats. The purport of many of these telegrams can be gathered from the following:

"NEW YORK, NOV. 15, —6.

"*Governor L. F. Grover:*

"Upon careful investigation, the legal opinion is that votes cast for a Federal office-holder are void, and that the person receiving the next highest number of votes should receive the certificate of appointment. The canvassing-officers should act upon this, and the governor's certificate of appointment be given to the

---

1 S. Misc. Doc. No. 44, 44th Cong. 2d Sess., p. 31. This will be cited as "Testimony."

elector accordingly, and the subsequent certificate of the votes of the electors be duly made specifying how they voted. This will force Congress to go behind the certificate, and open the way to get into merits of all cases, which is not only just, but which will relieve the embarrassment of the situation.

"ABRAM S. HEWITT." [1]

The Eastern leaders by no means confined themselves to long distance messages of advice. They deemed the matter of such importance that they secured one J. N. H. Patrick of Omaha, Nebraska, to make the long trip to Oregon and see to it that no bungling was done by the supposedly inexperienced Democrats of the western coast. Mr. Patrick hastened westward, taking with him a copy of *The Household English Dictionary*, [2] which was to be used in certain activities in which he expected to engage. Arrived in Oregon, Mr. Patrick displayed much zeal if not discretion in forwarding the purpose for which he had been sent out. After consultation with leading Democrats, he proceeded, as one of his first acts, to retain in consideration of the sum of $3,000 the services of the Republican law firm of Hill, Durham, and Thompson; not, it appears, primarily for the sake of their legal assistance — there were enough Democratic lawyers to render all necessary aid in that connection — but because one of the firm was the editor of the two most

---

[1] Committee's Report, p. 29. For other dispatches see pp. 18-37.

[2] Testimony, pp. 441-455, and Report of Committee, p. 19.

influential newspapers in the state.[1] Some time later Mr. Patrick dispatched the following telegram:

"To W. T. Pelton, No. 15, *Gramercy Park, New York:*

"By vizier association innocuous to negligence cunning minutely previously readmit doltish to purchase afar act with cunning afar sacristy unweighed afar pointer tigress cuttle superannuated syllabus dilatoriness misapprehension contraband Kountze bisculous top usher spiniferous answer.
"J. N. H. PATRICK."[2]

When this dispatch was received, Mr. Pelton, or his secretary, took each word of the telegram in turn and found its position in another copy of *The Household English Dictionary,* and then sought out the word in the corresponding position in the eighth column ahead.[3] The result obtained by this process was as follows:

"Certificate will be issued to one Democrat. Must purchase a Republican elector to recognize and act with Democrat and secure the vote and prevent trouble. Deposit $10,000 to my credit with Kountze Brothers, Wall street. Answer."

---

1 Report of Committee, pp. 9-10; telegram to Pelton in Testimony, p. 449; testimony of Bellinger, pp. 300 *et seq.,* of Kelly, p. 332, and of others. The newspapers continued hostile, however.

2 Testimony, p. 448.

3 *Ibid,* pp. 439-468, 236, 247, 250, 351, 494. Patrick had at one time used practically the same cipher in business dealings with Alfred B. Hinman of Detroit. Hinman had explained the cipher to his agent and later partner Alfred W. Shaw. When the Senate committee had possession of the dispatches, some of them in their original form were given to the newspapers. Shaw saw one of them in a Detroit paper, and explained the key to the editor of the Detroit *Daily Post.*

Money to the amount of more than $15,000 in all was furnished Mr. Patrick,[1] but his scheme to purchase a Republican elector was not consummated.[2] How the other part of the plan was carried out will presently appear.

On the 4th of December the secretary of state canvassed the returns in the presence of the governor and found that the Republican candidates — Cartwright, Odell, and Watts — had received "the highest number of votes." But the governor then stated that a protest had been filed against the issuance of a certificate to Watts, and announced that on the following day he would hear arguments anent the matter. At the appointed time he took a seat on the bench in the room of the state supreme court. The three Republican electors then presented a protest denying his jurisdiction in the case, and insisting that, in the absence of judicial proceedings, his only power in the premises was to issue certificates to the persons receiving the highest number of votes as declared by the secretary of state. They took no further part in the hearing, but the Democratic counsel presented arguments which lasted far into the night.[3]

---

1 Testimony of Asahel Bush of the firm with whom the money was deposited.—*Ibid*, p. 284.

2 On the following day Mr. Pelton sent a dispatch stating that "If you make obligation contingent on result in March, it can be done, and [incremable] slightly if necessary." He testified before the committee that this did not refer to the purchase of an elector; but in view of later revelations, it may well be doubted whether he told the truth.—See *Ibid*, 502 *et seq.*

3 The protests and a summary of the proceedings are given in the Report of the Committee, pp. 7-9; see also Testimony, pp. 103, 120, 413.

Although his mind was already made up, [1] Governor Grover withheld his decision until the following day, which was the time appointed for the electors to cast their ballots. Shortly after noon of that day he delivered to the secretary of state certificates containing the names of Odell and Cartwright, the two Republican candidates whose eligibility was not questioned, and of Cronin, the Democratic claimant for Watts's electorship. The governor pretended to act on the theory that since Watts was ineligible the votes cast for him were void and hence the majority of legal votes were cast for his opponent. In order to escape the law providing for the filling of vacancies by the other electors, he argued that because Watts was ineligible he was never an "incumbent" and hence there could be no vacancy. This interpretation was plainly at variance with the state law defining vacancies, but as the election of a President was at stake the governor did not hesitate at a matter of such small importance as the law. [2]

Then ensued a scene which would have been farcical had it not been fraught with possibilities of grave danger to the peace of a great nation. The secretary of

---

1 See telegrams from Oregon to Pelton, Testimony, pp. 449, 464.

2 The state law provided that the governor should issue his certificate to the persons "having the highest number of votes," but as the state law by mistake said "two lists" while the Federal law said "three," he evaded the state law by claiming to act under the Federal law, which was more general. See his testimony in *Ibid*, pp. 103, 120, 202, 235, and especially his written defence, published in pamphlet form, and incorporated into his testimony, pp. 413-425. For the view of the committee see their Report, pp. 38-74. The law of the case will be considered in greater detail in Chapter XI.

state signed the certificates given him by the governor, and took them to the room set apart for the electors. There he found Odell, Cartwright, and Watts (who had now resigned his postmastership), and also Cronin and the other two defeated Democratic candidates. To Cronin he handed the envelope containing the three certificates, and then retired. When Odell and Cartwright asked for their certificates, Cronin refused to deliver them, but condescended to read part, or all, of one of the certificates aloud. Odell and Cartwright nevertheless proceeded to organize the college; Cartwright was elected president, and he then chose Odell as secretary. Cronin now again refused to hand over the certificates, and also refused to obey a resolution to that effect passed by Cartwright and Odell. At this point Watts, who hitherto had taken no part, presented his resignation, stating that the objections made to his eligibility were his reason for doing so. His resignation was accepted, whereupon Cronin exclaimed:

"I understand that by receiving Dr. Watts's resignation you refuse to act with me, and I shall proceed to fill these vacancies. I declare there are two vacancies, and I shall proceed to fill them." [1]

He then instructed Mr. Klippel, one of the defeated Democratic candidates, who now took charge of the door, to "call in Mr. J. N. T. Miller." Miller was waiting outside the door in readiness for such an emergency, and at once came in. Cronin thereupon

---

1 Testimony, p. 48.

appointed him to fill one of the "vacancies," after which the two chose a Mr. Parker to fill the other. After Parker had been called in the three proceeded to cast their ballots for President and Vice-President. Considering that all three were Democrats, they showed great forbearance in this matter, for they cast two votes for Hayes and Wheeler and only one for Tilden and Hendricks.

In the meantime Odell and Cartwright were not idle. They chose Watts to fill the vacancy caused by his own resignation, or disqualification, and then cast three ballots for Rutherford B. Hayes for President and three ballots for William A. Wheeler for Vice-President. [1]

Returns from both "colleges" were later forwarded, both by mail and by special messenger, to the president of the Senate. The Democratic returns, which were certified by Governor Grover, were conveyed to Washington by Cronin, who, however, first forced the Democratic managers to pay him $3,000 for doing so. [2] The Republican returns, which were not certified by the governor but which were accompanied by certificates of the results of the canvass furnished by the secretary of state, [3] were carried by Mr. Odell.

---

[1] My account of this whole transaction is based chiefly upon the testimony of the secretary of state, *Ibid*, pp. 19 and 66, of Odell, pp. 32, 37, 67, 392; of Cartwright, pp. 46, 181; of Watts, 59, 145, 203, 368, 391; of Cronin, p. 78; of Klippel, pp. 162, 249; of Miller, p. 175; of Laswell, pp. 252, 265, and of some other witnesses. Upon most of the essential facts the witnesses were in substantial accord.

[2] Testimony of Cronin himself.—*Ibid*, pp. 88 *et seq.*

[3] Three certificates were obtained from the secretary by a Mr. Dolph and were carried by him to the Republicans in the electoral room.—*Ibid*, pp. 25, 52.

The Republicans, both of the state and the nation, denounced the Democratic procedure as an "outrage" and an attempted "steal;" in Oregon itself the indignation ran so high that Governor Grover was burned in effigy. The Democrats, on the other hand, usually characterized the matter as a "good joke," or a "shrewd trick."[1] Not many of their leaders expected the Cronin return to stand, but they did believe it would secure a revision of other electoral returns by forcing the Republicans to set a precedent of going behind the certificate of the governor. They were now confident that whatever course the Republicans should take, Tilden was sure of the necessary number of electoral votes.

But their rejoicing was premature. As was almost immediately pointed out, they failed to discern a radical distinction between the Oregon question and the questions raised in the Southern states. In the latter the issue arose regarding the manner in which the board of state canvassers discharged their duties. To go behind their returns would require a recount of the popular vote in those states, a revision of the application of state registry laws, and a decision as to the facts and effects of intimidation and fraud. Such action would lead to a substitution of national for state authority, in violation of the Federal Constitution, which says that each state shall appoint its electors "in such manner as the legislature thereof may direct."

---

1 *Daily Oregonian,* Dec. 8th; New York *Times,* Dec. 7th to 10th.

The Oregon question, on the contrary, was one which would not lead to any such investigation. The dispute there began at a point subsequent to where the Southern questions ended. It would not lead to any inquiry or judgment as to how or why the people voted or neglected to vote. It would not touch the action of any state canvasser in canvassing the votes. It would simply relate to the unauthorized interference of the governor of Oregon and his man Cronin with the action of the college of electors at a time when they were assembled to discharge their duty under the United States law and Constitution, as the law of Oregon expressly declared they should do, and could hardly, if at all, go beyond facts appearing upon the face of the returns made by the duly elected electors. [1]

In this clear and undeniable distinction between the domains of state powers and Federal powers lay momentous possibilities. Out of the failure, either through mental obtuseness or willful obstinacy, on the part of many persons to perceive this nice distinction there later originated much unjustifiable criticism of the constitutional stand taken by eight men who were to decide one of the most momentous controversies which judges have ever been called upon to decide.

[1] See an article by Dorman B. Eaton in the New York *Times* for Dec. 14th. In the light of subsequent events this article was prophetic.

CHAPTER X

COMPROMISE OR CIVIL WAR?

Few of the generation which has grown up since then will ever have any but the faintest conception of the gravity of the situation existing during the winter of 1876-77. In the end the question at issue was settled peaceably without leaving many traces that could easily be remarked by future observers. But at the time probably more people dreaded an armed conflict than had anticipated a like outcome to the secession movement of 1860-61.[1]

In fact, it was difficult to see how the dispute could be settled in any other manner. Both parties seemed equally determined; both professed to be thoroughly confident of the justice of their cause. There was intense bitterness of feeling on both sides, but especially on the part of the Democrats. They had thought themselves about to enter the Promised Land, when, lo, a possibility had arisen that they might be excluded from it. They at once began to cry out that a conspiracy was on foot to cheat Tilden out of the Presidency; hot-heads were loud in asserting their deter-

---

[1] Senator Hoar, Autobiography, I, p. 369, says that in his opinion there would have been a resort to arms had it not been "for the bitter experience of a few years before."

mination to resist to the uttermost the consummation of the "plot." Threats of force were freely indulged in. The phrase, "Tilden or blood," was heard in some quarters.[1] "Tilden has been elected," said the Evansville, Indiana, *Courier;* "and by the Eternal he shall be inaugurated." The New York *World* declared that in case Republican returning boards should count in Hayes, "many times

> "Forty thousand American men
> Will know the reason why."[2]

The New York *Express,* which was said to be the property of John Kelly and other prominent Democrats, talked about "tea duties" and "the use of the sword" and indulged in a torrent of incendiary insinuations and assertions.[3] Similar expressions appeared in hundreds of other Democratic newspapers in all parts of the country.

But happily some of the persons who had supported Tilden were less violent. Speaking for this class, the New York *Herald* gave the radical element in the party some excellent advice. "Let us," it said on November 10th, "be as calm as we can. . . . . There must be no violence. . . . . This is not Mexico. . . . . As the Democratic party is that which feels itself likely to be aggrieved in this matter, we beg them to remember that the danger which

---

1 Quoted in the New York *Times,* Dec. 19th.
2 Nov. 16th.
3 Cited in the *Herald* of Nov. 16th.

now stares the country in the face is but one of the results of the rebellion which they encouraged, and in which the largest part of them engaged in 1861. That rebellion was causeless and unreasonable to the last degree; to their folly and wickedness in beginning and encouraging it are due the multitude of evils which have rested upon the country since, and of which this present emergency is another. The country has not forgotten their agency in these matters. It is not unwilling once more to trust them with political power; the present vote shows this. But it will not tolerate for an instant anything which looks to a disorderly or violent attempt to grasp power, or even anything which could be construed into a threat to do so. The American people will make extremely short work of any party, be it the Democratic or the Republican, which attempts or threatens civil disorder hereafter on any plea or pretext whatever." Other Democratic journals gave similar counsel. The New York *Sun,* for example, said on November 21st that it would be better to "submit to wrong for the time, however gross, than to appeal to any but legal, constitutional, and peaceful remedies."

The Republicans, while equally determined, were in general much more conservative in their utterances than were the Democrats.[1] They made no threats of "Hayes or war." They merely asserted that in case he should be found to have a majority of the electoral vote, he would be inaugurated. They sneered

---

[1] New York *Times,* Dec. 4th.

at the Democratic "vaporings," and in reply remarked significantly that General U. S. Grant, not Buchanan, was in charge of affairs at Washington. [1]

The contest absorbed the attention of the country to the practical exclusion of every other subject. Each day the newspapers were filled with conjectures, rumors, and long editorials. Few attempts were made to present the truth on both sides of the question. The Democratic press represented that during the campaign peace and good-will towards all had reigned in the South, with the exception that many good Democratic negroes had been wickedly intimidated by colored Republicans and United States troops. [2] The returning boards they characterized as the special device of the devil. The Republican press, on the other hand, spoke of Wells, Anderson, and the rest as gentlemen of the highest character, only a "little lower than the angels," and gave harrowing accounts of political murders and proscriptions committed without doubt at the direct instigation of Tilden and other leaders. For having sent troops to preserve the peace in the disputed states, the President was lauded by Republicans, and was threatened with impeachment by Democrats. [3] There was much talk about ineligible electors in Vermont, New Jersey, Missouri, Oregon

---

1 *Harper's Weekly*, XX, p. 965.
2 They misrepresented in the most absurd way the Pinkston story.—New York *World* of Nov. 29th, 30th, and Dec. 1st.
3 The New York *Herald*, however, approved the sending of the troops.—See issue of Nov. 12th. The impeachment talk was most pronounced after the troops had been used to support the Chamberlain legislature.—See New York *World* of Dec. 1st and 2d; *The Nation*, XXIII, pp. 337-338.

and elsewhere. There was the widest possible difference of opinion regarding who possessed the power
to count and declare the electoral vote. Republicans
asserted that this power belonged to the Republican
president of the Senate; Democrats were equally confident that the right resided in the ultimate analysis in
the Democratic House. The newspapers were filled
with long and learned discussions of the points of
law involved in the various questions at issue; cases
were cited in the most elaborate and conclusive
manner. The Democrats made much of the fact that
they had received a majority of "200,000" of the popular vote;[1] the Republicans retorted that Presidents
are not elected by popular vote, that there had been
several minority Presidents, and that, anyhow, with a
free election in Mississippi, Alabama, Georgia, and
elsewhere in the South, the majority would have been
reversed.[2] All sorts of stories were afloat. Because
the President ordered some companies of troops to
Washington, it was alleged he intended to seat Hayes
by force, or else to declare himself dictator.[3] Hayes
was reported to be arranging a trade with the Southern Democrats.[4] It was said that the Democrats
were attempting to bribe returning boards, that they
were attempting to bribe electors,[5] that at the last

---

[1] See almost any issue of the *World* or *Sun*. The *Herald*
deprecated this sort of talk as likely to stir up violence. The
popular vote, it pointed out, was altogether "irrelevant."
[2] This was no doubt true. For a convincing demonstration
see New York *Times* of Dec. 10th.
[3] *Sun*, Dec. 18th.
[4] *Times*, Dec. 3d, 4th, 5th.
[5] *Ibid*, Dec. 7th.

moment they would send out a false telegram purporting to be from Zach. Chandler informing the Republican electors that Hayes had withdrawn, and instructing them to vote for Blaine.[1] When *The Nation,* which was extremely anxious for a peaceful solution of the difficulty, suggested that some Republican elector give a casting vote for Tilden, the story immediately started that James Russell Lowell, who was one of the Massachusetts electors, intended to adopt this advice; Mr. Lowell had some difficulty in convincing anxious Republicans that he had no intention of doing so.[2]

On Monday, December 4th, two days before the electoral colleges voted, Congress assembled. As the solution of the great problem lay with that body, its composition was a matter of the highest importance. The Senate was decidedly Republican; the House decidedly Democratic. The presiding officer of the Senate was Thomas W. Ferry of Michigan; the speaker of the House, now chosen to succeed Mr. Kerr, who had died during the recess, was Samuel J. Randall of Pennsylvania.

Neither body had been long in session before the all-absorbing question was taken up. On the very first day the House passed without debate a resolution providing for three committees, one of fifteen members, one of six members, and one of nine members, to proceed to Louisiana, Florida, and South Carolina re-

1 *Times,* Dec. 5th.
2 *Ibid, The Nation,* XXIII, pp. 322-323, 334-335.

spectively, and investigate the "recent elections therein and the action of the returning or canvassing boards in the said states in reference thereto."[1] Next day the Senate likewise passed a resolution directing the Committee on Privileges and Elections to examine into the elections in the states of South Carolina, Georgia, Florida, Alabama, Louisiana, and Mississippi, in order to ascertain whether in those states the right of citizens to vote had "been denied or greatly abridged;" and also directing the committee to "inquire into the eligibility to office under the Constitution of the United States" of any electors who were alleged to have been ineligible, and as to whether the appointment of any electors had been made by force, fraud, or other illegal means.[2] On the 22d the same committee was given instructions to investigate the situation in Oregon.[3]

The various committees soon entered upon their labors.   With the exception of the Senate subcommittees on Oregon, Alabama, and Mississippi, which summoned witnesses to Washington, all the committees and subcommittees proceeded to the states in dispute.[4] There they examined witnesses of all kinds,

---

1 *Record*, pp. 11-16.

2 *Ibid*, pp. 18-21, 33-40. It will be noticed that the resolution of the Senate was strictly consistent with the stand later taken by the Electoral Commission.

3 *Ibid*, pp. 90 and 365-367.

4 A later committee on the privileges, powers, and duties of the House in counting the electoral votes took testimony at Washington. See H. R. Mis. Doc. No. 42, 44th Cong. 2d Sess. Exclusive of the debates in Congress and of several thousands of pages of testimony regarding contested seats in the House, the government ultimately published more than 20,000 pages of material bearing upon the election.

conditions, and colors, and after several weeks of work accumulated about 13,000 pages of testimony, which are of great value to the historian, but which exercised little or no influence upon the outcome of the controversy. Each committee and subcommittee, with the exception of the Senate subcommittees on Oregon, Mississippi and Alabama, brought in two reports. The majority members of the House committees reported that the electoral votes of Louisiana, Florida, and South Carolina belonged of right to Tilden and Hendricks; the minority members, from the same testimony, reported exactly opposite conclusions. The same state of affairs obtained with the Senate committees, except that with them the majority reports were favorable to Hayes, the minority reports to Tilden.

Congress by no means allowed the matter to rest with the mere appointment of investigating committees. The election, in all its varying aspects of intimidation, murder, returning boards, ineligible electors, and governors' certificates, was discussed day after day with great warmth in both houses, without either party being budged one iota from its claim that its own candidates had been elected.

Urged on by the New York *World* and other newspapers, some of the Democratic leaders attempted to carry through a plan to impeach President Grant for his alleged unconstitutional use of the army and for other offenses. A caucus to consider the advisability of beginning such proceedings and also to determine the general line of party procedure met on the 6th of December and again on the 7th.[1] At the first meeting Mr. Fernando Wood, then a representative in Congress but now chiefly remembered as the mayor of New York who in 1861 proposed that the metropolis should secede and set up as a city state, moved that impeachment proceedings should at once be instituted. Other leaders also spoke in favor of such action; but the majority of those present opposed it, and argued that it would serve to raise a distracting issue, and might lead to violence. The opposition on the part of the Southern members to anything which might lead to a civil war was particularly decided. In reply to a good deal of incendiary talk which certain Northern members indulged in, some of the Southern leaders were refreshingly sensible and frank. They declared that the South had had its fill of war. If, said John Young Brown of Kentucky, there should be a war, it would be the work of the Northern Democrats; while Benjamin Hill of Georgia referred cuttingly to a section of the party who were "invincible in peace and invisible in war." He was also reported to have said that Mr. Wood and others of those counselling armed resistance had "no conception of the conservative influence of a 15-inch shell with the fuse in process of combustion."[2]

As time passed it became more than ever apparent

---

1 For accounts see *World*, Dec. 7th, 8th, 9th; *The Nation*, XXIII, pp. 337-338; *Harper's Weekly*, XX, p. 9; *Times*, Dec. 7th and 8th.

2 *Ibid*, Dec. 14th; H. R. Mis. Doc. No. 31, 45th Cong. 3d Sess., I, p. 885.

that the crux of the whole contest lay in the question of the power to count and declare the electoral vote. Unfortunately the constitutional provision on the subject was so indefinite as to leave room for decidedly different interpretations. The Constitution provides, it will be remembered, that the certificates of the votes of the electoral colleges shall be transmitted sealed to the seat of the government, "directed to the president of the Senate," and that "the president of the Senate shall, in the presence of the Senate and House of Representatives, open all the certificates, *and the votes shall then be counted."* Upon the interpretation of the last clause seemed to hinge the question of who was to be the President of the United States. If, as some of the Republicans contended, the clause meant "counted by the president of the Senate,"[1] then there was little doubt that Mr. Ferry, who was a partisan, would decide that the returns sent in by the Republican claimants constituted the true vote and would declare a majority of one for Hayes. If, as the Democrats asserted, the counting was to be done under the direction of the two houses, then a deadlock seemed likely to ensue. Such a deadlock, they contended, would throw the election into the Democratic House.[2]

Nor did the precedents seem to furnish any way

---

[1] *Atlantic,* LXXII, p. 522.

[2] One Democratic theory was that upon disputed questions the two houses should vote together. This would have meant that the Republican majority in the Senate would be overcome by the Democratic majority in the House.—*Atlantic,* LXXII, p. 523.

out of the difficulties of the situation.[1] They did, however, throw light on some of the disputed points. Down to 1865, excluding a temporary expedient used in 1789,[2] the process of counting had been practically the same. Prior to the day appointed the two houses had always passed concurrent resolutions regulating the procedure. Before meeting in the joint session, which sometimes was held in the Senate chamber but oftener in the hall of the House, the Senate had invariably chosen one teller, and the House two. The duties of these tellers had been to make a list of the votes and deliver the result to the president of the Senate. That officer had on every occasion opened the certificates, but in no instance had he attempted, basing his claim on the ambiguous clause, "and the votes shall then be counted," to exercise the power of counting votes or rejecting votes. Clearly, therefore, the precedents were against the theory that the president of the Senate could arrogate to himself the now much coveted power of counting.

But were there any precedents to guide Congress through the other difficulties which would inevitably arise even though the Republican contention on this particular point should be abandoned? The answer is: None that were conclusive. At the first elec-

---

1 For all the proceedings and debates of Congress relating to counting the electoral votes down to 1876 see H. R. Mis. Doc. No. 13, 44th Cong. 2d Sess.

2 John Langdon was chosen president of the Senate "for the sole purpose of receiving, opening, and counting the votes." This was done in accordance with a resolution of the Convention of 1787, later ratified by the Congress of the Confederation.—*Ibid*, pp. 3-8.

tion of Monroe objection was made to counting the votes of Indiana on the ground that Indiana was not a state of the Union at the time her electors were chosen. But as senators and representatives from the state had been admitted to Congress, her votes were received and counted.[1] Four years later a similar question arose regarding the votes of Missouri; as the result of the election did not hinge upon that state, the issue was evaded by counting the votes in the alternative, — that is, 231 for Monroe with the votes of Missouri, and 228 without those votes.[2] In 1837 the same objection was made to the vote of Michigan, and again the issue was evaded by counting in the alternative.[3] Twenty years later, at the time of Buchanan's election, objection was made to the vote of Wisconsin on the ground that the electors had voted on the day after that prescribed by law. Her vote was, however, declared by the Vice-President as it was reported to him in the certificates; not because he claimed the right to pass upon the validity of the election, for he later expressly disclaimed any such authority, but merely because the two houses failed to decide the matter.[4]

The count of 1865 took place under exceptional circumstances. A week previously Congress passed a joint resolution excluding the eleven seceded states

---

1 H. R. Mis. Doc. No. 13, 44th Cong. 2d Sess., pp. 46-47.
2 *Ibid*, pp. 49-56.
3 *Ibid*, pp. 70-76.
4 *Ibid*, pp. 86-144.

from participation in the choice of the President, [1] and by another joint resolution prescribed a mode of procedure to be used in counting the votes from the other states. [2]   This second resolution was the famous Twenty-Second Joint Rule, which provided that in case objection should be made to the vote of any state, the two houses should separate, and, without debate, decide upon the question of receiving such vote, and no vote was to be counted except by consent of both houses.   Of the states excluded by the law none except Louisiana and Tennessee had chosen electors; the Vice-President, in obedience to the law, refrained from presenting their returns to the convention; and, as no objection had been made to any other return, no resort to the most vital part of the rule was necessary. [3]

Four years later, at the first election of Grant, objection was made to the vote of Louisiana on the ground that no valid election had been held in that state, but the two houses concurred in counting her vote. [4]   The vote of Georgia was also objected to because the electors had not been chosen on the day required by law, because at the date of the election the state had not been readmitted to representation in Congress, because she had not complied with the Reconstruction Act, and because the election had not

---

1 H. R. Mis. Doc. No. 13, 44th Cong. 2d Sess., pp. 149-223. President Lincoln signed this resolution, although he expressed the opinion that it was unnecessary for him to do so.—*Ibid*, pp. 229-230.

2 *Ibid*, pp. 147-149, 223-225.

3 *Ibid*, pp. 225-230.

4 *Ibid*, pp. 238-244.

been "a free, just, equal, and fair election." The two houses, under a special joint rule already provided for the case, counted the vote in the alternative.[1]

Four years later the situation in the states of Louisiana and Arkansas was such that Senator Sherman moved an investigation to ascertain whether the choice of electors in those states had been conducted "in arcordance with the Constitution and laws of the United States, and what contests, if any, have arisen as to who were elected electors in either of said states, and what measures are necessary to provide for the determination of such contests, and to guard against and determine like contests in the future election of electors."[2] In the discussion which followed a number of opinions were advanced which are of interest in connection with the controversy of 1876. Thurman of Ohio said he would vote for the resolution, but expressed a belief that it seemed "to imply that there is a broader jurisdiction in Congress over the election than I have been accustomed to suppose is vested in Congress." He thought that the only power over electors bestowed upon Congress was the power to "determine the time of choosing electors and the day on which they shall give their votes," and held that to the states belonged the right to determine the validity of the claims of different persons to the position of electors. "We may," he however admitted, "be compelled possibly from

1 H. R. Mis. Doc. No. 13, 44th Cong. 2d Sess., pp. 244-266.
2 *Ibid,* p. 336.

necessity to determine which of the two sets of electors has the official evidence that entitles their certificates to be received, and votes given by them to be counted." [1] Other Democrats, as well as many Republicans, expressed similar views upon the power of Congress to go behind the returns. Trumbull of Illinois said: "I think where there are two bodies claiming to be electors of a State we must necessarily have the right to inquire which is the electoral college of the state; but I question whether we could go so far as to go behind the election." [2] Other speakers, including Senator Conkling, [3] interpreted the powers of Congress somewhat more broadly.

The resolution was adopted, and a month later the committee, through Senator Morton, reported upon the situation in Louisiana but not upon that in Arkansas. The report in part was as follows: "The committee are of the opinion that neither the Senate of the United States nor both houses jointly have the power under the Constitution to canvass the returns of an election and count the votes to determine who have been elected Presidential electors, but that the mode and manner of choosing electors are left exclusively to the states. And if by the law of the state they are to be elected by the people, the method of counting the vote and ascertaining the result can only be regulated by the law of the states. Whether it is competent for the two houses, under the Twenty-

---

1 H. R. Mis. Doc. No. 13, 44th Cong. 2d Sess., pp. 336-337.
2 *Ibid*, p. 343.
3 *Ibid*, pp. 343-345.

Second Joint Rule (in regard to the constitutionality of which the committee here give no opinion), to go behind the certificate of the governor of the state to inquire whether the votes have ever been counted by the legal returning board created by the law of the state, or whether, in making such count, the board had before them the official returns, the committee offer on suggestions." [1]

In the end the votes of neither Arkansas nor of Louisiana were counted. Three votes from Georgia were also thrown out because they had been cast for Horace Greeley after that gentleman was dead. Objections were made to the votes of yet other states, but none of these objections were sustained by either House. [2]

Prior to 1876 two unsuccessful attempts to regulate the counting of the electoral votes had been made. In 1800 a bill was introduced into the Senate providing for a Grand Council, composed of six senators, six representatives, and the chief justice, or in his absence the senior associate justice, which should "have power to examine and finally decide all disputes" relative to the count. In so doing the tribunal was to have power to take testimony upon questions of the eligibility of electors, the truth of their returns, and such matters, but was expressly denied the power to go behind the action of canvassing officers. This bill, which in some of its main features was not unlike

---

1 H. R. Mis. Doc. No. 13, 44th Cong. 2d Sess., pp. 358-363.
2 *Ibid*, 357-408.

the act creating the Electoral Commission, was passed in amended form by the Senate, [1] but was defeated in the House. [2]

The other unsuccessful attempt to regulate the count occurred after the count of 1873, already described. Although the general public had taken little interest in the complications of that count, for the simple reason that whatever the decision upon the disputed points might be the general result would not be changed, some of the members of Congress had been awakened to the possibility that the system then in force might in case of a close election lead to a national disaster. Foremost among these persons was Senator Morton of Indiana, who, with wonderful prescience of the dangers soon to arise, began, even before the count of 1873 was made, to urge upon Congress the advisability of changing the method of electing the President, or at least of regulating more effectually the process of the count. [3] The Twenty-Second Joint Rule he denounced as "the most dangerous contrivance to the peace of the nation that has even been invented by Congress — a torpedo planted in the straits with which the state may at some time come into fatal collision." [4] His first effort was directed to securing a constitutional amendment providing for the choice of all but two of the electors apportioned to a state by con-

---

1 One of these amendments substituted a senator chosen by the House from among three nominated by the Senate for the chief justice.

2 H. R. Mis. Doc. No. 13, 44th Cong. 2d Sess., pp. 16-29.

3 *Ibid*, pp. 345-355.

4 *Ibid*, p. 417.

gressional districts; the two others to be chosen by the state at large.[1] When, early in 1875, it became apparent that this plan would fail, he attempted to carry through a bill to govern the count. The bill provided that the vote of no state from which there was but one return should be rejected except by concurrent vote of both houses; but that in case of two or more returns only that one should be counted which each house, acting separately, should decide to be the true one. In the end the bill also failed, partly because of opposition to its provisions, but largely owing to the fact that the Democrats, to their later regret, were unwilling to have it pass until the House chosen in 1874 should be installed.[2] When this had occurred, the matter was again taken up, but nothing was accomplished.[3]

In the debates upon both the proposed amendment and the bill many widely different opinions upon the subject of the power to count were expressed, and some of these opinions are interesting in view of the stand later taken by the statesmen uttering them. Morton himself was by no means consistent in his attitude on the matter of the power to count. He held at first that the president of the Senate must *ex necessitate rei* decide between returns.[4] Later he said that while the constitutional provision might be construed either as giving the power to the president of the Senate

---

1 H. R. Mis. Doc. No: 13, 44th Cong. 2d Sess., pp. 408-458.
2 Senator Thurman, for example, favored the bill but wished to postpone its passage.—*Ibid*, p. 505.
3 *Ibid*, pp. 520-689.
4 *Ibid*, p. 416.

or as giving it to the Congress, he adopted the latter construction as the more reasonable and as more in accord with the spirit of our government.[1]

Numerous devices which have a somewhat similar interest were proposed for settling disputes about the count. One, which was brought forward by Senator Edmunds of Vermont, was for a commission of four members from each House.[2] Senator Frelinghuysen introduced an amendment providing that disputes should be referred to the supreme court.[3] Later he suggested a commission to be composed of the president of the Senate, the speaker, and the chief justice.[4]

But, as already stated, Congress utterly failed to put any authoritative interpretation upon the question of the power of counting. Furthermore, the Senate in January, 1876, on the motion of Senator Morton, refused to readopt the Twenty-Second Joint Rule.[5] Thus there remained nothing to regulate the count in the present crisis save the bare constitutional phrase and the precedents. And unfortunately the precedents were not such as to settle conclusively any of the controversies likely to arise.

Circumstances were therefore favorable for the advocating of extreme measures by hot-heads in both

---

1 H. R. Mis. Doc. No. 13, 44th Cong. 2d Sess., pp. 565-566.
2 *Ibid*, p. 498.
3 *Ibid*, p. 345.
4 *Ibid*, p. 549.
5 *Ibid*, pp. 782-794. The claim was made after Congress reassembled in December that the rule was still in force, but as most of the Democratic senators took the opposite view, the claim came to nothing.

parties. Extremists on the Republican side continued to assert that in case the House and Senate disagreed upon the question of what were the true returns the president of the Senate would count the votes and declare the result. The Administration, they openly announced, would see to it that the man thus chosen was inaugurated. The Democratic extremists, on the other hand, continued to declare that to the House belonged at least equal power in the count, that that body possessed the right to decide when a choice had not been made, and that when such a decision was made, the House would proceed to choose the President as the Constitution directed.

The newspapers continued to publish stories about the impending conflict. In furtherance of a Republican plot General Hancock, who was in command of the Department of the East, was to be sent off to the Pacific coast, his place was to be taken by the terrible Phil. Sheridan, and New York City was then to be "bulldozed" by troops and warships.[1] The bloodthirsty and dictatorial Grant had sworn that if the Democrats in Congress attempted to impeach him, he would clap them all into Fortress Monroe.[2] Senator Sherman was to supplant Ferry as president of the Senate, and with his brother Tecumseh, commander-in-chief of the army, was to set up a sort of duumvirate.[3] Republican newspapers discovered circulars

[1] The story appears to have first been published in the Albany *Argus* of Dec. 11th. There was truth in part of it.—See Reminiscences of Hancock by his wife, pp. 158-162.
[2] *World,* Dec. 12th.
[3] *Ibid,* Dec. 14th.

directing Southern rifle-clubs to assemble in Washington and assist in inaugurating Tilden, [1] and asserted that the treasonable organization known as the Knights of the Golden Circle, or Sons of Liberty, was being revived for the same purpose. [2]

Unquestionably there were some Democrats who were prepared to go to any lengths in order to seat their candidates. Resolutions to the effect that usurpation must be resisted were passed by various state committees, and calls were issued for conventions to consider what should be done. [3] Steps were taken toward organizing the members of the state and county committees — especially those members who were ex-soldiers — into an organization to be used in case force should become necessary, and in some places Tilden and Hendricks "minute-men" appear to have been enrolled. This work was carried on in large measure through the Democratic Veteran Soldiers Association, and the activity appears to have been greatest in the Middle West, where General J. M. Corse of "Hold the Fort" Allatoona fame was in control. [4]

The Republicans were not at all dismayed by these preparations on the part of their opponents. Since

1 *Times*, Dec. 10th.
2 *Ibid*, Dec. 16th *et seq.*
3 Indianapolis *Journal* and *Sentinel*, Dec. 14th.
4 New York *Times*, Dec. 13th *et seq.* Dec. 6th Corse telegraphed to Col. Pelton: "Glory to God. Hold on to the one vote in Oregon. I have 100,000 men to back it up." Three weeks before he had telegraphed to Perry H. Smith: "We have 160,000 ex-soldiers now enrolled." Evidently the general had a poor head for figures, or else some of his men had deserted. Corse later testified before a Senate committee that the dispatches were intended as a piece of "badinage," and said that he "never contemplated" raising troops, but some of his testimony was conflicting. S. R. No. 678, 44th Cong. 2d Sess., pp. 409-413.

the electoral colleges had met and voted they would admit of no doubts as to the election of their candidates. Hayes himself now expressed the opinion that he had been honestly elected, and said, "I fully expect to be inaugurated." [1]

The Democrats abated not one jot nor tittle of their claim of victory, and on December 13th National Chairman Hewitt issued at Washington an announcement of the election of Tilden and Hendricks. This drew from Zach. Chandler a rather saucy reply, [2] and from the New York *Herald,* which deplored such *pronunciamentos* as tending to stir up violence, a statement to the effect that "there is a gentleman in Utica, the inmate of a public institution, who regards himself as the Emperor of China, and issues edicts by the score, but we have never heard that he enjoys the revenues of the Celestial kingdom." [3]

But fortunately the American people possessed too much hard sense to allow themselves to be carried away by the counsels of extremists on either side. The recent bloody conflict served as an excellent object lesson of what might be expected in case the hot-heads should be allowed to have their way. Good men and true in both parties set themselves to work to evolve a compromise. Warlike speeches were frowned upon or laughed down. Petitions began to flow into Congress imploring that body to find means for adjusting the contest. [4]

1 *World,* Dec. 12th.
2 *Ibid,* Dec. 14th; *Herald,* Dec. 14th.
3 Dec. 14th.
4 See, for example, *Record,* p. 72.

Happily the men in Congress whose patriotism rose higher than their partisanship proved equal to the occasion. Despite the wrangling in both houses, proposals looking to a peaceful settlement had already been made. One of these, introduced by Senator Edmunds, provided for a constitutional amendment placing the count in the hands of the supreme court. The proposal was debated on a number of occasions, but ultimately failed to pass even the Senate.[1] Far more important in its results was a resolution introduced into the House on the 7th of December by George W. McCrary, a Republican member from Iowa, who was later a member of Hayes's cabinet and then a Federal judge. The resolution was as follows:

"Whereas, There are differences of opinion as to the proper mode of counting the electoral votes for President and Vice-President, and as to the manner of determining questions that may arise as to the legality and validity of returns made of such votes by the several states:

"And whereas, It is of the utmost importance that all differences of opinion and all doubts and uncertainty upon these questions should be removed, to the end that the votes may be counted and the result declared by a tribunal whose authority none can question and whose decision all will accept as final: therefore,

"Resolved, That a committee of five members of this House be appointed by the Speaker, to act in conjunction with any similar committee that may be appointed by the Senate, to prepare and report without

1 *Record*, pp. 117-128, 140-144, 157-163.

delay such a measure, either legislative or constitutional, as may in their judgment be best calculated to accomplish the desired end, and that said committee have leave to report at any time."

The resolution was referred to the House judiciary committee, of which J. Proctor Knott, afterward governor of Kentucky, was chairman.[1] The fate of the resolution depended upon the attitude taken by the Democratic leaders toward compromise. If Mr. Tilden had had his way, doubtless it would never have been reported, for he was strongly averse to any surrender; but the leaders at Washington, many of whom were jealous of him, were not much inclined to heed his wishes.[2] His influence was further weakened by the fact that neither at this time nor later was it ever definitely known exactly who represented him. Mr. David Dudley Field, a well-known lawyer, had accepted an election to Congress at a special election for the purpose of looking after Mr. Tilden's legal interests; but neither Field nor Colonel Pelton, nor Hewitt, nor Randall, were ever thoroughly trusted by Tilden. Furthermore, shortly before the resolution was introduced in the House President Grant, who was anxious for compromise, summoned Mr. Hewitt, who as national chairman, was naturally regarded as the Democratic leader at Washington, to an interview, as a result of which Mr. Hewitt became anxious to play the rôle of a Henry Clay. Consequently no considerable hostility toward the resolution developed. The judiciary com-

---

1 *Record,* pp. 91-92.
2 Bigelow, II, p. 63; personal statement by same author.

mittee did, however, amend it in such a way as to provide for a committee of seven instead of five, and for another committee of seven to report upon the powers, privileges, and duties of the House in counting the electoral vote. Thus changed, it was on the 14th of December reported to the House by Mr. Knott, and was at once passed without debate under the previous question. [1]

On the following day the resolution was taken up in the Senate. Senator Edmunds thereupon offered the following:

"Resolved, that the message of the House of Representatives on the subject of the Presidential election be referred to a select committee of seven Senators with power to prepare and report without unnecessary delay such a measure, either of a legislative or other character, as may in their judgment be best calculated to accomplish the lawful counting of the electoral votes, and best disposition of all questions connected therewith, and the due declaration of the result; and that said committee have power to confer and act with the committee of the House of Representatives named in such message and to report by bill or otherwise." [2]

Three days later the resolution was passed without debate and without opposition. [3] On the 21st the president of the Senate announced the committee as follows: Mr. Edmunds of Vermont (chairman), Mr. Morton of Indiana, Mr. Frelinghuysen of New Jersey, Mr. Logan of Illinois, — Republicans; and Mr. Thur-

1 *Record*, pp. 197-199.
2 *Ibid*, p. 221.
3 *Ibid*, p. 258.

man of Ohio, Mr. Bayard of Delaware, and Mr. Ransom of North Carolina, — Democrats. As General Logan was in the midst of a contest for re-election, he found it expedient to look after his political "fences" in Illinois, and asked to be excused.[1] The vacancy thus made was filled by the appointment of Mr. Conkling of New York.

On the 22d Speaker Randall announced the House committee as follows: Henry B. Payne of Ohio (chairman), Eppa Hunton of Virginia, Abram S. Hewitt of New York, William M. Springer of Illinois, Democrats; and George W. McCrary of Iowa, George F. Hoar of Massachusetts, and George Willard of Michigan, Republicans.

Although nothing of much importance[2] was done by the committees until after the holidays, the effect of their appointment upon the public mind was quieting. People "began to get out of the Mexican and into the Anglo-Saxon frame of mind." In a much applauded speech delivered in New York at the New England Society's dinner on Forefathers' Day George William Curtis unquestionably expressed what were coming to be the sentiments of the thoughtful, prudent, and patriotic men of all parties when he said: "The voice of New England, I believe, going to the Capitol, would be this, that neither is the Republican Senate to insist on its exclusive partisan way, nor is the Demo-

---

1 *Century*, XL, p. 924.
2 A subcommittee of the House committee compiled the proceedings and debates of Congress relating to the electoral votes in the past. The result of their labors constitutes the volume already referred to as Debates on Electoral Count.

cratic House to insist on its exclusive partisan way;
but the Senate and House, representing the American
people and the American people only, in the light of
the Constitution and by the authority of law, are to
provide a way over which a President, be he Republican or be he Democrat, shall pass unchallenged to the
chair." [1]

But despite the growth of a spirit of compromise,
there were many evidences that the situation was still
fraught with dangers. The enrolling of Democratic
minute-men went forward until military organization
to a certain degree had been effected in eleven states, [2]
and a commander-in-chief, namely General Corse, [3] had
been tentatively agreed upon. Republican leaders still
defiantly asserted that the president of the Senate
would count the vote, and Mr. Ferry let it be known
that he "would shirk no responsibility." [4] The inaugural address of Governor Robinson of New York contained a long argument, written by Tilden himself,
setting forth the opposing Democratic view of the
right of the House to elect in case of a deadlock. [5] In
the South, although the chief leaders were generally
for peace, expressions like, "We'll try them this time
with Tilden and New York to help us," were frequently heard; [6] while some of the more excitable of

---

1 *The Nation,* XXIII, p. 375.

2 *McClure's Magazine,* XXIII, p. 77. Statement of Hewitt.

3 So says Henry Watterson. John Goode of Virginia says that
Gen. Franklin of Connecticut was mentioned for the place.
Hancock was no doubt considered.

4 *World,* Dec. 26th; *The Nation,* XXIII, p. 375.

5 Bigelow, Tilden, II, pp. 66-74; *Times,* Jan. 3d and 4th.

6 *Atlantic,* XXXIX, p. 190.

the local leaders wrote all sorts of wild promises of assistance to their compatriots in the North. [1]   On the 8th of January conventions of Democrats were held at Washington, Richmond, and at the capitals of several of the states of the Middle West. [2]   At the Washington meeting a fiery Louisville editor, whose opinions are always interesting but whose advice if followed would have wrecked this Republic a score of times, declared that 100,000 Kentuckians would see that justice was done Tilden. [3]   At Indianapolis the orator of the day, Mr. George W. Julian, once candidate on the Liberty Party's ticket for Vice-President, "warned" the Republicans "that, millions of men will be found ready to offer their lives as hostages to the sacredness of the ballot as the palladium of our liberty.   Whosoever," he concluded, "hath the gift of tongues, let him use it; whosoever can wield the pen of the ready writer, let him dip it into the inkhorn; whosoever hath a sword, let him gird it on, for the crisis demands our highest exertions, physical and moral." [4]   Similar speeches were made at the other meetings, and more or less warlike resolutions were passed; but, in general, the meetings proved much less impressive than their promoters had hoped.   Far more dangerous to the peace of the country than mass meetings or the utterances of fiery editors was the situation in two of the disputed states of the South.

---

1 *The Nation*, XXIV, p. 38.
2 *World, Times* and *Herald* of Jan. 9th and 10th.
3 *Times* and *World* of Jan. 9th.
4 Indianapolis *Journal* and *Sentinel* of Jan. 9th.

From the last of November there had been a dual legislature and from the 10th of December a dual executive in South Carolina, and a similar condition of
affairs obtained in Louisiana. [1] While peace was to
a certain extent maintained between the rival factions
by Federal troops, no man could feel sure that some
violent incident might not occur which would prove a
spark sufficient to fire the whole magazine.

After the holidays the two congressional committees, working first separately, later together, and all
the time in secret, began trying to evolve some plan
for a peaceful settlement. [2] At first there was much
uncertainty and floundering about. In the House
committee, for instance, the first session was devoted
to considering such questions as: What are the
powers of the president of the Senate in counting
the vote? Could the counting of the vote be referred
to an independent tribunal? Should a new election
be held? What would be the situation on the 4th of
March if no person has been declared elected by Congress or has been chosen by the House of Representatives? [3]

The divergence of opinion between the two factions

[1] For a more extended account of these matters see Chap.
XII.

[2] The Senate committee met in the room of the Senate
judiciary committee; the House committee in the room of the
House committee on banking and currency or in the chairman's private apartments in the Riggs House. The joint meetings were held in the room of the Senate judiciary committee.

[3] My account of the work of the committees is based chiefly
on an article by Milton H. Northrup, secretary of the House
committee, published in the *Century*, XL, pp. 923-934. The
article is in large part made up of notes taken by Mr. Northrup
at the time. In addition, I have received information from
ex-Senator Edmunds on a few points.

proved almost as pronounced in the committees as elsewhere. At the second meeting of the House committee on the 4th of January the Democratic chairman introduced a resolution to the effect that the power of the president of the Senate was confined to opening the returns; while on the 10th Mr. McCrary introduced one to the effect "that the certificates of the proper state authorities, executed according to law, ... if not conclusive, are at least *prima facie* evidence, and cannot be set aside or disregarded by one House without the concurrence of the other." These two widely divergent resolutions indicate clearly that in a week's time nothing definite had been accomplished. Still "the work of crystallization" had been progressing, and the time had not been wholly wasted, for to the same meeting of the 10th Mr. McCrary brought a plan which was in many respects similar to that finally adopted.

His plan, which in some of its features was not unlike the bill of 1800, provided for an independent tribunal, to be composed of the chief justice and a certain number of associate justices, whose decisions were to be final unless overruled by the concurrent vote of both houses. After a futile debate that night on the Payne resolution, the plan was taken up and discussed for some time. On the following day, with the consent of the Republican members, it was amended so that the decisions of the tribunal were not to be final unless concurred in by both houses. Another amendment excluded Chief Justice Waite, because he was thought to be hostile to Tilden. It was then informally agreed that the commission ought to consist of the five senior associate justices, namely Clifford, Swayne, Davis, Miller, and Field.

Meanwhile the Senate committee had also evolved a plan. Their plan had grown out of a proposition introduced by Senator Edmunds in the Senate committee about the same time that Mr. McCrary introduced his into the House committee.[1] Unlike the House proposal, the Senate plan provided for a commission of thirteen, composed of nine members of Congress and the four senior associate justices. In choosing the nine each house was to choose five, and then one of the ten was to be eliminated by lot.

On the 12th the two plans were presented to the two committees at a joint session held in the Senate judiciary room. On the following day at a second joint session the House committee consented to adopt that feature of the Senate committee's plan which provided for a tripartite commission; while the Senate committee, in turn, agreed that the number of members should be fifteen instead of thirteen, and that the "lot" feature should be applied only in choosing the judges. Before the meeting adjourned all the members, except Mr. Springer, who wished time to consider, had agreed that the names of the six senior associate justices were to be put into a hat, one was then to be drawn out, and the persons whose names

---

1 Mr. Edmunds says that, as he remembers it, Mr. McCrary and he did not work together.

remained were to constitute the judicial portion of the commission.

This meeting took place on Saturday, January 13th. Before the following Monday, through some "leak" in the committees, the plan became known to the public. The result was that much opposition, particularly to the "lot" feature, developed among the Democrats who saw that under it the chances would be against them. Mr. Tilden, who was personally consulted by Mr. Hewitt in New York, utterly declined to approve the plan. He opposed compromise of any sort, and insisted that the House should stand out for its right to participate in the actual counting and to proceed to elect in case no one received a majority of the electoral votes. Mr. Tilden placed much faith in the effect of the publication of a compilation of the precedents which Mr. John Bigelow had been preparing, and which was published about this time under title of *Presidential Counts.* He believed that if the Democrats held firm the Republicans would not dare to carry through their plan for having the president of the Senate declare the election of Hayes. The plan which, without his approval, the Democratic leaders were considering at Washington, was, he said, "a panic of pacificators. They will act in haste and repent at leisure." "Why surrender now?" he asked. "You can always surrender." He was especially hostile to the "lot" device, and is reported to have said next day regarding it: "I may lose the Presidency, but I will not raffle for it." [1]

When the committees met again on Monday, Mr. Payne therefore announced on behalf of the Democrats that the six-judge plan would have to be dropped, for the opposition to it was so strong that it could never pass the House. Mr. Tilden's influence, however, was by no means great enough to induce the Democratic leaders to give up the idea of compromise. They merely endeavored to evolve a less objectionable plan, and Mr. Payne, speaking for the Democrats of the House committee, proposed in lieu of the six-judge plan, "the selection of the five senior associate justices outright, as in the original House bill. The committee earnestly believes that the selection of these five, two being understood to be in sympathy with the Republicans, two with the Democracy, and the fifth [Justice David Davis of Illinois] leaning no more to one side than the other, would assure the non-partisan character of the commission, and give the odd number without a resort to the 'lot' system to which there is in many minds a very serious objection."

"This," says Mr. Northrup, the secretary of the House committee, "precipitated a discussion of the political bias of Justice David Davis. The distinguished Illinois jurist whom Abraham Lincoln had placed on the supreme bench was thenceforth, till the committees had come to a final agreement, the storm-center of earnest disputation. The Republicans tena-

---

[1] Bigelow, Tilden, II, pp. 75-76; Marble, A Secret Chapter of Political History; statement of Mr. Bigelow to the author.

ciously argued that Justice Davis was, to all intents
and purposes, a Democrat, and that his selection should
be charged up against the Democrats. Just as stren-
uously the Democratic committeemen insisted that he
occupied a midway position between the parties, and
therefore could with entire propriety serve as the fifth
wheel of the commission coach. Senator Edmunds
promptly took issue with Mr. Payne's characterization
of Justice Davis as an Independent. 'Judge Davis,'
said the cynical Edmunds, 'is one of those Independents who stand always ready to accept Democratic
nominations. It is my observation that such men are
generally the most extreme in their partisanship. I
would rather intrust a decision to an out-and-out Democrat than to a so-called Independent.'"   Mr.
Springer, on the other hand, said: "Judge Davis is
just about as much a Democrat as Horace Greeley was
in 1871; he is not and never was a Democrat. His
most intimate friends, among whom I may count my-
self, don't know to-day whether he favored Tilden or
Hayes. He didn't vote at all. Our people in Illinois, when he was mentioned for the Presidency, were
utterly hostile to his nomination because he was not a
Democrat, and had no standing in that party. They
only know that he is absolutely honest and fair."

All the next day, January 16th, was spent in discussion without any agreement being reached. The
Democrats of the House committee tendered the five-
senior-justices plan, with the concession that the decisions of the tribunal should be final unless overruled

by both houses, but the Republicans could not bring themselves to accept Davis. Various other proposals were made. Mr. Hoar suggested an evenly divided commission, with power to call in an outsider in case of a deadlock. Senator Thurman proposed an even number of judges, say four to six; he believed they would not "range themselves on party lines. No doubt they would decide as they believed right." Mr. Hewitt said he would be willing to let four judges select a fifth, and the suggestion found favor with Mr. Hoar. After rejecting the five-senior-justices plan, the Senate committee tendered a counter-proposition along the line of Hewitt's suggestion; the new scheme provided for a commission composed of five senators, five representatives, and the four senior justices (Clifford, Davis, Swayne, and Miller), who should name a fifth. To this Payne demurred, saying Davis was not a Democrat and ought not to be charged to the Democrats as one. Senator Bayard, however, being very anxious for a compromise, supported the proposition. He thought it "rather saddening that the agreement should hinge on the *quantum* of bias in Judge Davis;" he believed "that in this hour of great danger to the institutions of this country there will be evolved a feeling above party."

At the joint meeting on the following day Mr. Payne announced that the majority (meaning, of course, the Democrats) of his committee were unwilling to assent to the proposal which required them to take Judge Davis as a Democrat. He then said that Mr. Hewitt would make "a proposition which at first blush had the unanimous approval of the House committee." Mr. Hewitt thereupon stated that he believed none of the propositions thus far made could pass, because each leaned one way or the other. As an "absolutely just" plan he therefore suggested that the two senior justices, Clifford and Swayne, should each select another justice and that these four should then select a fifth.

The Senate committee, however, rejected Mr. Hewitt's proposition, and submitted yet another one, which was to take the associate justices from the first, third, eighth, and ninth circuits, and let them select a fifth. In supporting this plan Senator Edmunds urged that it had the merit of being based on geographical considerations — Justice Clifford representing New England, Justice Strong the Middle States, Justice Miller the Northwest, and Justice Field the Pacific slope — while at the same time maintaining the desired political equipoise of the commission.

After a conference among themselves the House committee, with the exception of Mr. Hunton, who wished to consider the matter over night, agreed to the plan. The two chairmen thereupon began to compare the bills in the hands of each, and, with the assistance of other members, to perfect the phraseology. Senator Edmunds also read a draft of an address prepared by him to accompany the report of the bill to the two houses. On motion, Senator Thurman was appointed to act with him in completing the address, which was to be signed in the morning.

Several of the members expressed great relief at the successful outcome of their labors. Senator Thurman said the agreement would be hailed with joy from one end of the country to the other, and the effect on business would be immediately felt. Mr. Hewitt thought it was "worth five hundred millions to the country at once." Mr. Hoar not unjustly said that "this committee's action will be considered as one of the important events in history."

But one senator, namely Morton, was far from being so well satisfied. He objected especially to certain features which might perhaps be taken as conferring power upon the Commission to go behind the returns. In reply to this objection Senator Thurman made a statement which, in the light of subsequent events, possesses considerable importance. "The bill," declared he, "decides no disputed questions, creates no new power, but submits all disputes to this tribunal with the same powers, no more, no less, than belong to Congress, jointly or severally. It is as near a non-committal bill, as to disputed questions, as could be made." But Morton continued to frown upon the bill; and when on the following day the report to accompany it was in readiness,[1] he alone, of all the members of the two committees, refused his signature.

The report[2] justified the bill both on constitutional

---

[1] When the report was being discussed, Mr. Hoar objected to the phrase that it was "comparatively unimportant" who became President, and declared that in his opinion it was of "immense importance." Senator Conkling criticised the phrase, "If such jurisdiction is not vested by the Constitution, this bill creates it." Both phrases were accordingly stricken out.

[2] For the report see *Record*, pp. 713-714.

grounds and on grounds of expediency. The bill, it argued, "is only directed to ascertaining, for the purpose and in the aid of the counting, what are the constitutional votes of the respective states; and whatever jurisdiction exists for such purpose, the bill only regulates the method of exercising it. The Constitution, our great instrument for liberty and order, speaks in the amplest language for all such cases, in whatever aspect they may be presented. It declares that Congress shall have power 'to make all laws which shall be necessary and proper for carrying into execution the foregoing powers, and all other powers vested by this Constitution in the Government of the United States, or in any department or officer thereof.' " "It is impossible," the report continued, "to estimate the material loss that the country daily sustains from the existing state of uncertainty. It directly and powerfully tends to unsettle and paralyze business, to weaken public and private credit, and to create apprehensions in the minds of the people that disturb the peaceful tenor of their ways and mar their happiness. It does far more; it tends to bring Republican institutions into discredit and to create doubts of the success of our form of government and of the perpetuity of the Republic. All considerations of interest, of patriotism, and of justice unite in demanding of the law-making power a measure that will bring peace and prosperity to the country and show that our Republican institutions are equal to any emergency."

The bill itself, unquestionably one of the most important measures ever considered by an American Congress, regulated in detail the whole procedure of the count. It provided that the two houses should meet in joint session in the hall of the House of Representatives on the first Thursday in February, two weeks earlier than had been the practice under the then existing law. The joint sessions were to be presided over by the president of the Senate, and each House was to be represented by two tellers. In case objections should be made to the votes of a state from which there was but one return such objections were to be in writing, signed by at least one member of each House. The two houses should then vote separately upon the question at issue, and no vote or votes should be excluded except by concurrent action. In cases where more than one return had been received these were to be opened and read, and then submitted to a tribunal of fifteen, composed in the manner already described. Provision was made for filling any vacancy which might occur in the tribunal. In the disputed cases all the papers together with written objections were to be submitted to the tribunal, "which shall proceed to consider the same, with the same powers, if any, now possessed for that purpose by the two houses acting separately or together, and, by a majority of votes, decide whether any and what votes from such state are the votes provided for by the Constitution of the United States, and how many and what persons were duly appointed electors in such state, and may therein take into view such petitions, depositions, and other papers, if any, as shall, by the Constitution and now existing law, be competent and pertinent in such consideration." The decision of the commission in disputed cases was to stand unless an objection, signed by at least five senators and five representatives, should be sustained by the separate vote of both houses. To facilitate the count, there was to be no debate at joint sessions, and debate at the separate sessions was limited to two hours. The joint meeting was not to be dissolved until the count should be completed; and recesses, except when a case was before the commission, were not to be taken beyond ten A. M. the following day, or from Saturday to the following Monday. Lastly the bill disclaimed any infringing upon any right, if such existed, to question in the courts the title of any person to the Presidency or the Vice-Presidency. [1]

The news that the committees had at last agreed upon a plan was received with much satisfaction in all parts of the country. A large portion of the press spoke favorably of the bill; the business interests were delighted at the prospect of a peaceful settlement; and petitions in its behalf began to pour in upon Congress.

Most of the Democrats both in and out of Congress at once showed themselves favorable to the bill, while perhaps a majority of the Republicans showed themselves inclined to oppose it. The Democrats were the more inclined to treat, not because they had more grace, but because, despite their pretended confidence,

---

1 *Record*, p. 713.

they were at a disadvantage and knew it.[1] Mr. Ferry
had all the returns in his possession, and was a partisan
Republican. President Grant was also a Republican;
and, although anxious for a peaceful settlement,[2] he
had given out that he intended to see his duly declared
successor inaugurated. It was well known that in
case the two houses were unable to come to an agreement Mr. Ferry would proceed to count the votes, and
would declare Hayes the President-elect. Mr. Hayes
would then be inaugurated under the protection of the
United States army. Even though the House should
refuse to recognize his election and should proceed to
choose Tilden, that gentleman would be unable to set
himself up as more than the *de jure* President. His
opponent would have control of the official machinery,
with appropriations sufficient to last until the first of
July. Mr. Tilden and his supporters would thus be
put in the position of opposing the regular government.[3] Such a position, as many independent and
even Democratic journals pointed out, was one which
the party, with its recent antecedents, could not afford
to assume.[4] It could safely be forecast that in case
the Democrats should resort to force, the majority of
the people would take the side of the government
whose seat was at Washington.[5] For this reason, if
no other, force could not succeed. Another reason

---

1 *The Nation*, XXIV, p. 4.
2 Recollections of George W. Childs, pp. 77-81.
3 *Herald*, Dec. 23d.
4 *The Nation*, XXIII, p. 364; files of *Herald* and *Sun*.
5 Some prominent Democrats had publicly stated that they
would not stand by the party in a resort to force. See *Herald*
of Dec. 19th. Some of these were ex-Confederate generals.

why it could not — a reason which brought to pause
hot-heads with whom other considerations weighed
but little — was that at the head of the government
was a man, who, whatever might be said of his capacity
as a civil administrator, was known beyond all cavil
to be a peerless leader on the field of battle.

The Democrats were influenced by yet other motives
to support the compromise plan.[1] Many favored it
out of genuine patriotism; while some disliked the idea
of the election devolving upon Congress, since though
that would result in the election of Tilden by the
House, it would also result in the choice of a Republican Vice-President by the Senate. These last and
most others believed with Senator Gordon of Georgia
that with the compromise plan both Democratic candidates were certain of election. They reasoned that
only one more vote was needed, that twenty were
in dispute, and that, out of so many, the Commission,
with Justice Davis as the fifth judge, would surely
award the Democrats at least one.[2]

The very considerations which caused Democrats to
favor the compromise led many Republicans to oppose
it. To them the chances for success looked extremely
dubious. To elect their candidates, they must take
every trick. If Tilden should receive so much as a
single one of the disputed votes, the game was up. And
Republicans looked forward with reluctance to such an
outcome. Some groaned at the thought of losing the

1 For an analysis of Democratic motives see **Bigelow, Tilden,**
II, p. 63.
    2 *The Nation,* XXIV, p. 19.

fat patronage of a hundred thousand offices. Others were more concerned at the thought of relinquishing the reins of power to men whom they believed to be at heart disloyal to the Union. It is not strange, therefore, that the most radical opposed a plan which looked not unlike "giving up the fort." They believed that in case no compromise were made Hayes would be peacefully inaugurated — at any rate he would be inaugurated. Mr. Hayes himself believed the bill unconstitutional, and opposed it, though not actively. [1]

On the other hand, a considerable portion of the party were unwilling to support the extremists. Chief among those favoring a compromise was the President himself. He had all along been working to secure a peaceful settlement, and he now used his influence in behalf of the bill. As a result of his urging Senator Conkling of New York, and doubtless others undertook to work for its passage. [2]

When the bill came up in the Senate on the 20th of January, Senator Edmunds, chairman of the Senate committee, made a powerful and patriotic plea, singularly free from partisanship, in its behalf. He argued that it was constitutional, that it did not take away from either the president of the Senate or the House of Representatives any power which the Constitution "vested in them free from limit and free from

---

1 Hayes thought the power to count belonged to the president of the Senate.—Letter to Sherman in John Sherman's Recollections, I, p. 561; to Carl Schurz, Jan. 17th and 23d, and to Alonzo Taft, Jan. 26th, in the Hayes Papers.
2 George W. Childs, Reminiscences, pp. 77-80.

regulation." He urged its passage as a wise measure
of public policy. [1]

The opposition in the Senate was led by Morton.
On Monday, the 22d, although ill and scarcely able to
attend, he made a bitter speech against it. He declared in opening that the bill was a "literal product
of 'the Mississippi plan;' that the shadow of intimidation" had entered the Senate; that members of Congress were "acting under the apprehension of violence, of some great revolutionary act" which would
"threaten the safety and continuance of our institutions." He did not believe "in the reality of the danger." He regarded the bill as a compromise which
would "take its place alongside of the Compromise of
1820 and the Compromise of 1850." He contended
that Rutherford B. Hayes had been elected President;
that if he should "be counted in, as eighteen Presidents were successively counted in from the beginning of this government," there would be "no violence
and no revolution." In discussing the constitutional
question he admitted that Congress had power to leg-
islate upon the subject, "yet in the absence of legislation, the President of the Senate must count the votes"
in order "to prevent a deadlock." In support of his
view he quoted from Chancellor Kent a statement to
the effect that "in the absence of all legislative provision on the subject, ... the President of the
Senate counts the votes and determines the result, and
. . . . the two houses are present only as spec-

1 *Record*, pp. 767-771.

tators to witness the fairness and accuracy of the transaction and to act only if no choice be made by the electors." Morton asked whether the five judges would be "officers," and whether, if so, they must not be appointed as the Constitution prescribes. He questioned the power of Congress to delegate its authority in the premises, pronounced the whole scheme a patched-up "contrivance," and finally was forced to conclude from sheer physical exhaustion. [1]

Frelinghuysen of New Jersey refused to follow Morton's lead, and spoke in behalf of the bill. [2] After a few other speeches had been made, Edmunds asked for an immediate vote, but the matter was held over till the next day. [3]

On that day, after a speech in opposition by Sherman, [4] Senator Conkling began an elaborate and characteristic speech, which filled the galleries with spectators and consumed the greater part of two days. He reviewed the precedents in great detail to show that in no instance had the president of the Senate assumed of his own authority to do anything beyond opening the certificates. He referred to the Twenty-Second Joint Rule, to the Sherman Resolution of inquiry in 1872, and to Morton's own bill as serving to show that Congress could regulate the count. He accused Morton and the other extreme Republicans of seeking to provoke a deadlock as a result of which the

1 *Record,* pp. 799-801.
2 *Ibid,* pp. 801-805.
3 *Ibid,* pp. 805-808.
4 *Ibid,* pp. 820-825.

president of the Senate must act. "If," he exclaimed,
"there was ever a political Hell-Gate paved and honeycombed with dynamite, there it is." He pointed out
that only a few months before Morton himself had
voted for a proposition to import the chief justice into
a similar tribunal. He said he would vote for the bill
because it was constitutional, would prevent disorder,
and would be to the lasting benefit of the people. [1]

Bayard, Christiancy, Thurman, and others spoke in
behalf of the bill. At half-past twelve o'clock A. M.
of January 25th Morton, after an ineffectual attempt
to secure an adjournment on the plea of being too ill
and worn-out to speak, began his closing argument
against it. In the course of his speech he once more
advanced his theory of the power of the president of
the Senate. It was impossible, he asserted, to consider such a body as the proposed Commission a mere
committee of Congress. He admitted that perhaps his
views upon the count had not always been consistent;
but, said he, "there are no popes in this body." He
could show that every member of the committee had
expressed sentiments different from those contained in
the bill, and he quoted a statement by Conkling entirely
at variance with a portion of it. Any measure, declared
he, which might result in the seating of Tilden and
Hendricks ought to be opposed, because the welfare of
humanity demanded that the Republican party remain
in power. "It is not to our interest," he frankly

1 *Record,* pp. 825-831, 870-878.

stated, "to depart from that method pursued for seventy-five years simply to give our political opponents advantages and chances which they now have not." [1]

But all the efforts of the extremists against the bill proved unavailing. [2] An amendment forbidding the Commission from going behind the returns and another granting it that right were voted down. [3] A final vote was taken at 7 A. M. after an all night session, and resulted in the passage of the bill by 47 to 17. [4]

Although the bill had been reported to the House on the same day as to the Senate, its consideration was not begun by the former body until some days later. From the 17th to the 24th of January the House devoted most of its time to debating a set of resolutions reported by the committee which had been directed to investigate and report upon the powers, privileges, and duties of the House in counting the electoral vote. These resolutions, which were really the work of Mr. Tilden, [5] denied the power of the president of the Senate to do more than receive and open the certificates; they asserted that, on the contrary, the two houses have the power to examine and ascertain the vote, and held that no return could be counted against the judgment and determination of the House. [6]

On the 25th of January, however, the electoral bill

---

1 *Record,* pp. 894-898.
2 For a speech by Blaine against the bill see *Ibid,* p. 898.
3 *Ibid,* p. 911-912.
4 *Ibid,* p. 913.
5 Bigelow, II, pp. 65-66. They were slightly changed by the committee.
6 *Record,* p. 609.

was at last taken up. Mr. McCrary opened the debate with a plea in behalf of favorable action.[1] He emphasized the fact that there was "widespread, honest difference of opinion." He pointed out that many Democrats, including Senators Bayard, Whyte, and Stevenson, had at one time or another held that in the absence of legislation the power to count inhered in the president of the Senate; while many Republicans, including Senators Boutwell, Dawes, and Christiancy, had opposed that theory. He showed also that Democrats like Bayard, Maxey, Whyte, and others, were on record as opposing the right of one house to throw out the vote of a state; while many Republicans were on record as supporting the contested right. When there was such difference, there might well be compromise.

Lamar of Mississippi, Harrison and Springer of Illinois, Watterson of Kentucky, and many others of both parties made speeches in behalf of the bill. Hunton of Virginia cited the plan of 1800, the Twenty-Second Joint Rule, and other precedents in order to show that the bill was constitutional.[2] Hewitt of New York said that "a hundred thousand place holders *in esse* and an equal number of place hunters *in posse* were busily attacking the bill for the same reason as did the " 'Ephesian worker in copper' the early Christians" — it threatened "to spoil their trade." The very fact that it was said on the Republican side that the bill was a scheme to make Tilden President, while

1 *Record*, pp. 930-935.
2 *Ibid*, pp. 935-939.

it was said on the Democratic side that it was a plan to make Hayes President, was, he thought, sure proof of the plan's fairness. [1] Other speakers expressed the belief that the bill offered the only hope of escape from a dual government and civil war. [2] Hill of Georgia said the South was for peace, [3] and the sentiment was approved by most of the speakers from that section.

Hale of Maine, Knott of Kentucky, Monroe of Ohio, Townsend of New York, Mills of Texas, Hurlbut of Illinois, Garfield of Ohio, and others spoke against the bill. Mills declared that the Democrats should have taken a bold stand on the powers of the House; he objected chiefly to the provision that no vote could be excluded except by the concurrent vote of both houses.[4] Hurlbut thought that in arranging for the choice of the fifth judge Congress had "gravely inaugurated the great national game of draw." [5] One of the chief speeches in opposition was that by Garfield. He said in part:

"The Senate at Rome never deliberated a moment after the flag was hauled down which floated on the Janiculum Hill across the Tiber. That flag was the sign that no enemy of Rome breathing hot threats of war, had entered the sacred precincts of the city; and when it was struck, the Senate sat no longer. The reply to war is not words but swords.

"When you tell me that civil war is threatened by any party or State in this Republic, you have given me a supreme reason why an American Congress

1 *Record*, pp. 946-948.
2 See, for example, Watterson's speech, *Ibid*, p. 1007.
3 *Ibid*, pp. 1008-1009.
4 *Ibid*, pp. 979-982.
5 *Ibid*, p. 1008.

should refuse with unutterable scorn to listen to those who threaten, or to do any act whatever under the coercion of threats by any power on the earth. With all my soul I despise your threat of civil war, come it from what quarter or what party it may. Brave men, certainly a brave nation, will do nothing under such compulsion." [1]

But, just as in the Senate, the opponents of the bill found themselves powerless. The pressure of public opinion in favor of compromise was well-nigh irresistible, and a perfect hurricane of petitions was sweeping into Congress. [2] The Democrats were almost unanimous in favor of the bill, and the Republicans were not able to muster their full strength against it. When a vote was taken on January 26th, the bill was passed by the overwhelming majority of 191 to 86. [3]

A study of the vote in both houses shows unmistakably that the bill succeeded by grace of the support given it by most of the Democratic members and by a comparatively small number of Republicans. In the Senate 26 Democrats supported it, and only one opposed it; in the same body 21 Republicans supported it, and 16 opposed it. In the House 160 Democrats supported it and 17 opposed it; while only 31 Republicans supported it, and 69 opposed it. In the light of these figures it seems almost fair to call the act a Democratic measure. [4] Whatever, therefore, should be the outcome of the labors of the tribunal thus created, it could reasonably be held that the Democrats were in

---

1 *Record*, p. 968.
2 *Ibid*, pp. 913, 946, 948, 949, 1024, 1049, etc.
3 *Ibid*, p. 1050.
4 For a discussion of this matter see Blaine II, p. 587.

honor bound to accept its decisions and abide by them.

Unquestionably one of the chief factors in the Democratic support of the measure and the Republican opposition to it lay in the prevailing belief that Justice David Davis would be the fifth representative of the supreme court. "In the ponderous Illinois jurist were centered the hopes of Democracy, the apprehensions of Republicanism." But it has well been said that all things are uncertain in love, war and politics—especially in politics. At the capital of Illinois while the bill was still pending occurred one of those unexpected events which so often seem to change the course of history.[1] In that city the supporters of General Logan had for some time been vainly trying to secure his re-election to the Federal Senate. The situation was complicated by the presence in the legislature of five Independents, who held the balance of power. For more than a week the balloting proceeded without result. During that time a few votes were cast for Judge Davis. On the 24th, the day before the electoral bill came up in the House at Washington, the Democrats at Springfield, with strange fatuity, began to regard him as the proper man on whom to form a combination;[2] and on the following day he received

---

1 Assuming, of course, that Davis would have voted with the Democratic members in at least one case. In a letter written to Mr. Joseph M. Rogers the late Senator Hoar expressed the belief that since Davis "was a great lawyer and at heart a very earnest Republican, ... he would . . . . have never agreed to any other decision than that to which the majority of the Commission came."

2 Mr. Hewitt believed to the day of his death that the election of Davis was the result of a corrupt bargain engin-

the votes of three Independents and of the 98 Democrats, making exactly a majority.[1]

The news came as a stunning blow to the Democratic leaders in Congress; for they realized that the
election rendered him in a certain sense ineligible for
a place upon the Commission, and that the fifth judge
would of necessity be chosen from out-and-out Republicans.[2] But they had committed themselves too far
to recede; and, still hoping for the best, they voted for
the bill. Later they realized more fully that this bit
of *gaucherie* on the part of their compatriots on the
broad prairies of the West had probably exercised a
determining influence in deciding whether the Republican or the Democratic party should during the ensuing four years control the government of the American people.

---

eered by Sen. Morton to get Davis off the Commission and secure a Democrat in his place. Mr. Hewitt left an article on
the disputed election, which is sometime to be published, in which
he gives his view of this matter. See also Bigelow, II, p. 64.
Mr. Foulke, Morton's biographer, says he has found no evidence to support the story. It seems entirely improbable.

1 New York *World* and *Times* of Jan. 25th and 26th; *Annual
Cyclopaedia*, 1877, p. 383.

2 "The writer," says Mr. Northrup, "will never forget the
drop in the countenance of the Hon. Abram S. Hewitt, who had
charge of Tilden's campaign, when, meeting him in the hall of
the House of Representatives, he informed him of Judge Davis's
transfer from the Supreme Court to the Senate."—*Century*, XL,
p. 983.

CHAPTER XI

President Grant approved the Electoral Commission bill on the 29th, and in doing so expressed to Congress his great satisfaction at the adoption of a measure that affords an orderly means for deciding "a gravely exciting question." [1]

On the following day each House proceeded by a *viva voce* vote to designate five of its members to sit upon the Commission. [2] The House chose Payne of Ohio, Hunton of Virginia, Abbott of Massachusetts, Democrats; Hoar of Massachusetts and Garfield of Ohio, Republicans. The Senate selected Edmunds of Vermont, Frelinghuysen of New Jersey, Morton of Indiana, Republicans; Thurman of Ohio and Bayard of Delaware, Democrats. All these gentlemen had, of course, been previously designated in party caucuses. [3]

Naturally each caucus had done its work with extreme care. It occasioned some remark at the time that the caucus of Senate Republicans had not chosen Conkling. The claim was later made that the reason why he was not chosen was that he believed Tilden

---

1 *Record*, p. 1081.
2 Proceedings of the Electoral Commission, pp. 5-6.
3 *World* and *Times* of Jan. 28th, 29th, and 30th.

had been elected. But this seems not to be the correct explanation. A more probable one is that first of all he was a "Conkling man;" his popularity in the Senate was not great; he had been indifferent to Hayes even during the campaign;[1] and it was known that he thought it would be better politics, since the title was in doubt and there had been fraud on both sides, to yield the Presidency to the Democrats.[2]

On the same day the four justices — Clifford and Field, Democrats; and Strong and Miller, Republicans — while not greatly relishing the work they had been called upon to perform, met together to select the fifth justice. It appears that they offered the place to Justice Davis, but that he, being averse to accepting the responsibility, refused it and based his refusal on the fact that he had just been elected senator by the Democrats. The justices were then for some time unable to agree upon a substitute; there seemed a possibility that the whole plan of settlement might be blocked;[3] but at length they selected Justice Joseph P. Bradley, of the fifth judicial circuit. Justice Bradley was the most acceptable to the Democrats of any of the remaining justices; for he was by no means a partisan, and in some of his opinions had shown himself out of sympathy with the radical Republicans.[4]

---

1 *Ante*, p. 36, note.
2 Conkling, Life and Letters of Roscoe Conkling, p. 528. Later, when he was completely estranged from Hayes, he took a more pronounced view.—Hoar, II, p. 44.
3 *McClure's*, XXIII, p. 83.
4 New York *World* of Feb. 1st. In the opinion of that paper Bradley was not satisfactory to the Republicans. It expressed pleasure over his choice. See also *Atlantic*, LXXII, p. 529.

Thursday, February 1st, the day set by the law for the count to begin, saw a great crowd of sightseers in the hall of the House of Representatives. In the diplomatic gallery were Sir Edward Thornton, the English minister; the Japanese and German ministers, and other foreign representatives, together with their suites and members of their families. In the other galleries sat the wives and relatives of congressmen and of the cabinet officers, and persons of lesser note. On the floor itself were Justices Field and Miller of the Commission, Jeremiah S. Black, jurist and member of Buchanan's cabinet, J. D. Cameron, the secretary of war, Charles O'Conor of the New York bar, George Bancroft, diplomatist and historian, General Sherman, and many other distinguished visitors.

At one o'clock the door-keeper of the House announced the Senate of the United States. That body then entered the hall, preceded by their sergeant-at-arms, and headed by their president and secretary, the members of the House standing to receive them. Upon reaching the desk the president, Mr. Ferry, in accordance with the law, took the speaker's chair; Mr. Randall, the speaker, occupied another immediately on his left; the senators seated themselevs in the body of the hall on the right of the chair; the representatives and visitors filled the remaining floor space; the tellers, — Messrs. Ingalls and Allison for the Senate and Messrs. Cook and Stone for the House — the secretary of the Senate, and the clerk of the House took seats at the clerk's desk; the other officers were accommodated in front of the clerk's desk and on each side of the speaker's platform.[1]

Mr. Ferry then called the joint session to order, and the historic count began. The votes of Alabama, Arkansas, California, Colorado, Connecticut, and Delaware were declared and counted without special incident; the proceedings were somewhat tedious, and there was considerable talk and confusion on the floor and in the galleries. But as the count of the votes of Delaware was completed a hush fell over the hall, and there was a great craning of necks in the galleries. Florida had been reached.

From Florida there were three certificates: one from the Hayes electors, regular in form because certified by Governor Stearns and Secretary of State McLin; one from the Tilden electors, dated December 6th, but confessedly irregular in form, though certified by Attorney-General Cocke; one from the same Democratic electors, dated January 26th, 1877, certified by the new governor, Drew, and containing a copy of the act of January 17th, the certificate of the state canvassers who recanvassed the vote under that act and a reference, in the governor's certificate, to the judgment of the circuit court in the *quo warranto* proceedings against the Hayes electors.[2]

Objections were at once filed against each of the certificates, and the Democrats also filed a special objection against the reception of the vote of F. C.

---

1 Proceedings, pp. 5-9.
2 *Ibid,* pp. 10-24.

Humphreys, one of the Hayes electors, on the ground
that he was a Federal office-holder, and was therefore
ineligible. The certificates, objections, and all other
papers were then, in accordance with the law, referred
to the Electoral Commission. [1]

That tribunal had already met and organized, with
the venerable Justice Clifford, the justice "longest in
commission" as president. [2] The sessions were held
in the room usually occupied by the supreme court.
For the sake of the future historian the spectacle presented by the Commission should have been a splendid one, but it was not. If the official painting, which
now hangs in the Capitol, be a true representation, the
sight was far from imposing. [3] We are distinctly told
by an eye-witness that the proceedings furnished little
that was "unusual, unique, picturesque, or dramatic." [4]
Attempted descriptions along the line of Macaulay's
passage on the trial of Hastings are therefore misleading. [5] To be sure, the room itself was the same which,
as the Senate chamber of other days, had "resounded
with the eloquence of Clay and of Webster;" but it
was much too small for the audience which now filled
it, and even the bench was insufficient to accommodate
all of the fifteen judges. [6]

---

1 For the objections see Proceedings, pp. 24-28.

2 *Ibid,* pp. 8-9. The law so provided.

3 Painted by Mrs. C. Adele Fassett, who made sketches during
the sessions and later secured sittings from most of the distinguished participants. For an account of the painting and a
'key" see *Magazine of American History,* XXVII, pp. 81-97.

4 *Times* of Feb. 6th.

5 *Herald* of Feb. 11th.

6 Owing to lack of lighting facilities in the court room, some
of the evening sessions were held in the Senate chamber.

The proceedings were more notable for the eminent character of the participants than for any dramatic or spectacular interest. All the members of the Commission were men of broad experience and high legal attainments. Of the five from the Senate, two, Thurman and Edmunds, were unsurpassed as constitutional lawyers; a third, Bayard, was to be a secretary of state, a minister to England, and several times a formidable candidate for the Presidential nomination; while a fourth, Morton, had approved himself the greatest of "war governors," [1] and now, though partially paralyzed, possessed a will which triumphed over all the infirmities of the body and made him one of the most feared leaders of his party. Of those from the House, one was soon to be honored with the exalted position for which the contest was now raging; while another, who has but recently gone from among us, was a man who in spotless integrity and singleness of devotion to his country's service was the peer of any man who has ever represented the great state of Massachusetts.

The counsel who appeared for the contending parties were scarcely less eminent than the Commission itself. Among those for the Democrats were Charles O'Conor, Jeremiah S. Black, John A. Campbell, once associate justice of the supreme court, ex-Senator Lyman Trumbull of Illinois, William C. Whitney of New York, and Richard T. Merrick of Washington. Foremost among the Republican counsel was the astute

---

[1] So thought Stanton and Chase.—Letter of Chase to Morton given by Foulke, I. p. 456. See also Hoar, II, p. 75.

and learned William M. Evarts, leader of the New York bar, defender of Andrew Johnson, ex-attorney-general, and soon to be secretary of state. He was ably assisted by Edward M. Stoughton of New York and by Samuel Shellabarger, the personal representative of Hayes, and by Stanley Matthews of Ohio. Some of the best known of the senators and representatives including Montgomery Blair, J. Randolph Tucker, George W. McCrary, David Dudley Field, John A. Kasson, and William Lawrence, appeared before the Commission as objectors to the various certificates.

The objections to the Florida certificates were heard on the 2d. The Democratic objections were presented by David Dudley Field of New York and by J. Randolph Tucker of Virginia. Mr. Field, who was the first to speak, asserted that in a peaceful and orderly election the Tilden electors had been chosen by a majority of the votes, but that through a "sort of jugglery" a false certificate signed by the former governor of the state had been sent up by the Republican candidates. He then entered upon a detailed account of the sharp practices resorted to by the Republican canvassing officers in Baker county and charged that the returning board had manufactured a majority for Hayes. He also laid stress upon the *quo warranto* proceedings which had resulted in a decree by a district court in favor of the Tilden electors, and told of the later canvass of votes by the new returning board created for the purpose by the new legislature. The certificate of Governor Stearns, he argued, formed no barrier against the investigation of the facts by the Commission, for the governor's certification was done in accordance with a Federal law which did not provide that his certificate should be conclusive evidence. The Commission could, therefore, go behind the certificate and overthrow the "fraud." [1] Mr. Tucker, the other objector, pointed out that the powers of the tribunal, in accordance with the act creating it, were exactly those of the two houses of Congress; these powers, he thought, "are not less than the powers of a court upon a *quo warranto* proceeding." In every appointment or election, he argued, there are two elements: first, the elective function, and second, the determining function. Whenever the determining authority acts illegally such action must be set aside. The determining authority in Florida had so acted, and its action must be set aside by the Commission. Since the canvass made by the returning board had been declared illegal by a court in *quo warranto* proceedings, the judgment of the court must be accepted as final. He closed by stating the Democratic objection to the vote of the alleged ineligible Republican elector. [2]

Representatives Kasson and McCrary appeared as the Republican objectors. [3] The certificate sent by the Hayes electors, argued Mr. Kasson, was the only regular one. The second was irregular, because

---

1 Proceedings, pp. 35-45.
2 *Ibid*, pp. 45-52.
3 For their respective speeches see *Ibid*, pp. 54-64 and 64-72.

"signed by an officer not recognized by the laws of the United States nor by the statutes of Florida as a certifying officer." The third was "still more extraordinary . . . . a certificate which is thoroughly *ex post facto,* certified by an officer not in existence until the functions of the office had been exhausted; a certificate which recites or refers to posterior proceedings in a subordinate court and in a superior state court, the latter expressly excluding the electoral question; a certificate which is accompanied by that sort of a return which a canvassing board might under some circumstances report to the state officers, but which has never been sent to the Congress of the United States or to the President of the Senate for their consideration in the hundred years in which we have been a Republic." The Republicans were prepared to meet the charges of fraud that had been brought. The Democratic objectors had spoken of Baker county but had neglected to mention the trainload of non-resident Democrats who had voted in Alachua county. He denied, however, that the Commission had power to investigate such matters; it must accept the regular return certified by the state authorities; it could not go behind the action of the state canvassers because the Constitution provides that each state shall appoint its electors "in such manner as the legislature thereof may direct." Mr. McCrary, in his speech, attacked the theory put forward by his opponents that the Commission possessed the judicial powers attributed to it by his opponents. He held also that the Republican electors, under color of title, had met and voted on the 6th of December, and had thereupon become *functi officio;* all subsequent proceedings were of no effect; the acts of the electors, in accordance with the law of officers, must stand, even though it be admitted for the sake of argument that they were only officers *de facto* and not *de jure.* While contending that the Commission should not take cognizance of the proceedings in *quo warranto,* he said that if the Commission did decide to do so, the Republicans were prepared to show that an appeal to a higher court was then pending. As regarded the case of the alleged ineligible elector, Humphreys, he stated that it could be easily proven that Mr. Humphreys had resigned the office before the election; he objected, however, to the subject coming before the Commission because there were "no papers accompanying any of the votes, or papers purporting to be votes," that related to the matter.

When the counsel began their arguments on the following day, this vital question of the reception of evidence at once arose, and as it had to be decided before any progress could be made, the whole attention of the Commission was turned to it. In their arguments [1] the Democratic advocates showed themselves, for once, strangely indifferent to the sphere of state powers. The evidence they wished to bring in was of two

---

[1] For the Democratic arguments see Proceedings, pp. 64-101, 124-136. For their briefs see pp. 729-774. None of these briefs was devoted entirely to this matter of the reception of evidence, but all touched upon it.

kinds: first, that which was contained in the various certificates received from Florida; and, second, extrinsic evidence taken by the investigating committee of the House of Representatives, or evidence to be taken by the Commission itself. The certificate of the governor, argued they, was not conclusive; it was merely required by a Federal statute, which must have been passed as a precautionary measure, for the Constitution itself provides for the return by the electors themselves. Under the circumstances of the present case the Commission must make an investigation in order to determine what votes should be counted; "any legitimate evidence going to determine the true votes is," they held, "proper and competent evidence before this tribunal." They pointed out that in 1873 a Senate committee had gone behind the certificate of the governor of Louisiana, had found that the returns "had never been counted by anybody having authority to count them," and that with this report before them Congress had excluded the vote of the state. This precedent, the Democrats contended, was sufficient proof of the right of Congress and the Commission to receive both kinds of evidence; but they said they would, in the case of Florida, ask the reception of no extrinsic evidence save upon the rejection of certain returns by the returning board and upon the ineligibility of Mr. Humphreys. They suggested that the Republicans would need to offer in rebuttal no extrinsic evidence save upon these matters and upon the fact of the appeal from the decision in *quo war-*

ranto. This was intended to meet the Republican argument that, aside from constitutional reasons, the reception of extrinsic evidence would from the very vastness of the labor involved be impracticable.

The Republican advocates, on their part, advanced "strict construction" views which were quite as unwonted as were the "loose construction" arguments put forward by their opponents. [1] With admirable acumen and calculation they placed themselves squarely upon the line of division between Federal and state powers. They accepted the position so painfully constructed by the Democrats on the question of the power to go behind the governor's certificate; this could be done, said they, because the governor acts in that matter in obedience to Federal law and his action is therefore reviewable by Federal authority. But, they pointed out, this does not apply to the *choice* of the electors; that is a matter wholly under state control, for the Constitution expressly declares that electors shall be appointed by each state "in such manner as the legislature thereof may direct."

Up to "the completion and consummation of this appointment," argued Matthews, "the state alone acts. That last act completes the appointment, and that appointment completed and finished is unchangeable except by state authority exerted upon that act within an interval of time; and what is that? Congress, under the Constitution of the United States, has

---

1 For the Republican arguments see Proceedings, pp. 101-124 and 136-137.

had reserved to it control in certain particulars over this appointment; that is to say, it may designate the day on which the appointment may be made, and it shall designate the day on which the electors so appointed shall deposit their ballots for President and Vice-President. In that interval I do not know and I do not care to discuss, I will neither deny nor affirm, but I am willing to admit, any and everything that may be claimed on the other side as to the existence of state authority to inquire into and affect that record." But he contended that once the day had passed when the body which according to the forms of law had been invested with the apparent title to act had accomplished the purpose for which it had been brought into being, then that transaction, so far as state authority was concerned, had passed beyond the limits of its control. [1]

In case of conflicting returns Congress might investigate to see which one was the true one, but its investigation must stop with ascertaining the determination reached by the authority empowered by state law with that function. Its duty was merely "to count the electoral vote, and not to count the votes by which the electors are elected." To attempt to do the latter would not only be unconstitutional but would involve difficulties which would be insuperable.

On the question of receiving extraneous proof regarding the eligibility of electors the Republican counsel held that while Congress had power to make a law

---

1 Proceedings, p. 103.

providing for the reception of such proof, there was no such law and therefore such proof must not be received. The injunction against appointing persons holding Federal offices, they argued, "does not execute itself under the Constitution, and if unexecuted in the laws of the state, is only to be executed by laws of Congress providing the means and time and place for proof and determination on the fact of disqualification." [1]

The hearing on the question of receiving evidence was concluded on the afternoon of Monday, February 6th. The Commission reserved its decision until the following Wednesday. In the meantime there was great impatience in Washington and elsewhere to learn what stand the Commission would take, for upon that stand hinged, it was believed by many, the final decision.

Through a peculiar misapprehension the Democrats believed for a time that their cause was won. In making up his mind, Mr. Bradley, following a not uncommon custom among jurists, wrote out what were in effect two opinions giving the arguments on both sides. A Democratic member learned of the opinion giving the Democratic arguments and inferred that Justice Bradley was siding with the Democrats. The joyful news was carried to Mr. Hewitt. There was jubilation among the Democrats. Bradley was a just judge — a veritable "Daniel come to judgment." But hasty inferences are apt to prove mis-

1 From speech by Evarts, Proceedings, pp. 117-118.

leading. On the following day, when Justice Miller moved, "that no evidence will be received or considered by the Commission which was not submitted to the joint convention of the two houses by the president of the Senate with the different certificates, except such as relates to the eligibility of F. C. Humphreys, one of the electors," Bradley voted with the Republicans; and the order was carried by 8 to 7.[1] From that time forward Justice Joseph P. Bradley was in the eyes of Democrats an "unjust judge," a "partisan," and the cry went forth from the house-tops that he had been bribed. To give color to the bribery story, it was alleged that on the night prior to the decision his house had been surrounded by the carriages of Republican politicians and Pacific Railroad magnates, and that as a result of "pressure" brought to bear upon him at this time he had changed his views. There was not one iota of proof brought forward in support of the charge, but Democratic newspapers took up the story, and Justice Bradley's whole after-life was embittered by it.[2]

Upon one question, however, namely that of receiving extraneous evidence relating to the alleged ineli-

1 Proceedings, pp. 138-139.

2 The New York *Sun* was especially active in keeping the story alive. See Lewis, Miscellaneous Writings of the Late Hon. Joseph P. Bradley, pp. 220-222, for a letter written by Bradley to the Newark *Daily Advertiser* of Sept. 5, 1877. Bigelow, Tilden, II, p. 95, states that Tilden told him that he had been offered the vote of a member of the supreme court (presumably Bradley) on the question of going behind the returns for $200,000. If there was such an offer, it was made by one of those irresponsible persons who were so active just then in trying to engineer corrupt bargains without any authority from those concerned.

gibility of Mr. Humphreys, Mr. Bradley voted with the Democrats. On the following day the evidence was taken. It showed conclusively that Mr. Humphreys had been shipping commissioner of the port of Pensacola, but that on the 24th of September he had sent a letter of resignation to the Federal circuit judge, who was then on a visit to Ohio. The resignation had been accepted on the 2d of October, and Mr. Humphreys had turned over the books and records to the collector of customs and had ceased to perform the duties of the office. The Democratic counsel did not deny these facts; but they raised the technical objection that the resignation was not valid because made, not to the appointing power, the circuit court, but to the absent judge.

In the final hearing upon the Florida case the counsel for both parties made use of substantially the same arguments that have already been set forth.[1] The Republicans once again claimed that theirs was the only regular certificate; that the first Democratic certificate was confessedly irregular; that the second was "a posthumous certificate of a *post-mortem* action, never proceeding from any vital or living body of electors, but only from the galvanic agency of interested party purpose, taking effect after the whole transaction was ended."[2] The *quo warranto* proceedings, they held, were not before the Commission;

---

[1] For the final arguments on both sides see Proceedings, pp. 145-193. See also Democratic briefs Nos. 2, 3, and 4, pp. 745-774.

[2] Evarts, *Ibid*, p. 179.

even if they were, they were wholly *post hoc*
and, furthermore, had been appealed from. If such
post hoc proceedings were to be of any effect,
it lay in the power of any partisan *nisi prius*
court to reverse an election and even to un-
seat a President after he was inaugurated. In reply,
the Democrats admitted that the *quo warranto* had
been decided after the electors had voted, but they
claimed that service had been made before the act.
The Tilden electors, they declared, had been recognized by all the departments of the state government;
and their votes must be received and counted.

The hearing in the Florida case was closed on
Thursday, February 8th. Next day the Commission
met behind closed doors and argued the question for
many hours.[1] On one point, namely the eligibility
of Mr. Humphreys, there were three Democrats —
Thurman, Bayard, and Clifford — who were willing
to take the Republican view;[2] but upon every other
important question the Commission divided on strict
party lines. And on strict party lines the Republicans
had a majority of one. By a vote of 8 to 7 it was
therefore ordered that the four electoral votes of Florida should be counted for Hayes and Wheeler.[3] The
grounds of the decision, as stated in the report to
Congress, were as follows:

---

1 Proceedings, p. 194. For the opinions in the Florida case
see pp. 817, 833, 844, 855, 901, 932, 955, 959, 974, 994, 1006,
1019, 1042. These opinions were delivered orally. Each member later wrote out what he had said.

2 *Ibid*, pp. 194, 871, 1059.

3 *Ibid*, pp. 195-196.

"That it is not competent under the Constitution and the law, as it existed at the date of the passage of said act, to go into evidence *aliunde* the papers opened by the president of the Senate in the presence of the two houses to prove that other persons than those regularly certified to by the governor of the state of Florida, in and according to the determination and declaration of their appointment by the board of state canvassers of said state prior to the time required for the performance of their duties, had been appointed electors, or by counter-proof to show that they had not, and that all proceedings of the courts or acts of the legislature or of the executive of Florida subsequent to the casting of the votes of the electors on the prescribed day, are inadmissible for any such purpose.

"As to the objection made to the eligibility of Mr. Humphreys, the Commission is of the opinion that, without reference to the question of the effect of the vote of an ineligible elector, the evidence does not show that he held the office of shipping-commissioner on the day when the electors were appointed." [1]

When the report of the Commission was read in joint session on Saturday, February 10th, Mr. Field at once submitted an objection, signed by the requisite number of senators and representatives. [2] The two houses accordingly separated to decide upon the objection. The Senate soon decreed by 44 to 25 that the decision should stand. [3] But in the House the Democratic majority were much exercised over the decision; and against the protests of the Republicans,

---

1 Proceedings, p. 196.
2 *Ibid*, pp. 200-201.
3 *Record*, pp. 1473-1477.

a recess was taken over Sunday in order that the Democrats might have more time for deliberation.[1] On Monday some of the more indignant members irregularly attempted to have the questions resubmitted to the Commission.[2] Others were for not having anything further to do with the tribunal. After much denunciatory talk the report was rejected by 168 to 103.[3] But, as the act provided that a decision should stand unless overruled by both houses, the votes of Florida were, when the joint convention reassembled, counted for Hayes.[4]

The count of the states then proceeded unchallenged until Louisiana was reached. From Louisiana there were four certificates, or papers purporting to be such.[5] The first was the original certificate made by the Republican electors on December 6th and certified by Governor Kellogg; only one copy of it was in the hands of the president of the Senate, for, as already explained, the copy sent by messenger had been carried back to Louisiana. The second, of which there were two copies, was from the Tilden "electors," and was certified by "Governor" McEnery. The third, of which there were also two copies, was the antedated Republican certificate, in which, although the Democrats knew it not, two signatures were forged. The fourth, received by mail only, was from "John Smith,

---

1 *Record*, p. 1487.
2 A resolution to that effect was offered by Proctor Knott.— *Ibid*, pp. 1489-1490.
3 *Ibid*, p. 1502.
4 *Ibid*, p. 1503.
5 Proceedings, pp. 205-212.

bull-dozed governor of Louisiana," certifying that the
vote of Louisiana had been cast for Peter Cooper.
This certificate was suppressed, but its announcement
created considerable merriment, and the Democrats
later claimed that it had purposely been sent in in
order to distract attention from the Republican certificates. [1] Three objections were submitted against
the Republican certificates, one against the Democratic,
and the whole case was then transferred to the Commission. [2]

The objections offered to the Republican returns
before the Commission were many, complicated, and
not entirely consistent with one another. [3]   It was
claimed that at the time of the election there had been
no law "in force directing the manner in which electors for said state should be appointed."   In the election which had taken place the Democratic electors
had received a majority of votes; hence "the lists
of names of electors made and certified by the said
William P. Kellogg, claiming to be, but not being,
governor of said state, were false."   The canvass
made by the returning board was illegal and void —
because the statutes gave that body no power to canvass the vote for electors; because such "statutes, if
construed as conferring such jurisdiction, give the returning officers power to appoint electors, and are void,
as in conflict with the Constitution, which requires

1 H. R. R. No. 140, 45th Cong. 3d Sess., p. 58.

2 Proceedings, pp. 212-217.

3 For the written objections see *Ibid*, pp. 212-216; for the oral
ones, pp. 221-243.

that electors shall be appointed by the state;" because
the board had no right to exercise discretionary
powers; because the board consisted of but four
persons instead of five, as the law provided;
because the board usurped jurisdiction in cases where
protests had not been properly filed; because the board
illegally and fraudulently changed the result; and because a member offered to receive a bribe. The votes
of A. B. Levissee and O. H. Brewster were of no
effect, because on the 7th of November both were Federal office-holders and therefore ineligible; the votes of
Oscar Joffrion, J. H. Burch, Morris Marks, and W. P.
Kellogg were likewise void because all of these four
persons held state offices and were ineligible under
state law. None of the Republican votes should be
counted because at the time of the appointment of the
Republican electors the state did not have a republican form of government.

The Republicans brought forward no such complicated and elaborate list of objections against the Democratic certificate. [1] They contented themselves with
defending their own certificates and with pointing out
that the Tilden electors had not been declared elected
by any state authority, that McEnery, who certified
their vote, was not governor, for Kellogg was the
real governor, having been recognized by the state
authorities and by every department of the Federal
government. [2] While asserting that the Commission

1 For written protest see Proceedings, p. 217; for oral objections see pp. 243-261.
2 *Ibid*, pp. 244-246, 253-254.

must accept the returning board's decision and must not attempt to investigate the conduct of the election, the Republican objectors took time to reply with vigor to the Democratic assertions regarding fraud. Senator Howe, who had been one of the Senate investigating committee, vividly described the intimidation in some of the parishes. There was, he admitted, in reply to a statement made by one of his opponents, "more than one foul stream to be found in the state of Louisiana. Coming right from that state, I know of other and larger streams which are not merely dirty but are very bloody. I would be glad if in this tribunal or in any there was power to say that only pure water should run anywhere; but the power does not reside in any human tribunal. I want your streams all purified as soon as it can be done. If you can aid in that direction, cleanse the bloody before you attempt the muddy streams."[1]

As in Florida, the real struggle was over the admission of evidence. The matter was again debated at great length;[2] Democratic offers to prove their contentions were many and insistent; but again the majority of the Commission refused to trench upon the domain of state powers by examining into such matters as the proceedings of the returning board and the ineligibility of electors holding state offices. Upon the other questions, such as whether the board was a lawful agent of the state, whether the vacancy

---

1 Proceedings, p. 261.
2 For the arguments in this case see *Ibid*, pp. 261-415; for the Democratic briefs see pp. 772-778.

vitiated its proceedings, and whether any of the electors were ineligible under the Federal Constitution,
the Republicans were on tolerably firm ground. The
law did provide for the returning board and gave it
power over "all elections held in the state;" the two
electors who had held Federal offices had not claimed
to vote by virtue of having been elected on November 7th but by virtue of appointment by the college
on December 6th after they had removed their dis-
qualifications by resigning; lastly, on the question of
the effect of the vacancy in the board, one opinon
could be defended about as successfully as the other.[1]

On the 16th the Commission met in secret session
to make its decision. After debate a great variety of
resolutions — to admit evidence showing that the returning board was unconstitutional, to admit evidence
to prove that the board was not legally constituted,
to receive testimony on the fraudulent acts of the returning board, and even to reject all the votes from
Louisiana — were offered by the desperate Democratic members. All were relentlessly voted down by
8 to 7.[2] Then the deciding vote was taken on a
resolution introduced by Senator Morton. Morton
had been informed by Kellogg that something was
wrong with certificate No. 3, so he was careful in
his resolution to stipulate that the votes certified in

---

1 In fact, the Republicans had slightly the stronger position because of the decisions of the state supreme court referred to above, pp.
115-116.
2 For all these resolutions with the votes see Proceedings, pp.
416-423.

No. 1 should be counted. [1] The resolution was carried by the usual vote of 8 to 7. The Commission explained its action to Congress as follows:

"The brief ground of this decision is that it appears, upon such evidence as by the Constitution and the law named in said act of Congress is competent and pertinent to the consideration of the subject, that the before mentioned electors appear to have been lawfully appointed such electors of President and Vice-President of the United States for the term beginning March 4th, A. D. 1877, of the state of Louisiana, and that they voted as such at the time and in the manner provided for by the Constitution of the United States and the law.

"And the Commission has by a majority of votes decided, and does hereby decide, that it is not competent, under the Constitution and the law as it existed at the date of the passage of said act, to go into evidence *aliunde* the papers opened by the president of the Senate in the presence of the two houses to prove that other persons than those regularly certified to by the governor of the state of Louisiana, on and according to the determination and declaration of their appointment by the returning officers for elections in the said state prior to the time required for the performance of their duties, had been appointed electors, or by counter-proof to show that they had not, or that the determination of the said returning officers was not in accordance with the truth and the fact, the Commission by a majority of votes being of opinion that it is not within the jurisdiction of the two houses of Congress assembled to count the votes for Presi-

---

1 Foulke, Morton, II, p. 470; H. R. R. No. 160, 45th Cong. 3d Sess., p. 60.

dent and Vice-President to enter upon a trial of such question.

"The Commission by a majority of votes is also of opinion that it is not competent to prove that any of said persons so appointed electors as aforesaid held an office of trust or profit under the United States at the time when they were appointed, or that they were ineligible under the laws of the state, or any other matter offered to be proved *aliunde* the said certificates and papers.

"The Commission is also of opinion by a majority of votes that the returning officers of the election who canvassed the votes at the election for electors in Louisiana were a legally-constituted body, by virtue of a constitutional law, and that a vacancy in said body did not vitiate its proceedings." [1]

Owing to a dilatory recess taken by the House against the protests of the Republican members, it was not until Monday, February 19th, that the joint session convened and received the report. The reading of the report was not greeted with many cheers from the Democrats. An elaborate objection, sufficient to fill pages 426 to 438 of the Proceedings, was at once presented by General Gibson of Louisiana, and shorter ones were offered by Senator Wallace and Representative Cochrane. [2] The two houses then separated in order to deliberate and decide upon the objections.

From the speeches in the debates which followed, it

---

1 Proceedings, p. 422. For Bradley's opinion on the constitutionality of the board see pp. 1028 *et seq.* There was no inconsistency in passing upon this point. The Commission naturally had the power to ascertain whether the returning board was the legal agent of the state.

2 *Ibid,* pp. 439-440.

is easy to infer that the Democrats had lost much of their pristine enthusiasm for the Electoral Commission. In the Senate Mr. Maxey declared that "the judgment in effect exalts fraud, degrades justice, and consigns truth to the dungeon."[1] "Deep indeed," said Bayard, "is my sorrow and poignant my disappointment. I mourn my failure for my country's sake; for it seems to me that not only does this decision of these eight members destroy and level in the dust the essential safeguards of the Constitution, intended to surround and protect the election of the Chief Magistrate of this Union, but it announces to the people of this land that truth and justice, honesty and morality, are no longer the essential bases of their political power."[2] In arguing that the Commission ought to have received evidence, Senator Wallace pointed out that one argument made by Morton, Garfield, and other Republicans against the bill had been that it might be interpreted as conferring power to go behind the returns.[3]

The decision did not, however, lack defenders among the Republican senators. Boutwell suggested that the opinion of the Republican "eight" was entitled to at least as much weight as that of the Democratic "seven," and expressed confidence that the people would accept the award.[4] "Mr. President," exclaimed Sherman, "a good deal is said about fraud,

---

1 *Record,* p. 1675.
2 *Ibid,* p. 1678.
3 *Ibid,* p. 1679.
4 *Ibid,* p. 1681.

fraud, fraud — fraud and perjury, and wrong. Why, sir, if you go behind the returns in Louisiana, the case is stronger for the Republicans than upon the face of the returns. What do you find there? Crime, murder, violence, that is what you find. . . . . I say now, as I said two months ago, that, while there may have been irregularities, while there may have been a non-observance of some directory laws, yet the substantial right was arrived at by the action of the returning board." [1]

None of the speeches made on either side had any effect on the vote. After two hours of debate the decision was concurred in by the Senate by 41 to 28. [2]

In the House the waves of Democratic declamation and vituperation ran even higher than in the Senate. The Democrats were, as Mr. McMahon admitted, [3] almost without hope, and they sought what little consolation they could find in flaying the wicked "eight." If, said New of Indiana, no evidence was to be received, what was the use of these many thick volumes of reports made by investigating committees and "visiting statesmen?" [4] There was much talk about the "ten thousand sovereign voters" who had been disfranchised by the returning board. [5] Solemn warnings were given of the terrible wrath which an outraged nation would visit upon the party which upheld such fraud. "There is yet much to live for in this rough

---

1 *Record*, p. 1677.
2 Proceedings, p. 440.
3 *Record*, p. 1688.
4 *Ibid*, p. 1685.
5 *Ibid*, 1701.

world," said Watterson, that fiery editor whose dream
of "a hundred thousand" had now been supplanted by
the dream of a *revanche,* "and among the rest that day
of reckoning, *dies irae, dies illa,*

> "When the dark shall be light,
> "And the wrong be made right." [1]

"Ah," cried the gentleman so justly famous for his
description of a sunset, "they called in the ermine to
help them. The ermine is a little animal. It is an
emblem of purity; it would rather be caught than be
bedraggled in the mire. Hunters put mud around its
haunt to catch it. But where is the ermine now. Ah!
the fox has become the ermine. But no cunning, no
craft, no human law, no divine law, can ever condone
fraud. All codes and the histories of all nations cry
out against it. Crime cannot breed crime forever.
Ask the people of this country. Fraud is to them an
endless offense. I was about, Mr. Speaker, before
the hammer fell, to refer to the holy writ, so that
gentlemen on the other side may have time for repentance. With permission of the House, I will read
from Psalms, xciv, 20: 'Shall the throne of iniquity
have fellowship with thee, which frameth mischief by
a law?' "

Mr. Kelley.—I object.

Mr. Cox.—The Bible is *aliunde* with these gentlemen. [2]

---

1 *Record,* p. 1690.
2 As quoted in Three Decades of Federal Legislation, p. 659.

Two Republicans of the House, — Pierce and Prof. Seelye, both of Massachusetts, — while not accepting the Democratic view, refused to vote with their party on the Louisiana decision. Pierce believed that the evidence offered should have been received. In his opinion, the evidence collected was such as to render necessary the exclusion of the state from participation in the Presidential election; there was, he declared, more ground for such action than there had been in 1872.[1] Prof. Seelye said that the Commission had unquestionably "applied the Constitution and the laws to the question;" but he feared that a strict and accurate interpretation of the Constitution would, under the attending circumstances, imperil the vote of the future. "It seems to me perfectly clear," said he, in a speech which received the closest attention, "that the charges made by each side against the other are in the main true. No facts were ever proved more conclusively than the fraud and corruption charged on the one side and the intimidation and cruelty charged on the other. Which of the two sides went the further would be very hard to say. The corruption of the one side seems as heinous as the cruelty of the other side is horrible, and on both sides there does not seem to be any limit to the extent they went, save only where the necessities of the case did not permit or the requirements of the case did not call for any more. I find it therefore quite impossible to say which of the two sets of electors coming up here with their certifi-

---

[1] *Record*, p. 1701. Pierce later became an ardent Democrat. —Hoar, *Autobiography of Seventy Years*, I, p. 370.

cates voices the true will of the people of Louisiana in the late election, and therefore equally beyond my power to assent to the propriety of counting either. . . . . Granted that the decision reached is fairly within the bond; yet what if the pound of flesh cannot be taken without its drop of blood?" [1]

The other House Republicans stood by the decision. At heart they doubtless believed with Mr. Crapo [2] that the returning board of Louisiana was a suspicious body, but thought that the rifle-clubs of Ouachita and elsewhere were equally so, and as the rifle-clubs had been the original offenders, decided that the acts of the returning board formed an equitable set-off, and hence declined to give way and allow violence and murder to be rewarded. To the Democratic denunciations of fraud they replied with accounts of intimidation and talk of Oregon cipher telegrams. Some of their speeches were quite as denunciatory as any made by their opponents. One member declared that the Democrats had started out in their campaign for the "Grand Fraud of Gramercy Park" with "the impression that they could buy every man they could not frighten or delude." [3]

Upon the conclusion of the debate the House rejected the decision by 173 to 99. But, as the Senate had accepted it, the eight votes of Louisiana were counted for Hayes and Wheeler. [4]

---

1 *Record,* p. 1685.
2 *Ibid,* p. 1689.
3 *Ibid,* p. 1686.
4 Proceedings, p. 441.

The count then proceeded unchallenged until Michigan was reached. From Michigan but one return had been received, but objection was offered by Representative Tucker to counting the vote of one of the electors of that state. [1] The grounds of the objection were, however, so slight that after deliberation the houses concurred in receiving the vote. An equally baseless objection was submitted to the vote of one of the Nevada electors, but again both houses refused to sustain the objection. [2]

At last Oregon was reached. From that state there were two certificates: One from the Republican electors, Cartwright, Watts, and Odell; the other from Cronin, Miller, and Parker. [3] The first was not certified by the governor, but it did contain certified copies of the canvass of votes, furnished by the secretary of state, together with a statement of the resignation of Watts from the college and his subsequent re-appointment. The one made by Cronin *et al.* contained the governor's certificate, attested by the secretary of state; this certificate stated that "at a general election held in the said state on the 7th day of November, A. D. 1876, William H. Odell received 15,206 votes, John C. Cartwright received 15,214 votes, E. A. Cronin received 14,157 votes for electors of President and Vice-President of the United States; being the highest number of votes cast at said election for persons eligible, under the Constitution of the United States,

1 Proceedings, pp. 442-446.
2 *Ibid*, pp. 446-454.
3 *Ibid*, pp. 454-460.

to be appointed electors of President and Vice-President." Two objections were submitted against the Cronin certificate and one against the Republican certificate.[1] The case was therefore referred to the Commission.

The Democratic contention[2] in the Oregon case started with the premise that since Postmaster Watts had been ineligible the votes cast for him had been null and void, and Cronin, his opponent next highest on the list, had been elected. The governor, after a hearing, had so declared, and with the secretary of state had made out lists attesting the fact. Even if the claim of Cronin was not valid, the subsequent resignation by Watts of the postmastership and then of the office of elector had failed to make it legal for the other two electors to choose him, for as Watts could not be elected because of his ineligibility, there could be no vacancy, and hence no filling of a vacancy. To be sure, the statute of Oregon provided that "if there shall be any vacancy in the office of an elector occasioned by the death, refusal to act, neglect to attend, or otherwise," the electors should proceed to fill such vacancy; but, argued the Democratic counsel, the law of Oregon stated only seven cases in which an office should be deemed vacant, namely, upon "the death of the incumbent;" "his resignation;" "his removal;" "his ceasing to be an inhabitant of the district, county, town or village," in which the duties of

---

1 Proceedings, pp. 461-463.

2 For the Democratic oral objections and arguments see *Ibid*, pp. 466-488, 555-581, 623-636. For their brief see p. 778.

the office were to be exercised; "his conviction of an infamous crime;" "his refusal or neglect to take his oath of office;" "the decision of a competent tribunal, declaring void his election or appointment." Since Watts had never been an "incumbent," there had not, the Democrats argued, been any "vacancy" for the college to fill. Even should this line of reasoning be held to be erroneous, the Commission must, to be consistent with its stand in the Florida and Louisiana cases, receive the certificate or list signed by the governor and secretary of state, under the great seal of the state, as final and conclusive evidence of how the vote was cast. Whether or not the governor had acted legally, his action had served, the Democrats held, to give the Cronin college possession of the office as electors *de facto*.

But the Democratic position was badly shaken before the hearing was concluded. [1] The Republicans successfully combated the claim that Cronin had been elected, and in so doing quoted Thurman himself to the effect "that the weight of judicial decision in the United States is decidedly against the claim of a minority man to election." They met the Democratic non-vacancy argument by quoting the clause, "The decision of a competent tribunal declaring void his [the incumbent's] election or appointment," which, they justly pointed out, was conclusive that under the law even an ineligible person might temporarily be an "incumbent." This was conclusive against the theory

[1] For the Republican objections and arguments see Proceedings, pp. 461, 463, 488-549, 581-598, 609-623.

that Watts could not have been elected, because
whether Watts's incumbency was terminated by the
governor's decision — and this the Republicans stren-
uously denied — or by his resignation presented to the
college, there existed a vacancy which the statute said
should be filled by the other electors.

The Republicans were also able to show pretty
conclusively that the merits of the case could be arrived at by the Commission without any trenching
upon the domain of state powers. The constitution
of Oregon, they pointed out, declared that "the person
or persons who shall receive the highest number of
votes shall be declared duly elected," and a statute
provided that the canvass of votes should be made by
the secretary of state in the presence of the governor.
The secretary had canvassed the votes, and his certified statement, enclosed with the Republican return,
showed that Odell, Cartwright, and Watts had received
"the highest number of votes," and were hence "duly
elected." This constituted the appointment. All else
that followed was merely certification of the results of
the canvass. As the duties laid down by the section of
the law governing the certification were ministerial
only, any certificate not in accord with the appointment as shown by the canvass was mere usurpation
and should not be taken as paramount to the certificate
of the canvass. Furthermore, the matter of certification lay within the domain of Federal powers, for
the state law on the subject was merely a carrying
into effect of the Federal law governing the matter;

objection to this contention could not consistently be made by the Democrats, for Governor Grover, on the ground of non-agreement between the two, had claimed to ignore the state law and to act under the Federal law.[1] All other matters were likewise in the domain of Federal powers and could be examined into and the truth ascertained.

Following the line just indicated, the Republicans were able to make good their case. Evidence was taken which showed conclusively that Watts had resigned the postmastership before acting as elector.[2] The certificate showed that he had also resigned his electorship and had been rechosen by the other two electors. The certificate itself was regular except that it was not accompanied by the governor's lists. These lists, however, were a statutory, not a constitutional requirement; and the Republicans contended that as the certificate of the canvass furnished sufficient authentication, their absence was not vital.

The vote on the Oregon case was taken on Friday, February 23d, at the home of Senator Thurman, whither the Commission had repaired in order that

---

[1] The state law provided that "The secretary of state shall prepare two lists of the names of the electors elected, and affix the seal of the state to the same. Such lists shall be signed by the governor and secretary, and by the latter delivered to the college of electors at the hour of their meeting on such first Wednesday of December."

The Federal law provided that "It shall be the duty of the executive of the state to cause three lists of the names of the electors of such state to be made and certified and to be delivered to the electors on or before the day on which they are required by the preceding section to meet."

The governor claimed that because the state law through some mistake said "two lists" instead of three, he was justified in ignoring it.—Proceedings, p. 495.

[2] *Ibid*, pp. 602-609.

the senator, who was ill, might participate. Upon one conclusion, namely that the Cronin certificate did not contain the vote of Oregon, the Commission was unanimous; but upon the proposal to reject the vote of Watts there was the usual party division. By the same vote it was then decided that the Republican certificate should be received.[1] The defense transmitted to Congress was as follows:

"The brief ground of this decision is that it appears, upon such evidence as by the Constitution and the law named in said act of Congress is competent and pertinent to the consideration of the subject, that the before-mentioned electors appear to have been lawfully appointed such electors of President and Vice-President of the United States for the term beginning March 4, A. D. 1877, of the state of Oregon, and that they voted as such at the time and in the manner provided for by the Constitution of the United States and the law.

"And we are further of opinion —

"That by the laws of the state of Oregon the duty of canvassing the returns of all the votes given at an election for electors of President and Vice-President was imposed upon the secretary of state and upon no one else.

"That the secretary of state did canvass the returns in the case before us and thereby ascertained that J. C. Cartwright, W. H. Odell, and J. W. Watts had a majority of all the votes given for electors, and had the highest number of votes for that office, and by the express language of the statute those persons are 'deemed elected.'

"That in obedience to his duty the secretary made

[1] Proceedings, pp. 637-641.

a canvass and tabulated statement of the votes showing this result, which, according to law, he placed on file in his office on the 4th day of December, A. D. 1876. All this appears by an official certificate under the seal of the state and signed by him, and delivered by him to the electors and forwarded by them to the president of the Senate with their votes.

"That the refusal or failure of the governor of Oregon to sign the certificate of the election of the persons so elected does not have the effect of defeating their appointment as such electors.

"That the act of the governor of Oregon in giving to E. A. Cronin a certificate of his election, though he received a thousand votes less than Watts, on the ground that the latter was ineligible, was without authority of law and is therefore void.

"That although the evidence shows that Watts was a postmaster at the time of his election, that fact is rendered immaterial by his resignation both as postmaster and elector, and his subsequent appointment to fill the vacancy so made by the electoral college." [1]

In the joint session an objection to accepting the decision was submitted, and the two houses therefore separated as the law required. In the Senate [2] the Republicans defended the decision, denounced Grover and Cronin, and made frequent references to the cipher telegrams to and from 15 Gramercy Park. [3]   The Democratic speakers devoted much of their time to the Florida and Louisiana cases and to contending that the decisions of the Commission were not consistent. They did not attempt seriously to sustain

1 Proceedings, p. 640.
2 For the Senate debate see *Record,* pp. 1888-1896.
3 *Ibid,* p. 1894.

the theory that the Cronin certificate should be received, but did insist that only two votes should be counted for Hayes.[1] When the debate came to an end, however, a resolution to that effect was voted down, and the decision of the Commission was then sustained by 41 to 24.[2]

In the House the debate was preceded by a spirited parliamentary contest. Although a Democratic caucus held about a week before had decided that the count should be allowed to proceed,[3] a knot of representatives had made up their minds to delay the progress of the count by dilatory proceedings. These filibusters were of two classes. One class, numbering about forty members and composed of men like Blackburn of Kentucky, Springer of Illinois, Mills of Texas, O'Brien of Maryland, and Cox of New York, were those irreconcilables who were willing to resort to any measures to prevent the consummation of what they termed "the Fraud." The other class, composed in large measure of Southern members, were actuated chiefly by other motives. Most of them were desirous that the count should be completed in order to prevent anarchy; but before it was accomplished they wished to scare the Republicans, and particularly the friends of Hayes, into giving assurances that the new Administration would refrain from supporting the Republican claimants for state offices in South Carolina and Louisiana. This movement was organized

---

1 *Record*, p. 1896.
2 Proceedings, p. 645.
3 H. R. Mis. Doc. No. 31, 45th Cong. 3d Sess., I, p. 970.

shortly after the Louisiana decision had convinced most Democrats that the prospects of saving the national ticket were hopeless; those who entered it were inspired by the belief that it would be thrifty policy to save even a little out of the wreck.[1] Conditions seemed to favor the filibusters, for the parliamentary methods of "Czar" Reed had not then been introduced; and in the preceding Congress Mr. Randall, who was now speaker, had for seventy-two hours occupied the floor and had forced the Republicans to abandon their attempt to re-enact the Force Bill.[2]

But when the irreconcilables, led by such men as Clymer of Pennsylvania, Lane of Oregon, and Springer of Illinois, began their attempt to hold up the count by introducing dilatory motions, they discovered, to their surprise and indignation, that the speaker refused to entertain the motions. A scene of disorder followed, but the speaker stood firm. The Chair "rules," said he, "that when the Constitution of the United States directs anything to be done, or when the law under the Constitution of the United States enacted in obedience thereto directs any act by this House, it is not in order to make any motion to obstruct or impede the execution of that injunction of the Constitution and the laws."[3]

Thanks to this wise and determined stand, the House was then able to proceed to the consideration

---

1 H. R. Mis. Doc. No. 31, 45th Cong. 3d Sess., I, pp. 971, 980; III, pp. 595, 631-632.
2 *McClure's*, XXIII, p. 85; *American Law Review*, XXXVIII, p. 173.
3 *Record*, pp. 1905-1907.

of the Commission's finding. As in the Senate, the Democratic speakers did not display a great deal of enthusiasm for the Grover-Cronin proceedings. In fact, Mr. Le Moyne of Illinois said: "I have never believed in this Oregon road, and it does not satisfy me to say that it is only using the same means employed by the Republicans." The same speaker also showed considerable disgust at the Democratic management of affairs. "We of the West," he declared, "are done in politics with the domination of New York." Referring to the Oregon dispatches, he said: "If Mr. Tilden either directly or indirectly consented to the purchase of a Republican elector, he deserves double condemnation from every man who supported him." [1] Several speakers laid stress upon alleged inconsistencies in the Commission's rulings in the various cases [2] and upon inconsistencies in the positions taken by Republican members of that tribunal. In the latter connection Mr. Hewitt accused Mr. Hoar of having said in the debate on the bill that proof would be admitted; the charge brought a warm denial from Mr. Hoar, who proceeded to intimate, amidst laughter, that, as a result of the responsibilities imposed upon him, there was "a screw loose somewhere" in Mr. Hewitt. [3]

---

1 *Record*, p. 1913.
2 E. g., *Ibid*, pp. 1910-1911.
3 *Ibid*, pp. 1914-1915. A study of the *Record* will show that Hewitt's charge was not well founded. Not long before his death Mr. Hoar prepared a statement which is to be published in case the one left by Mr. Hewitt (see foot-note at end of preceding chapter) appears. Mr. Hoar's statement makes certain allegations which are designed to cast a decidedly unfavorable light on Mr. Hewitt's veracity.

The Republican "eight," and especially Judge Bradley, came in for much rabid denunciation. Referring to Bradley, Clymer of Pennsylvania said: "We in this House assisted in developing one the latchets of whose shoes even Wells, in all his moral deformity, is unworthy to unloose. Their precious names will go to posterity linked together, as those between whom, here in this Capitol, in the very temple of justice, the rights of the people were betrayed and crucified." [1] In reply to talk of this kind, Woodworth of Ohio said it was curious that "while the supposed partisanship of the eight who concur is denounced, there is a silence profound as the hush of death as to the at least equal partisanship of the seven who dissent."

The same speaker accused the Democrats of being poor losers. "Filibuster," said he, "has been called in to aid those who cannot accept defeat. I am not surprised at this, nor at the chagrin and natural wrath of our Democratic friends; for with everything to gain and nothing to lose, they cunningly set a trap and were themselves caught — caught by the act of God, who disposes of all human events, and by the act of the Illinois legislature, which disposed of Judge Davis [Laughter].

> "They digged a pit, they digged it deep,
> They digged it for their brother;
> But through their sin they did fall in
> The pit they digged for t'other." [2]

But, as usual, the debate had no effect upon the

---

1 *Record*, p. 1908.

2 *Ibid*, p. 1911.

vote. A resolution to accept the Commission's decision was so amended as to provide for rejecting the vote of Watts, and in this form was then adopted without a division. [1]

The count of the states in joint session then proceeded, but was much delayed by technical objections to votes from states in which there had been no contest. Such an objection was made to receiving one of the votes from Pennsylvania; but as, after debate, only the House sustained the objection, the vote was counted with the rest. [2] An equally futile objection — sustained by neither house — was made to one of the votes of Rhode Island; then, about six in the afternoon of February 26th, South Carolina was reached.

From South Carolina there were two certificates. The first, that from the Hayes electors, was certified by Governor Chamberlain and Secretary of State Hayne; the second, that from the Tilden "electors," was not certified by any one, but in it the "electors" claimed to have received a majority of the votes cast, alleged that they had wrongfully been deprived of their rights by the returning board, and referred to the *mandamus* and *quo warranto* proceedings which have already been described. Objections were submitted against both

---

1 Proceedings, pp. 645-646.

2 One of the electors, who was a centennial commissioner, had remained away from the college, and the other electors had chosen H. A. Boggs to fill the vacancy. The Democrats held that because the first elector was ineligible, he was never an incumbent, and that hence his resignation created no vacancy which the other electors had power to fill. The contention was not, however, sustained by all the Democrats.—E. g., speech of Cockrell, *Record*, p. 1905. For the whole matter see *Ibid,* pp. 1900-1905, 1919-1923, 1927-1938, and Proceedings, pp. 647-652.

returns, and the case was referred to the Commission. [1]

The contest before that body [2] was a rather perfunctory one. The Democratic objectors did not attempt to prove that the Democratic electors had been chosen, but took the ground that because the legislature had failed to provide a registration law as required by the constitution of 1868 there had been no legal election in the state. [3] They further contended that the vote of the state ought not to be received because at the time of the election there was not a republican form of government in the state. In support of this view they alleged that prior to and during the election Federal troops, without authority of law, had been stationed at or near the polling-places, with the result that no legal or free election could be held; that more than 1,000 deputy United States marshals, appointed under an unconstitutional law, had interfered with the full and free exercise of the right of suffrage by the voters of the state. In their anxiety to prove that a condition of anarchy had existed in the state the Democrats made some interesting admissions. "We propose to show," said Representative Hurd, "by testimony taken by the minority of the same committee [the House committee], that in the counties which gave large Democratic majorities the Democratic leaders and managers interfered with the freedom of the election by practicing intimidation upon their black

---

1 For the returns and the written objections see Proceedings, pp. 659-664.
2 Owing to the illness of Thurman his place on the Commission was now taken by Kernan of New York.—*Ibid*, p. 655.
3 For the Democratic oral objections see *Ibid*, pp. 666-678.

employés and those who might happen to live within
their districts. We propose to show that rifle-clubs
were organized which were not disbanded in accordance with the proclamation of the President of the
United States, and that under the effect of these
rifle-clubs and of the intimidation that was practiced
in that method large numbers of negroes who otherwise would have voted the Republican ticket voted the
Democratic ticket." [1]

As the Democrats did not attempt to prove that the
votes of the Tilden "electors" should be received, the
Republican objectors [2] confined themselves almost entirely to defending their own certificate and to com-
bating the argument that the vote of the state ought
to be thrown out. They contended that the constitutional provision requiring a registration was directory
only, that the legislature had in effect complied with
the requirement by enacting that a poll-list should be
kept, that the Democratic position on the matter was
untenable because otherwise all elections and all government in South Carolina during the last eight years
would be illegal and void. Upon the question of
whether the state possessed a republican form of
government they argued that the fact that the state
was represented in both houses of Congress must be
taken as conclusive; to sustain this contention they
quoted an opinion delivered in the case of Luther *vs.*

---

1 Proceedings, p. 669. In reporting his speech the New York
World of Feb. 28th represented him as saying that work of this
kind was done by "colored [sic] rifle-clubs."

2 For the speeches of the Republican objectors see **Proceedings**, pp. 678-688.

Borden. As regarded the use of troops and deputy marshals, they contended that the Commission was not competent to receive evidence; they pointed out, however, that both the troops and the marshals had been used in accordance with the laws of the United States and under the direction of the President and the attorney general.

In order to hasten the count, the Republicans submitted their case without any argument by counsel. [1] For the Democrats short speeches were made by Montgomery Blair [2] and Jeremiah S. Black. [3] Mr. Black made the closing address. As he expressly disclaimed any intention of arguing the case, it is evident that he was put forward for no other purpose than to damn the Commission. And damn it he did in a bitter invective, hardly to have been expected from the man who, in the greatest crisis of our history, had rendered to a weak President one of the mildest and most unfortunate opinions ever given by a public officer. [4] He was, he said, "fallen from the proud estate of an American citizen," and was "fit for nothing on earth but to represent the poor, defrauded, broken-hearted Democracy."

"We may," he continued, "struggle for justice; we may cry for mercy; we may go down on our knees, and beg and woo for some little recognition of our rights as American citizens; but we might as well put

1 Proceedings, p. 694.
2 *Ibid*, pp. 688-694.
3 *Ibid*, pp. 695-699.
4 Burgess, The Civil War and the Constitution, I, p. 80.

up our prayers to Jupiter, or Mars, as bring suit in
the court where Rhadamanthus presides. There is
not a god on Olympus that would not listen to us with
more favor than we shall be heard by our adversaries.
. . . Usually it is said that the 'fowler setteth not
forth his net in the sight of the bird,' but this fowler
set the net in the sight of the birds that went into it.
It is largely our own fault that we are caught. . . . .
They offer us everything now. They denounce
negro supremacy and carpet-bag thieves. Their pet
policy for the South is to be abandoned. They offer
us everything but one; but on that subject their lips
are closely sealed. They refuse to say that they will
not cheat us hereafter in the elections. . . . .

"If this thing stands accepted and the law you have
made for this occasion shall be the law for all occasions, we can never expect such a thing as an honest
election again. If you want to know who will be
President by a future election, do not inquire how the
people of the states are going to vote. You need
only to know what kind of scoundrels constitute the
returning boards, and how much it will take to buy
them.

"But I think even that will end some day. At
present you have us down and under your feet. Never
had you a better right to rejoice. Well may you say,
'We have made a covenant with death, and with hell
are we at agreement; when the overflowing scourge
shall pass through, it shall not come unto us: for we
have made lies our refuge, and under falsehoods have

we hid ourselves.' But nevertheless wait a little while. The waters of truth will rise gradually, and slowly but surely, and then look out for the overwhelming scourge. 'The refuge of lies shall be swept away, and the hiding place of falsehood shall be uncovered.' This mighty and puissant nation will yet raise herself up like a strong man after sleep, and shake her invincible locks in a fashion you little think of now. Wait; retribution will come in due time. Justice travels with a leaden heel but strikes with an iron hand. God's mill grinds slowly but dreadfully fine. Wait till the flood-gate is lifted and a full head of water comes rushing on. Wait, and you will see fine grinding then."

But the fiery words of the old Pennsylvanian did not suffice to melt the hearts of the Republican eight. Upon a proposal to receive evidence regarding the use of the troops and of the marshals they voted as usual. Then, after a resolution to the effect that the Democratic electors had not been chosen had been unanimously agreed to, they carried a resolution to count the votes of South Carolina for Hayes. They explained their action in the following words:

"The brief ground of this decision is, that it appears, upon such evidence as by the Constitution and the law named in said act of Congress is competent and pertinent to the consideration of the subject, that the beforementioned electors appear to have been lawfully appointed such electors of President and Vice-President of the United States for the term beginning March 4, A. D. 1877, of the state of South Carolina, and that they voted as such at the time and in the manner provided for by the Constitution of the United States and the law.

"And the Commission, as further grounds for their decision, are of opinion that the failure of the legislature to provide a system for the registration of persons entitled to vote, does not render nugatory all elections held under laws otherwise sufficient, though it may be the duty of the legislature to enact such a law. If it were otherwise, all government in that state is a usurpation, its officers without authority, and the social compact in that state is at an end.

"That this Commission must take notice that there is a government in South Carolina republican in form, since its Constitution provides for such a government, and it is, and was on the day of appointing electors, so recognized by the executive and by both branches of the legislative department of the government of the United States.

"That so far as this Commission can take notice of the presence of the soldiers of the United States in the state of South Carolina during the election, it appears that they were placed there by the President of the United States to suppress insurrection, at the request of the proper authorities of the state.

"And we are also of opinion that from the papers before us it appears that the governor and secretary of state having certified under the seal of the state that the electors whose votes we have decided to be the lawful electoral votes of the state, were duly appointed electors, which certificate, both by presumption of law and by the certificate of the rival claimants of the electoral office, was based upon the action of the state canvassers, there exists no power in this Commission, as there exists none in the two houses of Congress in counting the electoral vote, to inquire into the circumstances under which the primary vote for electors was given. *

"The power of the Congress of the United States in its legislative capacity to inquire into the matters alleged, and to act upon the information so obtained, is a very different one from its power in the matter of counting the electoral vote. The votes to be counted are those presented by the state, and when ascertained and presented by the proper authorities of the states they must be counted." [1]

While the South Carolina case was before the Commission other events of great significance had been taking place in secret. As already narrated, a movement had for some days been on foot to exact from the friends of Hayes pledges regarding the state governments in Louisiana and South Carolina. [2] This movement had created considerable alarm among Republicans. As early as February 23d, in an effort to conciliate the Southern Democrats, Mr. Charles Foster, representative from Hayes's own district, had stated in a speech in the Louisiana debate that it would be the policy of Mr. Hayes, if inaugurated, to wipe out sectional lines, that under him "the flag should wave over states, not provinces, over freemen and not subjects." [3] Negotiations were entered into between

---

1 Proceedings, 702.
2 An attempt to ascertain the probable attitude of Hayes toward the South had been made as early as the end of the preceding November. At that time Mr. W. H. Roberts of the New Orleans *Times* visited Columbus for that purpose. Hayes referred him to his letter of acceptance and also stated that in his opinion intelligence ought to govern. H. R. Mis. Doc. No. 31, 45th Cong. 3d Sess., I, pp. 875-899.
3 *Ibid,* III, p. 596; *Record,* p. 1708. On the 23d Hayes wrote to Foster commending this speech. He said that when the count was completed—if favorable—the public was to be informed that the Southern policy was to be as Foster had stated

the interested parties, and various conferences were held.[1] On the 26th of February there were three such conferences. One took place in the room of the House committee on appropriations between Mr. Foster, Representative John Young Brown of Kentucky, and Senator J. B. Gordon of Georgia.[2] Another occurred in the finance committee room of the Senate;[3] present, Major E. A. Burke, special agent for Louisiana, Stanley Matthews and ex-Governor Dennison of Ohio, and John Sherman.[4] The third took place that evening in the room of Mr. Evarts at Wormley's Hotel; present, Mr. Burke, Mr. E. J. Ellis and Mr. W. M. Levy, Democratic representatives from Louisiana, Mr. Henry Watterson, who represented the interests of South Carolina, Mr. Matthews, Mr. Dennison, Mr. Sherman, and Mr. James A. Garfield.[5]

The outcome of these conferences was to all intents

---

it. Foster showed this letter to Burke on the 25th. Burke "urged direct assurances or action before House yields."—See Burke's telegram to Nicholls, Report just quoted, p. 618.

1 Burke held an interview with Stanley Matthews as early as the night of February 16th, just after the Louisiana decision was announced. Bishop Wilmer of Louisiana was also in Washington trying to assist Nicholls and his associates. After an interview with Grant he visited Columbus. From there he telegraphed on Feb. 23d: "Peace not to be disturbed in Louisiana." —H. R. Mis. Doc. No. 31, 45th Cong. 3d Sess., III, p. 617.

2 Letter of Brown in Louisville *Courier-Journal* of March 29th. Given in New York *Times* of same date.

3 H. R. Mis. Doc. No. 31, 45th Cong. 3d Sess., III, p. 619.

4 Sherman had just returned from a visit to Hayes in Columbus. On the 15th Hayes had written Sherman that he preferred not to make any new declarations regarding his Southern policy further than to confirm what he had said in his letter of acceptance. "But you may say, if you deem it advisable, that you *know* that I will stand by the friendly and encouraging words of that letter and by all that they imply. You cannot express that too strongly."—John Sherman's Recollections, I, p. 561.

5 House document just cited, III, pp. 591, 619.

and purposes an agreement — "bargain" is perhaps
a more concise term — by which each contracting
party tacitly agreed to do certain things. [1] The Republicans, while expressly disclaiming any authority
to speak for him, in effect guaranteed that Mr. Hayes,
when he became President, would, by a gradual process of non-interference and withdrawal of troops,
allow the Republican governments in the two states
to disappear. They also agreed to use their best endeavors to induce President Grant to embark upon the
same policy before the end of his term. [2] The Democrats, on their part, promised to use their influence to
stop filibustering, and guaranteed peace, good order,
protection of the law to whites and blacks alike, and
no persecution for past political offenses.   In order to
avoid precipitating the whole issue upon the Senate
before the cabinet should have been confirmed and
thereby rousing up perhaps sufficient opposition to
prevent the confirmation of persons favorable to the
new Southern policy, the Democrats further agreed
that the Nicholls legislature should not elect the long-
term senator before March 10th. [3]

1 Many efforts were later made to show that no bargain was
made, but there is no evading the fact that in all essentials there
was an agreement. Hayes, however, was not a party to it.
He had steadfastly refused to authorize any one to represent
him, and had already made up his mind regarding his Southern
policy.   On Feb. 4th he wrote to Schurz in regard to the use of
the military as follows: "But there is to be an end to all that,
except in emergencies which I cannot think of as possible again."
2 The President had already declined to recognize either government.—See his telegrams to Kellogg and Gen. Augur in H.
R. Mis. Doc. No. 31, 45th Cong. 3d Sess., III, pp. 603-604. In
case one must be recognized, however, he intended to recognize
Packard.—Telegram to Augur just cited. As time passed he
became more favorable to Nicholls. See *Ibid,* pp. 604-631.
3 For accounts of the Wormley Conference see *Ibid,* I, pp.
978, 980, 981, 984, 990; III, pp. 595-633.

Certain details of the agreement were arranged next day. The Democratic assurances of peace, order, and equal rights were ratified by Governor Nicholls and by a legislative caucus, and a copy was sent by Burke to Matthews and his associates. Matthews, on his part, assured the Louisiana agents that Grant had promised that as soon as the count should be completed all orders heretofore issued in regard to preserving the *status quo* should be rescinded or modified so far as they were necessary for preserving the public peace.[1] Mr. Foster sought John Young Brown and gave to him the following unsigned letter addressed to Brown and to Senator Gordon:

"GENTLEMEN: Referring to the conversation had with you yesterday in which Governor Hayes's policy as to the status of certain Southern states was discussed, we desire to say in reply that we can assure you in the strongest possible manner of our great desire to have adopted such a policy as will give to the people of the states of South Carolina and Louisiana the right to control their own affairs in their own way; and to say further that we feel authorized, from an acquaintance with and knowledge of Governor Hayes and his views on this question, to pledge ourselves to you that such will be his policy."

After reading the letter Brown expressed the opinion that it might be "fuller and stronger," but that coming from the men it did it would be sufficient. Foster then saw Matthews, and an hour later Brown received from Foster the following:

---

1 See copy of written assurance given by Matthews to Burke and Levy, H. R. Mis. Doc. No. 31, 45th Cong., 3d Sess., III., p. 623.

"GENTLEMEN: Referring to the conversation had with you yesterday, in which Governor Hayes's policy as to the status of certain states was discussed, we desire to say that we can assure you in the strongest possible manner of our great desire to have him adopt such a policy as will give to the people of the states of South Carolina and Louisiana the right to control their own affairs in their own way, subject only to the Constitution of the United States and the laws made in pursuance thereof, and to say further, that from an acquaintance with and knowledge of Governor Hayes and his views, we have the most complete confidence that such will be the policy of his administration. Respectfully,

"STANLEY MATTHEWS,
"CHARLES FOSTER."

Brown did not like some of the generalities which this letter contained, but accepted it. By his request Foster affixed his signature to the first letter, and Brown retained that letter also. Later Brown gave copies to Ellis, to Burke, to M. C. Butler, of South Carolina, and to one or two other persons. [1]

While the personal friends of Hayes were striving in ways just described to lessen Democratic opposition to the completion of the count, other schemes were being devised for the contingency which would arise should the count not be completed. In the Senate Mr. Sargent on the 26th introduced a resolution to the effect that the Senate should proceed at once to elect a president *pro tempore* to succeed Mr. Ferry, whose

---

[1] See Brown's statement in the Louisville *Courier-Journal* of March 29th. The statement is given in the New York *Times* of the same date.

term as senator would expire on the 4th of March.[1]
The resolution was laid aside until the time should
come when its passage would be desirable. If that
time had come, it would probably have been passed,
and Morton would have been chosen. He would then
either have completed the count and declared Hayes
elected, or would himself have been installed as President under a forced construction of the law of 1792.[2]

In the House David Dudley Field on the 27th
reported from the committee on the powers, privileges, and duties of the House in counting the electoral vote a bill providing that, in case of a failure to
elect, the line of succession should be the president of
the Senate, the speaker of the House, and the secretary of state, and that the person who succeeded
should hold office until a successor had been duly
elected.[3] The bill was regarded by some as part of a
scheme to defeat the count and secure a new election.
Some Democrats opposed it because they preferred
Hayes to Morton;[4] but it was hurried through,[5] and
was then sent to the Senate, where it was referred to a
committee, and never came to a vote.[6]

---

1 *Record*, p. 1926; *Times* of 27th.
2 *Record*, p. 1983; *Times* of March 2d; letter of William Dudley Foulke to the writer. The law of 1792 provided, "That in
case of the removal, death, resignation, or disability both of the
President and Vice-President of the United States, the President
of the Senate, *pro tempore,* and, in case there shall be no President of the Senate, then the Speaker of the House of Representatives, for the time being, shall act as President of the United
States until such disability be removed, or until a President be
elected."
3 *Record*, p. 1980.
4 *Ibid*, p. 1983.
5 *Ibid*, p. 1984.
6 *Ibid*, p. 1974.

On the 28th the South Carolina decision was read in joint session. Objections were at once offered, and the houses separated to deliberate. After a short debate the Senate accepted the decision by 39 to 22.[1] In the House after the irreconcilables, led by Springer of Illinois and O'Brien of Maryland, had tried hard to secure a dilatory recess, but had been thwarted by the opposition of the Republicans, of the speaker, and of a number of Democrats under the leadership of Fernando Wood, who had now become a conservative, a debate was hãd, after which the decision was rejected.[2]

When the joint session had been resumed and Vermont had been reached, the proceedings entered upon a new and dangerous phase. After the regular return had been read, Representative Poppleton inquired whether any other return had been received. Mr. Ferry gave a negative answer. Mr. Hewitt, who up to this time had favored the completion of the count and had been much criticised by some rabid Democrats, then arose, and amidst breathless interest asked to be allowed to make a statement.

"I hold in my hand," said he, "a package which purports to contain electoral votes from the state of Vermont. This package was delivered to me by express about the middle of December last, and with it came a letter stating that a similar package had been forwarded by mail to the presiding officer of the

---

1 *Record*, pp. 1992-2002.
2 *Ibid*, pp. 2005-2020.

Senate; I called upon him and inquired whether any other than one certificate from the state of Vermont had been received by him by mail, and he informed me that there had been no other received by him than the one which was already in his possession. I then tendered to him this package, the seals of which are unbroken and which is now as it came into my possession. He declined to receive it, upon the ground that he had no authority in law to do so. Under the circumstances, I now tender this package to the presiding officer of the Senate as purporting to contain electoral votes from the state of Vermont." [1]

It was well known that the package had been sent in by a minority Democratic candidate who, although defeated by about twenty-four thousand votes, claimed to have been elected because one of the Republican candidates was a postmaster. Mr. Ferry pointed out that it would not be legal for him to receive the certificate because the law designated the first Thursday in February as the date on which certificates must be handed in; [2] but the opponents of the count, in accordance with a prearranged plan, were determined to make the most of the opportunity which they thought presented itself. Springer attempted to precipitate a debate in joint session, shrieked wildly, threw his arms about, and for a time refused to come to order. [3] After some minutes of excitement, however, quiet was restored, and the objections against the

---

1 Proceedings, p. 712.
2 *Ibid*, p. 712.
3 *Ibid*, pp. 712-714.

Vermont return were submitted.[1] The two houses then separated.

In the Senate a decision was soon reached by a unanimous vote to count the Vermont return,[2] but in the House an adjournment was decided upon before a vote had been taken.[3] The session of the following day was probably the stormiest ever witnessed in any House of Representatives. The irreconcilables were determined to force the president of the Senate to receive the certificate, and then to have the two certificates referred to the Commission. A resolution to that effect was introduced by Poppleton, but he shortly after accepted a substitute of the same tenor offered by J. Proctor Knott of Kentucky.[4] But the speaker was determined that the count should proceed, and therefore ruled that under the law the two hours' debate upon Vermont should begin. Then ensued a scene of the wildest excitement. Every possible device was resorted to by the filibusters. The speaker was assailed "with a storm of questions and reproaches. Would he not then put a motion for a recess? A motion for a call of the House? A motion to excuse some member from voting? A motion to reconsider? A motion to lay something on the table? He would not. Were not these motions in order under the rules? They were. Would he not then submit some one of them to the House? He would

1 Proceedings, 714-717.
2 *Record*, 2002-2004.
3 *Ibid*, 2024-2027.
4 *Ibid*, pp. 2027 and 2032.

not. Was he not an oppressor, a tyrant, a despot?
He was not. Would he not then put some dilatory
motion? He would not. Why would he not? Because of his obligation to the law." [1]

The occasion was rendered the more noisy and exciting by the presence on the floor of many persons
who had no right there and by the fact that the galleries were packed with a crowd who wildly applauded
each outbreak. Furthermore, some even of the conservative Democrats were angry and suspicious because the irregular certificate had temporarily disappeared. At one time the wrath of the filibusters became so great that they rushed forward shouting and
gesticulating; and one of them, Beebe of New York,
even sprang upon a desk, and, amid great uproar, demanded of the Chair why he declined to hear an
appeal. Pale but resolute, Mr. Randall still refused
to recede, and declared that he would no longer submit to the disorder. "If gentlemen forget themselves,"
said he, "it is the duty of the Chair to remind them
that they are members of the American Congress." [2]

After some further disorder the House quieted
down sufficiently for the debate to proceed. None of
the speeches made possessed any importance save one;
it was made by Levy of Louisiana, who, remembering
the Wormley compact, was anxious to stop the filibustering. "The people of Louisiana," said he, "have
solemn, earnest, and I believe truthful assurances from

---

1 *Atlantic,* LXXII, p. 533. The passage was written by James
Monroe, who was then a member of the House from Ohio.
2 *Record,* pp. 2033-2034.

prominent members of the Republican party, high in
the confidence of Mr. Hayes, that, in the event of his
election to the Presidency, he will be guided by a
policy of conciliation toward the Southern states, that
he will not use the Federal authority or the army to
force upon those states governments not of their
choice, but in the case of these states will leave their
own people to settle the matter peaceably, of themselves. This, too, is the opinion of President Grant,
which he freely expresses, and which I am satisfied he
will carry out and adhere to." Levy then announced
that because of these assurances he would throw no
obstacles in the way of the completion of the count,
and he called upon fellow-members who had been influenced in their action by a desire to protect Louisiana
and South Carolina to join him in opposing the filibusters. [1]

Shortly after this speech was made a vote was taken
on Knott's resolution regarding the bogus certificate. It was the decisive moment. If the resolution
was carried, there was no telling what might happen. There seemed to be danger that it might be
carried. Now that the end was at hand many conservative Democrats, badgered by their constituents
for having supported the Commission plan, felt desperate enough to vote with the filibusters. But some
of those members who were fully cognizant of the
agreement hurried about the hall appealing to their
fellows to vote in the negative; Hewitt and others

1 *Record*, p. 2047.

were brought over;[1] enough other Democrats were
sober-minded sufficiently not to stultify the party by refusing to carry out the terms of a law which they
had themselves helped to pass; and the resolution was
finally voted down by 116 to 148.[2]

With this vote the possibility of defeating the completion of the count disappeared. The strength of the
filibusters rapidly decreased. After some further delay the House voted to reject the vote of the postmaster-elector.[3] The Senate once more entered the
hall. The irreconcilables in their desperation even
attempted to get up an objection to receiving the vote
of one of the Virginia electors, but no senator would
lend himself to the scheme.[4] The votes of Virginia
were therefore counted; then those of West Virginia.
Wisconsin was reached. A final objection was then
offered; it alleged that Daniel L. Downs, one of the
electors, was an examining surgeon of the pension
office and was therefore ineligible.[5] The two houses

---

1 Speech of Hewitt in 45th Cong. 2d Sess. (*Record*, p. 1007);
McClure's, XXIII, p. 87. Hewitt later boasted that he forced
the Republicans to make concessions by his policy in the matter
of the Vermont return, and claimed that Levy came in just at
this time from the Wormley conference. This was impossible,
for Levy had just spoken. The assurances were exacted before
Hewitt became a filibuster, and Hewitt misrepresented his part
in the affair either through ignorance or in order to lessen Democratic criticism levelled against him for his failure to secure
the seating of Tilden. On Feb. 28th Burke telegraphed to
Nicholls: "Recent strength filibusters spasmodic.—Our leaders
have now no defined policy except prospect of anarchy, some
other Republican, or new election." On March 1st he telegraphed: "The weary struggle of aimless filibusters continues."
—See copies of the dispatches in H. R. Mis. Doc. No. 31, 45th
Cong. 3d Sess., III, pp. 624-625.
2 *Record*, p. 2049.
3 *Ibid*, pp. 2049-2055.
4 *World*, March 3d.
5 Proceedings, pp. 722-725.

separated. The Senate, without debate and without a division, agreed that the vote of Downs should be received.[1] In the house the filibusters made a last effort. Mills of Texas claimed the floor to submit, as a question of privilege, a resolution that the House should immediately proceed to elect a President of the United States.[2] The resolution was not allowed to come to a vote. Dilatory motions were not entertained. The indignation on the part of the filibusters against their Democratic brethren who refused to join them rose high. O'Brien caller Fernando Wood "the high priest of the Republican party."[3] At length the debate on Wisconsin began. After midnight on the morning of the 2d Blackburn of Kentucky rose and delivered the swan-song of the filibusters.

"Mr. Speaker," said he, "the end has come. There is no longer a margin for argument, and manhood spurns the plea of mercy, and yet there is a fitness in the hour which should not pass unheeded. Today is Friday. Upon that day the Saviour of the world suffered crucifixion between two thieves. On this Friday constitutional government, justice, honesty, fair dealing, manhood, and decency suffer crucifixion amid a number of thieves." [Applause on the floor and in the galleries].

The passage was not to go unanswered. After the gentleman from Kentucky had finished, Mr. Williams of Wisconsin arose. "I do not desire," said he, "to

1 *Record*, p. 2029.
2 *Ibid*, pp. 2055-2056.
3 *Ibid*, p. 2057.

retort in the spirit indulged in by the gentleman who
has just taken his seat. But if I did I might remind
him and this House that this is not only Friday but
hangman's day; and that there could be no more fit-
ting time than just after the hour of midnight

'When churchyards yawn, and Hell itself
breathes out
Contagion to this world.'

that this bogus, pretentious, bastard brat of political
reform, which for the last twelve months has affronted
the eyes of gods and men should be strangled to death,
gibbetted higher than Haman." [Great applause on
the floor and in the galleries].[1]

The end was indeed come. After a little more delay
the House voted to reject the vote of Downs; and then
the speaker, having received a telegram from Tilden
expressing his willingness that the count should be
completed,[2] sent a messenger to the Senate to announce that the House would once more receive them.

It was now four o'clock in the morning, but the
galleries still contained a crowd of tired sightseers
anxious to witness the final scene in the great contest
which had so long absorbed the attention of the American people. The session had lasted continuously for
eighteen hours, and the members were too weary to
make much of a demonstration of any sort. The Republicans were happy but not exultant; the Demo-

---

1 *Record*, p. 2062.

2 *McClure's*, XXIII, p. 87. This statement is made by Mr.
Rogers on the authority of Mr. Hewitt and confirmed from other
sources.

crats disappointed but on the whole good-humored.
The occasion was an extraordinary but by no means
a solemn one.   It was relieved by a final bit of pleas-
antry.   While the House was waiting a Democratic
member shouted to Henry Watterson to bring on his
"hundred thousand." [1]

The hundred thousand did not appear; instead the
Senate of the United States filed into the room in the
usual manner.   After the members were seated the
decisions in the case of the Wisconsin elector were
announced, and the votes of the state were counted.
Senator Allison, one of the tellers, then read the list
of all the votes, after which the president of the Senate arose to make the concluding statement.

"In announcing the final result of the electoral vote,"
said he, "the Chair trusts that all present, whether
on the floor or in the galleries, will refrain from all
demonstration whatever; that nothing shall transpire
on this occasion to mar the dignity and moderation
which have characterized these proceedings, in the
main so reputable to the American people and worthy
of the respect of the world."

Then, after announcing the total vote received by
each candidate, he continued:

"Wherefore, I do declare: That Rutherford B.
Hayes, of Ohio, having received a majority of the
whole number of electoral votes, is duly elected President of the United States for four years, commencing
on the 4th day of March, 1877.   And that William

---

1 *World,* March 3d.

A. Wheeler, of New York, having received a majority of the whole number of electoral votes, is duly elected Vice-President of the United States for four years, commencing on the 4th day of March, 1877."

Soon thereafter the Senate retired to its chamber. The galleries were quickly emptied. The House itself adjourned.[1] The greatest contest for an elective office in the history of popular government had been peacefully concluded.

---

[1] *Record,* pp. 2067-2068.

CHAPTER XII

THE ADJUSTMENT IN THE SOUTH

In the days preceding the final declaration of the result the bitterness of party feeling was so intense that not a few hot-headed partisans had sworn that even if "counted in," Hayes should never be inaugurated. A Washington newspaper, namely *The Capital,* edited by Don. Piatt, went so far as practically to counsel his assassination. [1] The President-elect received many letters containing threats of violence and "curiously drawn sketches of knives, daggers and revolvers." [2]

That there was no untoward incident during the long strain of waiting or after the result had been declared was unquestionably due in large measure to the firm hand of President Grant. His course during the whole trying crisis had been one which in the main merits the gratitude of his countrymen. His

---

[1] In issue of Feb. 18th. Quoted in New York *Times* of 19th.

[2] Quoted in *Record,* p. 1934, from a speech made by Hayes. One package, sent it would seem with no very serious intentions, contained "a knife about two feet long, one edge hacked like a saw, probably for sawing the bone, the other for cutting the flesh. This was wrapped in several thicknesses of paper, and inside was a note, as follows:

" 'This is the knife with which the editor of the *Capital* was to assassinate you as you went from the White House to the Capitol. It was taken from his pants leg while asleep'."

sending of troops to the disputed states brought upon him a storm of criticism, and the use to which they were put in at least one instance would be difficult to justify; but it is scarcely too much to say that their presence in all human probability prevented bloody collisions that might have led to yet more lamentable consequences. Throughout he had labored for a peaceful and legal settlement.[1] While in some things he showed himself perhaps too much the partisan, he afterwards said that had Tilden been declared elected he would have been quite as energetic in securing Tilden's inauguration as he was in securing that of Hayes. Unlike Buchanan, Grant "was quite prepared for any contingency. Any outbreak would have been suddenly and summarily stopped." He "did not intend to have two governments or any South American *pronunciamentos.*"[2]

Thus when a rumor spread abroad that Tilden intended to be sworn into office in New York, the President caused steps to be taken to declare martial law in that city in case the attempt should be made.[3] As it turned out, these preparations were utterly needless. Mr. Tilden was far from possessing the temperament of a revolutionist. Although some irresponsible persons urged him to take the oath and later criticised him for not taking it, and although on the 3d the House of Representatives passed a resolution

---

1 Church, Life of Grant, pp. 420-421.
2 Young, Around the World with General Grant, II, pp. 270-272. See also H. R. Mis. Doc. No. 31, 45th Cong. 3d Sess., III, pp. 884-885.
3 Church, p. 421.

declaring he had received 196 electoral votes and "was thereby duly elected President," [1] he saw clearly that he had no claim which would justify him in taking a course that would inevitably lead to civil war. There were, in fact, only two contingencies under which he would have asserted his claims: if Congress had declared him elected, or if the House, on the failure of a choice by the electoral colleges, had elected him. "No contingency provided by the Constitution," said one of his closest friends, "ever existed in which Mr. Tilden could lawfully or properly take the oath of office as President." [2]

So, despite the fact that some Democratic newspapers, such as the New York *Sun* and the Indianapolis *Sentinel,* came out in mourning and said much about "usurpers" and "the *de facto* President," Mr. Hayes was peacefully installed. He started for Washington before the result was finally declared, reached that city on March 2d, and was entertained at the home of Senator Sherman. As the 4th fell on Sunday, there was much curiosity and some uneasiness throughout the country regarding what means would be taken to guard against the danger of an interregnum. President Grant had taken it upon himself to solve this problem. On Saturday night, the 3d, in accordance with an invitation written on the 20th of February after the decision of the Louisiana case, the President-elect dined at the White House. Among the

---

1 *Record,* pp. 2225-2227.
2 Bigelow, Tilden, II, pp. 112-115. Mr. Bigelow gave this statement to a reporter at the time.

guests present was Chief Justice Waite. In the course of the evening General Grant sent his son Ulysses for a Bible. The two Grants, Mr. Waite, and Mr. Hayes then repaired to an unoccupied room, and there the chief justice administered the oath.[1] On Monday, the 5th, the new President was formally inaugurated.

One of his first and most trying tasks was to establish peace in the South. In order that the aspects of the settlement which was finally reached may be made clear, it will be necessary to go back in time and consider at some length certain events hitherto only referred to.

It will be recalled that in South Carolina the board of canvassers, before its hasty dissolution to avoid the action of the court, had thrown out the votes of the counties of Edgefield and Laurens because of gross frauds at the polls. Their canvass showed the election of all the Republican candidates for state offices excepting for the governorship and lieutenant-governorship, the returns for which were by law to be canvassed by the legislature; the choice of a House of Representatives composed of 59 Republicans and 57 Democrats, with eight vacancies from the two counties just named; and the election of enough Republican senators to give that party, with two vacancies from the same counties, a majority of five.[2]

The legislature met on Tuesday, the 28th of No-

---

1 Statement of Col. Webb C. Hayes.
2 Appendix to H. R. Mis. Doc. No. 31, 44th Cong. 2d Sess. pp. 118-122.

vember. On the night before a company of United States troops had occupied the Capitol, and these now assisted A. O. Jones, clerk of the last House, and John B. Dennis, who claimed to be acting as sergeant-at-arms, in excluding the Democratic claimants from Edgefield and Laurens from the hall of the House. The Democratic representatives, with one temporary exception, thereupon withdrew to the hall of a rifle company and organized with General W. H. Wallace of Union as speaker. The Republicans remained and organized with E. W. M. Mackey of Charleston as speaker. The important question then arose as to which body, if either, possessed a legal quorum of the members. The Democrats claimed to have 66 of the 124 members, but of these 66 only 57 had been declared elected by the canvassing board and held certificates from the secretary of state. The Republicans, on the other hand, had 59 certified members, and this number, they claimed, was a quorum of the 116 members who had been chosen. [1] The Senate, with Lieutenant-Governor Gleaves in the chair, organized with much less disturbance and with all hold-over members, and every newly elected member who had a certificate, present. The Democratic claimants from Edgefield and Laurens and a person who had been elected to fill the vacancy occasioned by the death

---

[1] See H. R. R. No. 175, Part 2, 44th Cong. 2d Sess., pp. 100-104, 126-129, 138-140 for the official journals and other papers bearing on these occurrences. Also *The Nation*, XXIII, p. 337; *Annual Cyclopaedia*, 1876, pp. 725-726; Allen, pp. 436-441; *Southern Historical Society Papers*, XIII, p. 66.

of a hold-over senator from Abbeville county were also present but were not allowed to vote.[1]

The Democrats protested vehemently against the use which had been made of the troops and managed to secure from General Ruger assurances that in the future his men would confine themselves to preserving the peace and would not assist in keeping the doors of the House.[2] On the morning of the 30th, therefore, the Democratic representatives all marched to the Capitol, and reached that building before many of the Republican members had arrived. Some of the Democrats who had certificates were allowed to enter; when they had done so, they turned, flung open the doors, placed their backs against them, and thereby, despite desperate efforts on the part of the doorkeepers, enabled all the Democratic claimants, including those without certificates, to get inside. Shortly afterwards the remaining Republican members appeared, and a scene of great confusion ensued which in all human probability would have resulted in bloodshed, had it not been for the restraining influence exercised upon the Democrats by the presence of the troops.[3]

For more than four days both bodies remained continuously within the hall, endeavoring from time to time to transact business, with dual speakers and frequently with dual debates. In this contest each side had some advantages. It was, says a South Caro-

---

1 H. R. R. No. 175, Part 2, 44th Cong. 2d Sess., pp. 104-109.
2 *Southern Historical Society Papers,* XIII, p. 69; *Annual Cyclopaedia,* 1876, p. 726.
3 H. R. R. No. 175, Part 2, 44th Cong. 2d Sess., pp. 101, 141; New York *Herald* for Dec. 1st.

linian, hard service for the Democrats "to be thus
shut up with these unwashed 'wards of the nation'
sending forth a stifling native perfume, when the pierc-
ingcold without prevented necessary ventilation. Sleep-
ing, too, on dirty floors, each with a single blanket,
would read well in a story of martyrdom, but their
heads and frames ached nevertheless. In all this the
negroes had the great advantage, as they were just
in their element. The perfume served but to stimu-
late them to song and jollity, and a blanket big enough
to cover the head was all that each needed. On the
other hand, in eating and drinking, the whites had
the incalculable advantage. While Sambo was munch-
ing his hardtack and cheese, he had to gaze wistfully
on baskets and boxes of fruit, and tempting viands,
furnished the other side in profusion by the rebel-
sympathizing merchants of Columbia and Charleston."[1]
Ultimately, however, the outcome of this novel contest
did not depend upon endurance; for the Democrats
learned that on the afternoon of the 4th a constab-
ulary force, backed up by the troops, would attempt
to eject the claimants from Edgefield and Laurens,
and rather than submit to this all the Democrats once
more withdrew to their former meeting-place. [2]

On the following day the Senate and the Republican
House, which had now by desertion lost its quorum,
met in joint convention and proceeded to canvass the
votes for governor and lieutenant-governor. In do-

[1] Leland, p. 170.
[2] H. R. R. No. 175, Part 2, 44th Cong. 2d Sess., pp. 101, 142.

ing so they threw out the returns from Edgefield and Laurens on the plea of violence and fraud, and declared Chamberlain and Gleaves elected by majorities of 3,145 and 4,099 votes respectively.[1] Two days later the two were inaugurated.[2]

Meanwhile the Democrats had attempted to secure a *mandamus* to compel Speaker Mackey to give up the election returns for governor and lieutenant-governor. The supreme court held, however, that a *mandamus* would issue only against a public officer, and that, as Mackey was not speaker of the House, the writ could not be issued against him. The decision was favorable to the Democrats in that it recognized the Wallace House, which had now been increased by desertions from the Republican camp to 63 members having certificates; but it was unfavorable in that it still left them without the official returns.[3] Nevertheless, on the 14th the Democratic House, together with the Democratic senators, proceeded to canvass the votes, using in that work tabular statements made from the county returns and from returns which had been in the possession of the board of state canvassers. As the result of their labors they announced the election of Hampton and Simpson, the candidate for lieutenant-governor, by majorities of 1,134 and 139 votes respectively. On the after-

---

1 H. R. R. No. 175, Part 2, 44th Cong. 2d Sess., pp. 114-121.
2 *Ibid*, pp. 136-138.
3 For court proceedings see Appendix to H. R. Mis. Doc. No. 31, 44th Cong. 2d Sess., pp. 137 *et seq.* The petition was also directed against Secretary of State Hayne, but he had turned over the returns to Mackey. See also *Southern Historical Society Papers*, XIII, p. 70, and *The Nation*, XXIII, pp. 338, 348.

noon of the same day these two also were inaugurated. [1]

Both governments asserted their claim to be the legal authority of the state, and peace was preserved only by the presence of the Federal troops. Not long after his inauguration Chamberlain attempted to pardon a prisoner in the penitentiary, with the result that the question of his right to the office of governor was brought up before Circuit Judge Carpenter. On the 1st of February the judge held that the recent proceedings gave neither Chamberlain nor Hampton a legal title and that Chamberlain, as the former governor, should hold over until his successor had been legally declared and inaugurated. [2] An appeal was taken to the supreme court, but before it was tried a new case came up before that court as a result of an attempt of Hampton to pardon Tilda Norris, another convict. After a long trial and much delay nothing remained save to pronounce judgment; but at this juncture Chief Justice Moses was stricken with an illness from which he never recovered, thus leaving but two judges, one being the negro Wright. On the 27th of February an order was finally signed for the release of Norris, but Wright asked that the filing and publication might be delayed for a few days, and Justice Willard consented. Two days later Wright, upon whom all possible influences had been brought to bear in the meantime, filed an opinion favor-

---

1 *Annual Cyclopaedia*, 1876,, pp. 726-727; H. R. R. No. 175, Part 2, 44th Cong. 2d Sess., pp. 154-157.
2 *Southern Historical Society Papers*, XIII, p. 72.

able to the legality of Chamberlain's claims and withdrew his signature from the order. Thus, although the convict was freed next day, the judgment of the court upon the merits of the claims of Chamberlain and Hampton was not entirely clear. [1]

However, the Hampton government had all the while been growing stronger, that of Chamberlain weaker. The supreme court had granted an injunction forbidding the banks which were depositories of public money from paying it out until further orders from the courts; and as property owners almost uniformly refused to recognize the authority of the Chamberlain government, the Republicans were left without the sinews of war. [2] In this respect the Democrats were more fortunate. Their House appealed to the people to pay to such receivers as Hampton should appoint twenty-five per cent. of the amount of taxes levied the preceding year. The appeal was answered with enthusiasm, and enough money was received to keep the government running. [3] In most of the counties the Democrats were strong enough to have their own way, and even at the Capital there were desertions from the Republican ranks. By the 4th of March, therefore, the Chamberlain government had dwindled to a mere shadow, and was saved from disappearing entirely only by the presence of the troops. [4]

---

1 *Southern Historical Society Papers*, XIII, p. 73; *The Nation*, XXIV, p. 141; New York *Herald* of March 2d; Reynolds, p. 467.
2 *Southern Historical Society Papers*, XIII, p. 71.
3 *Ibid*, pp. 71-72; H. R. R. No. 175, Part 2, 44th Cong. 2d Sess., pp. 163-167; *The Nation*, XXIII, p. 376. Hampton asked for only 10 per cent.
4 *Southern Historical Society Papers*, XIII, p. 83.

The situation of affairs in Louisiana can be explained in fewer words. On January 1st, the day for the assembling of the legislature, the state house was by Governor Kellogg's orders occupied by armed police and militia, and no persons were admitted to the legislative halls except those having certificates from the returning board. The Democratic members therefore withdrew to St. Patrick's Hall and organized separately, admitting not only those having certificates, but also those declared elected by the so-called Democratic Committee on Returns. The Republican members remained and organized with 19 senators and 68 representatives, which was, they claimed, a quorum in each House. The Democratic legislature consisted of 21 senators and 62 representatives, but of these 4 senators and 22 representatives had no certificates save from the Democratic committee. On the following day the Republican legislature in joint session, with, they claimed, a quorum in each House, received the election returns from the secretary of state, and declared Packard and Antoine elected; the Democratic legislature on the same day announced the election of Nicholls and Wiltz. On the 8th the Republican claimants were inaugurated at the Capitol; the Democratic claimants at St. Patrick's Hall. Next day a large force of armed White Leaguers, under pretense of acting as the state militia, gained possession of the police station and court-rooms, installed Democratic appointees as judges of the supreme court, captured the state arsenal, blockaded the state house, and would doubtless have over-thrown the Packard government entirely had it not been for the interference of United States troops.[1] From that time on until March the Federal govern-ment, without recognizing either claimant, preserved the *status quo*. As in South Carolina, the authority of the Republicans grew weaker and weaker; some of the parishes slipped out of their grasp, and there were numerous desertions from their legislature; the causes of this decline in their strength lay in the fact that their opponents were supported by the great mass of property owners and taxpayers and by prac-tically the whole of the stronger white race.[2]

Such then, was the situation in these two states when Hayes came to power. The South Carolina problem was the first solved. The initial step in its solution was a letter written on the 4th of March to Chamberlain by Stanley Matthews and indorsed by William M. Evarts, who had been selected by Hayes as his secretary of state. The letter asked the gov-ernor's concurrence and co-operation in some arrange-ment whereby the continued use of Federal troops might be rendered unnecessary and that government left to stand which should prove itself able to stand

---

1 My account of these matters is based upon files of the *World, Herald,* and *Times*; the legislative journals; a pamphlet entitled Legal Status of the Louisiana State Government, pub-lished by the Packard legislature; another entitled Organization of the House of Representatives, published by the adherents of Nicholls; testimony of Burke, Packard, Kellogg, and others be-fore the Potter Committee.

2 See H. R. Mis. Doc. No. 31, 45th Cong. 3d Sess., III, pp. 603-631.

of itself. [1] The proposal was indignantly rejected by Chamberlain, and no further steps of importance were taken for a fortnight. On the 23d of March, however, duplicate letters were by the President's order addressed to both claimants asking them to come to Washington and confer with the President upon the situation. [2] Both complied with the request, and while in Washington had protracted interviews with the President and members of the cabinet. Chamberlain and the two South Carolina senators proposed that the election controversy be submitted to a commission of five, but the Democrats had lost faith in commissions, and declined the offer. [3] By the President's request the Republican claimant also set forth in a letter his objections to the withdrawal of the troops; such action would, he said, inevitably result in the downfall of the Republican government before the superior physical force of its enemies and in "the quick consummation of a political outrage against which I have felt and now feel it my solemn duty to struggle and protest so long as the faintest hope of success can be seen." [4] Hampton, on his part, asked that the troops be withdrawn, and gave pledges that if it were done no violence would be used by his party and the constitutional rights of all parties would be respected. With the concurrence of the cabinet, the President at last decided to grant his request and

---

1 For this letter and Chamberlain's reply see Allen, pp. 469 and 470; Reynolds, pp. 451-453.
2 Allen, p. 472.
3 *Ibid*, p. 478.
4 *Ibid*, pp. 474-477.

bring Federal interference in South Carolina to an
end.[1] On the 10th of April, therefore, the troops
were withdrawn from the state house to the garrison
post; on the 11th Chamberlain, who had already announced that he would not prolong the contest further,
turned over the executive office to a representative of
Hampton; and, to the great rejoicing of the white
inhabitants, Radical rule in South Carolina came to
an end.[2]

The process of settlement in Louisiana was slower
and more complicated. In that state the problem
which faced the Administration was much more embarrassing; for while in South Carolina the Hayes electors had received a majority of the votes actually
cast and Chamberlain had not, in Louisiana Packard,
whom it was now proposed to sacrifice, had received
many hundreds of votes more than several of the
electors. How then could the Packard government be
allowed to fall and yet leave a semblance of title to
Hayes?[3] So perplexing did the problem prove that
after telegrams sent by President Grant on the 1st
and 2d of March to the effect that public opinion
would no longer support the maintenance of state
governments in Louisiana by military force,[4] no

---

1 Allen, p. 479; New York *Times*, April 3.

2 Allen, pp. 480-486; Leland, p. 173; *Southern Historical Society Papers*, III, p. 85; Reynolds, p. 460.

3 See Butler's report as a member of the Potter Committee,
H. R. R. No. 140, 45th Cong. 3d Sess., pp. 113-114.

4 The first telegram was sent by the President's private secretary to Packard on March 1st.—H. R. Mis. Doc. No. 31, 45th
Cong. 3d Sess., I, pp. 537, 890, 961, 1041, III, p. 33. The telegram was repeated to Gen. Augur by Gen. Sherman on the 2d
after, it has been claimed, Pres. Grant had had a personal inter-

further steps of importance were taken for almost
four weeks. Some of the Democrats who had been
parties to the "bargain" chafed exceedingly under the
delay. By the 28th of March Mr. John Young Brown
had become so impatient that he published the written
guarantees of Foster and Matthews in the Louisville
Courier-Journal and demanded of the President "ful-
fillment of the assurances" therein contained. [1]

On the same day, in accordance with a plan he had
already formulated, [2] the President appointed a commission to go to Louisiana and arrange matters. The
commission was composed of General Joseph R. Hawley of Connecticut, Judge Charles B. Lawrence of
Illinois, General John M. Harlan of Kentucky, ex-
Governor J. C. Brown of Tennessee, and Wayne Mac-
Veagh of Pennsylvania. The commission was directed to proceed to Louisiana and there ascertain what
were the hindrances to a peaceful conduct of the state
government without the interference of the Federal
authority. They were to devote their "principal attention to a removal of the obstacles to an acknowl-
edgment of one government;" but "if these obstacles
should prove insuperable from whatever reason, and
the hope of a single government in all its departments
be disappointed," it was to be their next endeavor to
accomplish the recognition of a single legislature as

view with Hayes.—*Ibid*, I, p. 537; III, pp. 628-629. These telegrams were intended to fulfil the agreement, but it is difficult
to see how they affected the status then existing in Louisiana.
1 New York *Tribune* and *Times* of March 29th.
2 *Times* of March 22d.

the depositary of the representative will of the people of Louisiana." [1]

Into all the details of their work it is unnecessary to enter here. They reached New Orleans on the 5th of April, and at once set to work. The Democrats did all in their power to further the performance of the task. Their legislature passed conciliatory resolutions indorsing the President's policy, promising to accept in good faith the Thirteenth, Fourteenth, and Fifteenth amendments, and guaranteeing school privileges to both races; these resolutions were transmitted by Nicholls, along with his own personal pledge, to the commission. [2] The Democrats rendered especially effective aid in securing the recognition of a single legislature, which was the goal towards which the commission found it expedient to direct its labors. The members of the Packard legislature who had received majorities of the votes actually cast were given to understand that upon joining the Nicholls legislature they would receive $8 per day for their previous services and forty cents per mile mileage. As the Packard government was bankrupt and as most of its legislators were poor negroes, the offer proved in many cases too strong to be resisted. [3] Some of the more important leaders are said to have been bribed directly with money coming from the Louisiana Lot-

1 For the full instructions, which were written by Secretary of State Evarts, see H. R. Ex. Doc. No. 97, 45th Cong. 2d Sess., p. 2.

2 H. R. Mis. Doc. No. 31, 45th Cong. 3d Sess., III, p. 28.

3 *Ibid*, I, pp. 835, 840, 908.

tery Company. [1] Other members who refused to be bribed but who feared for their personal safety in case they held out resigned, and by the 21st of April the Packard legislature had practically ceased to exist. [2] Three days later the troops were withdrawn to the post below the city; Packard and his remaining supporters gave up the struggle; and the authority of the Nicholls government was everywhere established without bloodshed. [3]

The settlement in South Carolina and Louisiana was not reached without arousing a storm of protest in the President's own party. Boutwell and Butler of Massachusetts, W. E. Chandler of New Hampshire, Blaine of Maine, Wade of Ohio, and others, together with a considerable portion of the Republican press, denounced the President's policy in unmeasured terms. The failure of the Administration to uphold the Republican claimants was characterized as a cowardly and treacherous abandonment of the Republicans of the South to their bitterest enemies. [4]

---

1 H. R. Mis. Doc. No. 31, 45th Cong. 3d Sess., III, p. 35; H. R. R. No. 140, 45th Cong. 2d Sess., p. 114; McClure, Our Presidents and How We Make Them, p. 267.

2 H. R. Ex. Doc. No. 97, 45th Cong. 2d Sess., p. 11; H. R. Mis. Doc. No. 31, 45th Cong. 3d Sess., I, p. 460; III, pp. 10 *et seq.*

3 For accounts of the whole Louisiana situation see testimony of Packard, Burke, Ellis, and others in *Ibid.* The testimony of Burke and Packard contains many important documents. In preparing my account I have also used the files of *The Nation, Harper's Weekly, The Times, Herald,* etc.

4 See *The Nation,* XXIV, pp. 154, 216, 242, XXV, p. 117; *Harper's Weekly,* XXI, pp. 282, 302, 558; Blaine, Twenty Years of Congress, II, p. 596; John Sherman's Recollections, I, p. 586; Hoar, Autobiography, II, p. 12; Congressional Record, 45th Cong. special sess. of Senate, pp. 16, 20, etc.; and a pamphlet by W. E. Chandler, entitled "Can Such Things Be and Overcome Us Like a Summer Cloud without Our Special Wonder?" The New York *Times* was one of the most active newspapers in attacking the Southern policy.

Nor was this feeling unnatural; for, from whatever point of view the settlements are regarded, they present some rather extraordinary aspects. In the case of South Carolina, to be sure, a fairly consistent defense could be made. On the face of the returns the Hayes electors had been chosen while Chamberlain had not been; the title given Chamberlain by the legislature was open to question; the courts had inclined to support Hampton's claims; and the Administration's part in the Republican downfall had been confined to refusing to decide between the claims of the two parties and to removing the troops and thereby allowing the stronger claimant to take possession. But in Louisiana the situation was more complicated. Upon the face of the returns Packard had received a considerably larger vote than several of the Hayes electors, and his claim had been favorably passed upon by a legislature containing an alleged quorum of members declared elected by the same returning board which had canvassed the returns for the electors. A possible escape from the conclusion that the claim of Packard was at least as good as that of Hayes would be to adopt the theory that since the state constitution provided that "each House of the General Assembly shall judge of the qualifications, election, and returns of its members," the law conferring upon the returning board the power to canvass the votes for members of the Assembly was unconstitutional, and that as a result the legislature which had

declared Packard elected had not been a legal one. [1]
Instead, however, of taking the attitude that Packard and he should stand or fall together, the President had, through a commission sent to Louisiana for
that purpose, worked to overthrow Packard and his
government. [2]

But there are other aspects of the case which must
be considered before any final conclusions are drawn.
While the title of Packard may have been fully as
good as that of Hayes, it does not necessarily follow
that because Hayes declined to support Packard in
maintaining his title he thereby acknowledged, as was
claimed by Democrats, the worthlessness of his own.
The conditions surrounding the two were entirely different.   At Washington Republican administrations
had no difficulty in maintaining themselves; but in
Louisiana for some years there had been Republican
governments which, while probably representing a majority of the inhabitants, had not represented the intelligence, the property, and above all the physical and
moral force of the state, and in consequence
had stood only by grace of support afforded by Federal bayonets.   Now, the Constitution provides that
the United States shall protect every state, "on application of the legislature, or of the executive (when
the legislature cannot be convened) against domestic

---

1 For a fuller statement of this theory see report of the commission to the President in H. R. Ex. Doc. No. 97, 45th Cong. 2d
Sess., p. 12.
2 Not only had the President sent the commission but after
its work was ended, in order to break up the Packard supreme
court, he appointed one of its judges, J. E. King, collector of
New Orleans.—*Tribune* of April 30th.

violence;" but it can hardly be held that the Constitution contemplates a situation of affairs such that protection, actually exercised in the form of military aid, shall be continuous. Common sense dictates that there must be an end to such aid sometime. It could reasonably be claimed that the proper time in Louisiana had now been reached. [1]

There were yet other considerations which rendered a policy of non-interference necessary. Even had the President not been bound by the promises of his friends, it would have been impossible for him to uphold the Republican claimants. Public opinion, as Grant himself had telegraphed [2] to Packard, would no longer support the maintenance of state governments in Louisiana by military force. The House had already refused to pass an army appropriation bill for the ensuing year, and would doubtless refuse to do so as long as there was danger that the troops would be used in the South. Under the circumstances to have attempted to maintain Chamberlain and Packard would have been to court governmental demoralization and inevitable defeat. [3] Even had he desired to do otherwise, prudence would therefore have dictated to the President that he acquiesce with the best grace possible in what in some respects may be regarded as a bloodless revolution in the states of Louisiana and South Carolina.

---

[1] *The Nation*, XXIV, pp. 172, 244.

[2] Under date of March 1.—H. R. Mis. Doc. No. 31, 45th Cong. 3d Sess., III, p. 33.

[3] Hoar, II, p. 13.

Whatever were the causes which produced it, the results of the new Southern policy were on the whole good.   It is true that the promises made by the Louisiana legislature, by Nicholls, and by Hampton were kept only in part by the white people of the two states; but it was something that such promises should be made, and, after all, the reaction which followed might have gone much farther.   It is also true that the Republican party practically disappeared in the South, and as a result the freedman in effect lost his political rights; but he preserved his civil rights, and he lived under a better government than when he himself had assisted in making and administering the laws.

Thus ended the story of Reconstruction.   It had been a lurid drama, but one which from the nature of things may be said to have been inevitable.   For on the one side had stood a class who were disinclined except under compulsion to concede to all men the basic rights of human liberty; while on the other had been a class who, though staunch advocates of liberty, were too unmoral, too ignorant, to govern either purely or efficiently.   Many lessons might be drawn from the period, but the chief is this:

"He who is unwilling to concede liberty to others deserves it not for himself, and under a just God cannot long retain it."

CHAPTER XIII

It would seem that after so perilous an experience as that through which the country had just passed statesmen ought never to have rested until the recurrence of such a crisis had been guarded against by the necessary legislation. Numerous proposals for changes in the electoral system were made in the years immediately following, but not one of the many bills and amendments brought forward was incorporated into the law of the land. Not, in fact, until a decade later, after two subsequent Presidential elections had occurred, did Congress pass a bill providing a permanent plan for counting the electoral vote. [1]

This bill was signed by President Cleveland on the 3d of February, 1887. In the main it was in accord with the principles laid down in the decisions of the Electoral Commission. It provides that a state may finally determine every contest connected with the choice of electors, but that such determination must be made in accordance with a law passed before the electors are chosen and that the decision must have been made at least six days before the meeting of the

---

1 For a synopsis of some of these proposals see Dougherty, The Electoral Commission, pp. 214, 354.

electors.[1] Where such a determination has been made, it must be accepted; but in cases where there is a conflict of tribunals that return is to be counted which the two houses concur in receiving. In no case is a return to be thrown out except by the consent of both houses; when the two cannot agree, that return is to be received which is certified by the executive of the state.[2]

The long delay in remedying the defects in the electoral machinery was in part due to the fact that both parties were far more concerned about the political effects of the great dispute than they were interested in statesmanlike efforts to secure the country from similar dangers in the future. *Revanche* in 1880 — that was the goal towards which all Democratic endeavors were directed. With this idea in mind, although yielding a grudging obedience to "the *de facto* President," they were careful not to allow the methods by which that President had been seated to drop out of the public's thought for an instant. In almost every issue of almost every Democratic newspaper there appeared at least one reference to the "Steal;" Hayes was a "Usurper," "the Boss Thief;" Liberty had been "stabbed by Radical Ruffians;" the "Death knell of the Republic" had sounded. Nor did the cry lessen in intensity as the months passed. Even

---

1 In order to give more time for such determination, the law provides that the electors shall not meet until the second Monday in January.

2 U. S. Statutes at Large, vol. 24, chap. 90, pp. 373 *et seq.* Even this law in many respects is unsatisfactory and in some respects is defective. For a detailed criticism see an article by Prof. Burgess in *The Political Science Quarterly,* III, p. 633.

after the quieting effects of a trip to Europe, Mr. Tilden himself proclaimed from the steps of his mansion
at 15 Gramercy Park that he had been deprived of the
Presidency by a "political crime," which the American people would not condone "under any pretext or
for any purpose." [1] This opinion he iterated and reiterated on all possible occasions. Of all those engaged in denouncing Republican wickedness and demanding the "keen, bright sunlight of publicity" none
was more insistent than Mr. Manton Marble, former
editor of the New York *World,* author of the famous
"Reform" platform of 1876, and himself one of the
Democratic visitors to Florida. [2]

In the hope of securing further evidence for political use, Mr. Clarkson N. Potter of New York, at the
instance of many leading Democrats, including, it
seems, Mr. Tilden himself, [3] introduced in the House
of Representatives on May 13th, 1878, a resolution
calling for the appointment of a committee "to inquire
into the alleged fraudulent canvass and return of votes
at the last Presidential election in the States of Louisiana and Florida." [4] The Republicans opposed the
resolution on the ground that, by reopening a question
once settled, it would harm the interests of the country; and they quite justly urged that if such an investigation must be undertaken it ought to be general in its scope and include a probing into the frauds

---

1 New York *Herald.* Oct. 28th, 1877.
2 See his letter to the *Sun* of Aug. 3d, 1878.
3 Charged by Blaine, II, p. 589.
4 As quoted at the beginning of the majority report of the
committee.

and violence in Mississippi, South Carolina, Alabama, Oregon, and elsewhere. But, despite all their efforts and also the opposition of a few Democrats,[1] the resolution was at length carried; and the committee was appointed.[2] It consisted of Clarkson N. Potter, Wm. R. Morrison, Eppa Hunton, Wm. S. Stenger, J. A. McMahon, J. C. S. Blackburn, and Wm. M. Springer, Democrats; of Jacob D. Cox, Thomas Brackett Reed, and Frank Hiscock, Republicans; and of Mr. Benjamin F. Butler, political affiliations at this time uncertain.

Conditions were not unfavorable for accomplishing the purpose for which the committee was created. By the President's policy towards the South many Republicans, both white and black, had been rendered his bitter enemies; others felt injured because, in their estimation, they had not been properly "rewarded;" yet others were anxious to make their peace with the now dominant party in that section; from among all these it proved easy to get any number of witnesses willing, nay, even anxious, to testify in detail to any amount of Republican rascality, both real and imagined.[3]

In Florida one of the chief witnesses was Samuel B.

---

1 *The Nation*, XXV, p. 333.
2 The debates on the resolutions are given in the *Record*, 45th Cong. 2d Sess., pp. 3438 *et seq.*
3 *The Nation*, XXVII, p. 217.   In their report the Democratic members of the committee said: "The character of persons engaged in conspiracies such as those in question in Florida and Louisiana requires that their statements, whether in confession or denial, should be received with suspicion.   It was unavoidable, from the character of those concerned, that the committee should be exposed to mistake and imposition."—H. R. R. No. 140, 45th Cong. 3d Sess., p. 4.   See also p. 3.

McLin, ex-member of the returning board. This gentleman was in exactly the proper frame of mind to
testify freely. After the inauguration of Hayes he
had been made associate justice of New Mexico *ad
interim,* but owing to the opposition of Senator Conover of Florida had not been confirmed by the Senate; after vainly waiting for some months in the hope
of receiving another appointment, he had decided that
duty demanded that he should tell the truth about the
election of the President who had "basely betrayed and
mercilessly destroyed the Republican party of the
South." Accordingly he had published an affidavit
in which he said:

"Looking back now to that time, I feel that there
was a combination of influences that must have operated most powerfully in blinding my judgment and
swaying my action. . . . . I was shown numerous
telegrams addressed to Governor Stearns and others
from the trusted leaders of the Republican party in
the North, insisting that the salvation of the country
depended upon the vote of Florida being cast for
Hayes. . . . . Following these telegrams trusted
Northern Republicans, party leaders and personal
friends of Mr. Hayes, arrived in Florida as rapidly
as the railroads could bring them. I was surrounded
by these men, who were ardent Republicans, and
especially by friends of Governor Hayes. One gentleman particularly, Governor Noyes of Ohio, was understood to represent him and speak with the authority
of a warm personal friend, commissioned with power
to act in his behalf. These men referred to the general destruction of the country should Mr. Tilden be
elected; the intense anxiety of the Republican party of

the North and their full sympathy with us. I cannot say how far my action may have been influenced by the intense excitement that prevailed around me, or how far my partisan zeal may have led me into error — neither can I say how far my course was influenced by the promises made by Governor Noyes, that if Mr. Hayes became President I should be rewarded. Certainly these influences must have had a strong control over my judgment and action."

In his testimony before the sub-committee which examined him Mr. McLin elaborated upon the statements made in his affidavit. [1] He stated that certain of the Republican visitors, and especially Mr. Noyes, W. E. Chandler, and General Lew Wallace, had assured him that if Hayes were elected he (McLin) would be well "taken care of." He also stated that since the contest was over an election officer named Joseph Bowes had confessed to him that at precinct No. 9 in Leon county he had stuffed the box with 74 "little jokers;" that L. G. Dennis, [2] county chairman of Alachua county, had boasted that he had secured the election of Hayes by causing 219 votes to be added to the returns of one of the precincts; that he had learned that in Jefferson county 100 Republican votes had been added in a similar manner; and that he had heard of other Republican frauds. From these facts McLin deduced the conclusion that the electoral votes of Florida had rightfully belonged to Tilden. Upon cross-ex-

---

1 For his affidavit see H. R. Mis. Doc. No. 31, 45th Cong. 3d Sess., II, p. 98. For his testimony, *Ibid*, and also pp. 116, 137, 150.
2 Dennis received a government position, but later lost it. He then made a "statement." His evidence bore out McLin's on the point referred to. He also made other revelations.

amination, however, he said that his decision had not
been swayed by offers of position, and admitted that
he had heard of other Democratic frauds. He also
made the interesting statement that while the case
was before the returning board he had been assured
by Mr. Manton Marble that should Tilden be elected
there would be no danger of McLin's dying poor. [1]

The Louisiana testimony, many of the facts in which
have already been used in this book, bore on such
subjects as the fraudulent registration in New Orleans, the "manufacture" of protests and affidavits, the
forgery and subsequent manipulation of the second
set of electoral certificates, the alleged promises made
by "visiting statesmen" to election officers, the Wormley Conference, and the work of the MacVeagh Commission. [2]

One of the chief witnesses in Louisiana was James
E. Anderson, ex-supervisor of the parish of East
Feliciana. Anderson had expected a reward for his
services and had been appointed consul to Funchal;
but representations regarding his character had been
made to the President by H. V. Boynton, and his
commission had been withheld.[3] After several of his

---

1 McLin admitted in his testimony that Noyes had never
promised him a reward before the contest was decided.—H. R.
Mis. Doc. No. 31, 45th Cong. 3d Sess., II, p. 101. Chandler denied having made him any promise.—*Ibid*, I, p. 468. Wallace
admitted having told McLin he had no doubt Hayes would take
care of his friends.—*Ibid*, I, p. 514.

2 For a Democratic summary of the Louisiana testimony see
H. R. R. No. 140, 45th Con. 3d Sess., pp. 23-67. References are
given to some of the most important testimony. The Republican
view is given on pp. 84-93.

3 H. R. Mis. Doc. No. 31, 45th Cong. 3d Sess., I, pp. 381, 384,
394.

attempts at blackmail had failed Anderson was ready
to make a confession.[1]   One of his stories was to the
effect that he and E. L. Weber, supervisor of West
Feliciana, had refused to make protests until they had
received definite promises of lucrative offices. He
claimed that a written promise had been given them
by John Sherman, who was now secretary of the
treasury. He was unable, however, to produce the
original letter, and claimed it had been on the person
of Weber when Weber was killed by political enemies,
and had then disappeared. Sherman denied ever having written such a letter, though he admitted there
were some things in it which he might have written
if he had been asked.[2] There is some reason to believe that it was forged by an eccentric adventuress
named Agnes D. Jenks, whose many examinations
before the committee were productive of much amuse-
ment but of very few facts.[3] There was probably
more truth in some of Anderson's other charges,[4]
though how much it is impossible to say, for he was a
self-confessed liar and later offered to make a counter-
confession.[5]

Much testimony was taken to prove that the affidavits to acts of violence and intimidation had been
falsely and fraudulently made. More than a dozen
negroes retracted either in whole or in part the affi-

---

1 H. R. Mis. Doc. No. 31, 45th Cong. 3d Sess., I, pp. 19, 24.
2 *Ibid*, pp. 16, 768.
3 *Ibid*, pp. 318, 357, 389, 422, 519, 554, 560.
4 For Anderson's testimony see *Ibid*, pp. 1, 38, 64, 72, 161,
583, 926.
5 *The Nation*, XXVII, p. 264.

davits signed by them.[1] Doubtless some of these re-
tractions were in accordance with the truth, but there
is reason to believe that some of them were the result
of fear or of the expectation of pecuniary reward.
Two witnesses who were expected to retract refused
to do so, and said that they, with other witnesses,
had been carefully watched and coached by a Democratic agent. One of them produced $35 which had
been given him as a part of his reward. The agent
later admitted giving the money, but took refuge in
the pretense of a "loan" and a "set-up job."[2] Whatever may be the truth about this particular matter,
it is certain that all the Democratic efforts did not
suffice to bring to life a single one of the negroes who
had been killed by the "bulldozers."

Even more effective than the testimony which has
been described were lists drawn up by the committee
of persons who had been connected with the canvass
in Louisiana and Florida and who had later received
Federal offices. Of the "visiting statesmen" Noyes
had been made minister to France, Kasson minister
to Austria, Stoughton minister to Russia, Lew Wallace governor of New Mexico, Coburn a commissioner of Hot Springs, and John Sherman secretary
of the treasury. Of the local politicians in the two
states, ex-Governor Stearns, Dennis, who had been
connected with the Alachua frauds, McLin, Wells,
T. C. Anderson, Kenner, Packard, and almost every

---

1 For some of this testimony see H. R. Mis. Doc. No. 31,
45th Cong. 3d Sess., III, pp. 294, 306, 319, 373, 471.
2 *Ibid*, pp. 342, 345, 365, 370, 374, 385, 394; I, p. 1195.

person engaged in making protests, getting evidence, making returns, and counting the votes had received offices, some of which were very lucrative.[1] There was no conclusive proof that these appointments were intended by the President or by any of his cabinet officers as rewards for questionable services, but the circumstances certainly lent themselves to that view. The most charitable construction is, in the words of Mr. Butler, "that *post hoc* is not always *propter hoc.*"[2]

The revelations resulting from the work of the Potter Committee were spread broadcast over the land by the Democratic press and gave promise of a bountiful political harvest. The Democrats were jubilant; the Republicans correspondingly depressed. The Republican leaders foresaw that unless something could be done to break the force of the disclosures their party would meet with overwhelming disaster in the approaching congressional elections. Furthermore, the Democrats would in 1880 renominate Tilden, and would, in truth, "right the Great Wrong." Of course everything possible was made out of the unquestionable fact that a great deal of the testimony was unreliable and that the investigation was extremely partisan and one-sided; but this, it was felt, was not sufficient. Something more must be done.

---

1 For these lists see report of the majority in H. R. R. No. 140, 45th Cong. 3d Sess., pp. 22, 48-49.

2 *Ibid*, p. 100. Some of the less prominent Republicans were unquestionably guilty of conferring rewards for corrupt practices. The mistakes made by the President in this respect seem to have resulted in part at least from following bad advice regarding persons concerning whom he knew little or nothing. When, as in the case of James E. Anderson, he became convinced of a man's dishonesty, he refused to go further.

An opportunity was long in coming, but come it did and in unexpected manner.

Back in January, 1877, the Western Union Telegraph Company had been ordered to deliver to committees of Congress all dispatches transmitted by Republican and Democratic leaders during the campaign and the exciting days which followed it. Of these dispatches, amounting in all to more than 30,000, many were in cipher. Out of the dispatches in their possession the Senate committee had unearthed the Democratic conspiracy, already described, to purchase the vote of a Republican elector in Oregon, — but otherwise the examination had not been searching enough to discover anything of much importance.[1] After a time all the dispatches, as was supposed, had been surrendered to the company and had been taken back to New York and burned.

Unknown to the company, however, some of the telegrams which had been in the hands of the Senate committee had not been given up. About 750 had been abstracted, and in May, 1878, were in the possession of Mr. George E. Bullock, who had been messenger of the committee and protégé of its chairman, Senator Morton. In the month mentioned Bullock went as United States consul to Cologne and left the dispatches in charge of Mr. J. L. Evans, who in turn gave them to Mr. Thomas J. Brady, second assistant postmaster general. Not long afterwards, in

---

1 For the details of the investigation by the House committee and the telegrams examined by it see H. R. Mis. Doc. No. 42, 44th Cong. 2d Sess.

ways which it is unnecessary to describe, a portion of them, either in the original or in the shape of copies, were put into the possession of the New York *Tribune*.[1]

That newspaper, then as now hotly Republican, was on the lookout for anything that gave promise of helping to bring about the discomfiture of the Democrats. But as all the important dispatches were in cipher, their possession for a considerable time resulted in nothing. Nevertheless, the managers of the paper proceeded, in the words of Mr. Whitelaw Reid, the editor, "to play about them for a little while. First, we threw a few of them out in editorials, trying to make a little fun out of them, and attract attention to them in the hope that somebody would turn up who could decipher them. Nobody came forward, however, and then we attacked them seriously."[2]

The problem to which the managers of the *Tribune* set themselves was a difficult one in the extreme, for in sending the telegrams at least six distinct systems of crytography, some of them very complicated, had been used. At last, however, Colonel William M. Grosvenor and Mr. John R. G. Hassard, by employing methods more suggestive of Poe's *Gold Bug* than of an event in real life, were able to discover the keys to all but a few messages. Nor were their results mere conjectures. So carefully was their work done and so thoroughly were the keys tested that, save in

---

[1] H. R. Mis. Doc. No. 31, 45th Cong. 3d Sess., IV, pp. 4, 9, 30, 46, 49, 63, 85, 319, etc.
[2] *Ibid*, p. 111.

a few cases, the translations were absolutely exact. [1]

And, as the translators had hoped, they found what they were seeking. Some of the telegrams revealed on the part of certain prominent Democrats conduct decidedly inconsistent with the manner in which the said Democrats had been "lifting up sanctimonious eyes to heaven and thanking God that they were not as these wicked Republicans."

The results were given to the world by the *Tribune* in a way skilfully calculated to arouse the public interest to the utmost. Hints were dropped that revelations were coming; then an announcement was made that the publication of the dispatches was about to begin. On the 7th of October a detailed account of how the translations had been made was published. On the following day the most important dispatches relating to Democratic negotiations in Florida appeared; eight days later came the yet more sensational ones relating to the negotiations in South Carolina.

The chief Florida dispatches thus published had passed between Manton Marble and C. W. Wooley, Democratic agents who had gone to Tallahassee, [2] and Colonel W. T. Pelton, acting secretary of the Democratic national committee. Colonel Pelton was Mr. Tilden's nephew and lived with him at the Tilden residence, No. 15 Gramercy Park, to which place many of the telegrams were addressed.

---

1 For the dispatches and translations made by Prof. E. S. Holden, U. S. Navy, for the Potter Committee, see H. R. Mis. Doc. No. 31, 45th Cong. 3d Sess., IV, pp. 325-385.

2 In the dispatches Marble was known as "Moses" and Wooley as "Fox."

The following was one of the most significant messages:

"Talla. *2.*

"Col. Pelton, No. 15 Gramercy Park, N. Y.:

"Certificate required to Moses decision have London hour for Bolivia of just and Edinburgh at Moselle had a any over Glasgow France rec'd Russia of." [1]

The translation of this dispatch read thus:

"Have just received a Bolivia [proposition] to hand over at any hour required Russia [Tilden] decision of London [canvassing board] and certificate of France [Governor Stearns] for Moselle [two] Glasgow [hundred] Edinburgh [thousand]. Moses [Manton Marble]."

To this the following reply was returned:

"Telegram here. Proposition too high (?)." [2]

On the 3d, the same day on which the reply was dispatched, Mr. Marble sent to Pelton another proposition for "giving vote of Republican of board or his concurrence in court action preventing electoral vote from being cast for half-hundred best United States documents" [$50,000 in U. S. notes]. Mr. Wooley also asked to be allowed to "give hundred thousand dollars less half for Tilden additional board member." [3] Pelton replied to Wooley telling him to consult Marble and act in concert with him; to Marble he sent a dispatch which could not be deciphered because four

---

1 H. R. Mis. Doc. No. 31, 45th Cong. 3d Sess., IV, p. 176.
2 There was some doubt about the exact translation of this dispatch. In his testimony, however, Pelton said: "I did send a dispatch declining the proposition made."—*Ibid,* p. 177.
3 *Ibid,* p. 179.

words had dropped out in transmission. At the request of Marble the message was repeated, this time correctly.[1] When translated it stood:

"Telegram here. Proposition accepted if done only once. Better consult with Wooley and act in concert. You can trust him. Time very important, and there should be no divided councils."[2]

But the returning board was just finishing its work, and the delay proved fatal.[3] Marble therefore reported that the plan had failed, and added, "Tell Tilden to saddle Blackstone;"[4] while Wooley telegraphed, "Power received too late."[5]

Eight days after the publication of the Florida dispatches the *Tribune* gave to the public those connected with the contest in South Carolina. In that state the chief Democratic negotiator was Smith Mead Weed, a prominent Tilden Democrat of New York. The dispatches revealed that on the very day he arrived in the state he transmitted two proposals for bribing the returning board. The last of these Colonel Pelton approved.[6] Negotiations were conducted for six days; then Weed transmitted the following:

"Majority of board have been secured. Cost is 80,000, to be sent as follows: One parcel of 65,000 dollars, one of 10,000, and one of 5,000, all to be 500 and 1,000 bills; notes to be delivered as parties accept

1 H. R. Mis. Doc. No. 31, 45th Cong. 3d Sess., IV, pp. 180, 241.
2 *Ibid*, pp. 242, 366.
3 *Ibid*, pp. 180, 352.
4 *Ibid*, pp. 243, 352.
5 *Ibid*, p. 351.
6 *Ibid*, pp. 132-133, 145-146, 181-182.

and given up upon vote of land of Hampton being given to Tilden's friends. . . . . Do this at once and have cash ready to reach Baltimore Sunday night. Telegraph decidedly whether this will be done." [1]

Weed and Hardy Solomon, who was supposed to represent the returning board, went to Baltimore, and were met by Colonel Pelton. What took place there the dispatches do not disclose. We only know with certainty that Pelton returned to New York accompanied by Weed, that Solomon also went to New York, but that in neither place was the deal consummated. The cause of failure will probably always remain a matter of some doubt; the Democrats claimed that it was because Tilden ordered Pelton home, the Republicans that it was because the returning board suddenly concluded its labors in order to evade the supreme court, or because its members had merely been playing with the Democrats. [2]

Not discouraged, however, Pelton later not only continued the negotiations already described in Florida but also entered into a new plot for capturing the electoral vote of South Carolina. One feature of this plot, which was a very complicated one, involved locking up the Republican electors in separate cells until after the legal day for casting their votes. [3]

The publication of the dispatches created a tremendous sensation. They were read throughout the coun-

---

1 H. R. Mis. Doc. No. 31, 45th Cong. 3d Sess., IV, p. 119.
2 For this matter see *Ibid,* pp. 116, 117, 124, 139, 145, 156, 186, 209, 211, 215, 217, 275, 284, etc.
3 *Ibid,* pp. 378-379.

try; every one marvelled at the ingenuity of the translators. Thousands of people made use of the keys and
tested the accuracy of some of the translations. The
Republicans jubilantly declared that Pelton had been
the agent of Mr. Tilden. The Democrats were at first
incredulous about the truth of the disclosures; some
claimed that the whole matter was a hoax. Then, when
the facts could no longer be denied, some of the party
organs displayed great indignation over the manner
in which the dispatches had been obtained; others
tried to minimize the importance of the revelations.
Mr. Tilden issued a skilfully drawn letter which
appeared to the general public to be a sweeping denial
of any prior knowledge of any of the dispatches or
of the South Carolina negotiations, or of any knowledge of the negotiations in Florida until some time
after their failure.[1] Nevertheless, Republicans continued to shake their heads sagely; while some of Mr.
Tilden's enemies in his own party expressed the opinion that even his denial would not save him the renomination in 1880.[2] Mr. Manton Marble also issued a
letter in which he violently denied having sent some of
the least important of the dispatches attributed to him,
or having engaged in any corrupt undertakings.[3]
The Republican press mentioned Mr. Marble frequently, along with "moral means" and the "keen, bright

---

[1] New York *Herald* of Oct. 18th. Mr. Tilden told the truth
so far as he went, but his letter conveyed an erroneous impression. Compare *The Nation,* XVII, p. 250, with *The Nation,*
XVIII, p. 112.
[2] See *Tribune* for Oct. 9th *et seq.* for many extracts from
other papers, along this line.
[3] See *The Nation,* XVII, p. 250.

sunlight of publicity." The other important parties refused to be interviewed.

Needless to say, the Republicans at once began to demand that the Potter Committee investigate the whole matter. But the Democratic leaders had no desire to stir up the unexpected hornet's nest any further. For some weeks after Congress met the Democrats of the House avoided the subject with great care.[1] But as the clamor increased rather than diminished, that body on January 21, 1879, reluctantly directed the committee to institute an inquiry.[2]

The committee's first efforts were directed to examining into the manner in which the dispatches had come into possession of the *Tribune* and to attempting to bring to light incriminating Republican dispatches. With this latter aim in view the committee examined in Washington some of the telegraph officials and a number of Republicans, including W. E. Chandler, ex-Postmaster General Tyner, and Second Assistant Postmaster General Brady. But aside from dispatches which had passed between the various Republican agents in the Southern states and between these agents and the party managers in the North on such matters as the chances for success in the various states and the transmission of money in comparatively small sums for the payment of legitimate expenses, nothing of importance was brought to light.[3] The fact was that the Re-

1 *Record,* p. 610, speech of·Conger of Michigan on Jan. 21.
2 *Ibid,* pp. 608-612.
3 Some of these dispatches had been explained by W. E. Chandler and others two years before.—See H. R. Mis. Doc. No.

publican dispatches remaining in existence were all innocuous. If there had ever been any of a different character — and naturally the Democrats made what they could out of the possibility [1] — they had been destroyed and proof of their having existed could not be found.

After this vain attempt to make counter revelations a subcommittee proceeded to New York city. This committee was composed of Messrs. Hunton, Stenger, and Springer, Democrats; and of Messrs. Hiscock and Reed (the later "Czar"), Republicans.

Among the persons examined in New York were Mr. Weed, Mr. Pelton, Mr. Marble, and Mr. Tilden. Neither Mr. Weed nor Mr. Pelton attempted to deny the essential charges made against them by the *Tribune,* but they tried to justify themselves on the ground that they merely intended to "ransom stolen goods from thieves." Mr. Marble, having expatiated so fully upon the exalted manner in which the Democratic campaign had been conducted, was somewhat more guarded in his admissions. He acknowledged certain of the telegrams attributed to him — he could do no less, for they were in his handwriting — but

---

42, 44th Cong. 2d Sess. The dispatches were in cipher, but in such "a feeble and worthless one" that almost anybody could tell what they meant; for example, "oranges" was substituted for Florida, "cotton" for South Carolina, "warm" for favorable, "cold" for hostile, etc. One object of the dispatches was to keep the workers in the various disputed states encouraged.

1 It was claimed by Democrats that Mr. Orton, the president of the Western Union allowed Republicans to remove incriminating dispatches.—Bigelow, II, p. 171. Another story was to the effect that Orton said the committees did not get *all* the dispatches.—McCulloch, Men and Measures of Half a Century, p. 420.

declared he had sent them merely as "danger signals." [1]
His statement on this point was received with peals
of derisive laughter. [2]

Two things were especially noteworthy about the
testimony of these witnesses. One was the remarkable
shortness of their memories. They were sure that
some of the dispatches were incorrectly translated, but
were unable to translate them correctly, for they had
both forgotten and lost the keys. Secondly, they all
strove anxiously to prove the innocence of Mr. Tilden.
While Pelton and Weed admitted having met each
other in Baltimore with the intention of consummating
a deal with Hardy Solomon, supposed agent of the
South Carolina returning board, they claimed that
Pelton had been summoned back to New York by Mr.
Tilden, to whom a knowledge of the affair had been
imparted by Mr. Edward Cooper, treasurer of the
Democratic national committee. Upon this point their
testimony was supported by that of Mr. Cooper. [3]

The climax of the investigation was the examination
of Mr. Tilden. [4] On the appointed day the parlor of
the Fifth Avenue Hotel in which the committee's
sessions were held was packed to the utmost with a
crowd anxious to see and hear the distinguished witness who had so narrowly missed occupying the Presidential chair. At half-past eleven o'clock Mr. Tilden

1 For Weed's testimony see H. R. Mis. Doc. No. 31, 45th Cong.
3d Sess., IV, pp. 114-166; for Pelton's pp. 166-221; for Marble's
pp. 221-272.
2 H. R. R. No. 140, 45th Cong. 3d Sess., p. 73.
3 H. R. Mis. Doc. No. 31, 45th Cong. 3d Sess., IV, pp. 156-157.
4 Tilden asked permission to be heard. However, he doubtless would have been summoned.

appeared, in company with his brother Henry and
ex-Secretary of State Bigelow.   Mr. Tilden was
dressed in black, and his face wore the solemn, sphinx-
like expression habitual to him.   Those who knew
him thought that he had aged greatly since his last
public appearance and that he looked ill and feeble.
"It was, indeed," wrote the *Herald's* reporter, "quite
a painful spectacle to see the slow, halting, lame walk
with which he passed the table and reached his seat.
His figure was stiffly drawn up and seemed incapable
of bending, as though he were suffering from a par-
alytic contraction of the limbs.   Not a muscle of his
face relaxed with animation or expression as he stiffly
extended his hand to Mr. Reed of Maine, who received
the salutation with something like a profound bow.
Then Mr. Tilden gave his hand to Mr. Hiscock, the
other cross-examiner, and after saluting the Democratic members took off his elegant, silk-lined overcoat,
stiffly turned round and seated himself at the table,
while settling at the same time a large handkerchief
in his breast pocket."

The examination lasted for two and one-half
hours, but was more remarkable as a contest of
wits than for sensational results.   Mr. Tilden was too
old and experienced a lawyer to betray himself into
any admissions (granting he had any to make),
even at the hands of such able and relentless
inquisitors as Mr. Hiscock and Mr. Reed.   He followed the line already laid down by the previous witnesses, asserted that he had in no case been privy to

any negotiations such as those described, and declared that where such negotiations had come to his notice he had at once put a stop to them. With these denials he intermingled emphatic expressions of a belief that he had been cheated out of the Presidency. The only point upon which the cross-examiners can be said to have scored was upon his misleading letter of the previous October. [1]

Opinions varied greatly as to the outcome of the investigations. The Democrats held, of course, that Tilden had been completely exonerated. They pointed to the fact that while, as they asserted, the returning boards could have been bought for sums that would have been mere bagatelles to Mr. Tilden, not a single such deal had been consummated; the boards had given their decisions to Hayes, and had been rewarded by offices. [2] The Republicans refused to admit that the boards had been as purchasable as the Democrats had believed, [3] and claimed that if the boards had been in the market, the failure of the attempts to purchase them had been due to other causes than reluctance of Mr. Tilden's agents to engage in such transactions. [4] In their efforts to fix a guilty knowledge upon Tilden they pointed out that he had always taken a close

---

1 For Tilden's testimony see H. R. Mis. Doc. No. 31, 45th Cong. 3d Sess., IV, pp. 272-294.

2 See Bigelow, II, pp. 170, 174.

3 They said the boards had merely been drawing the Democrats on. Against the Democratic claim that the boards had been purchased by the Republicans they argued that since the members were Republicans, they naturally gave their decisions for that party without reward.

4 *Tribune* and *Times* for Feb. 9, 1879, and days immediately succeeding.

interest in the details of his campaigns, that one of the ciphers had been used in his business, that he had misled the public in regard to the South Carolina negotiation, that after he knew of that attempted transaction he had not withdrawn his confidence from Pelton but had left him in such a position that he was able to make similar attempts in South Carolina once more and also in Florida and perhaps elsewhere. [1] In the absence of irrefragable proof on either side, the verdict of history will have to be that of "Not proven." At present the weight of opinion seems to be that at the worst he was not directly cognizant of the attempted bribery. He may have been entirely guiltless, but it is difficult to escape from the feeling that he was to a certain extent responsible.

But, while the measure of Mr. Tilden's participation remained a matter of doubt, the political effect of the cipher disclosures was enormous. The fact that the Democratic candidate had not been able to clear himself from suspicion militated against his chances as a candidate in 1880, and was doubtless one reason why the Democratic convention of that year accepted his "renunciation" without protest. [2] Even to those who believed him innocent it had been proved beyond the possibility of doubt that prominent Democrats, who were his close friends and one of whom was his nephew

---

1 Mr. Tilden also continued on the best of terms with Mr. Marble and Mr. Weed. As late as Mr. Cleveland's first administration he attempted, but without success, to secure the appointment of Weed as collector of the port of New York.

2 *The Nation* thought his renunciation freed the party of a heavy load.—XXX, p. 463.

had been guilty of attempting to purchase the Presidency for him; and it was pertinently asked whether, taking his own statement, a man so easily hoodwinked by those around him would prove any more successful as a "Reformer" than Grant had been.   And while the revelations did not remove from the skirts of the Republican party the mud that was attached to them they did open the eyes of independents to the fact that the skirts of Dame Democracy were not a whit cleaner. Unquestionably the publication of the dispatches had some influence upon the congressional election which came in the month following their appearance.   When the *Tribune's* statement of the case was substantiated by the admissions made in the following February before the Potter Committee, the "Great Steal," which had promised so much for the Democracy, at once ceased to be a living political issue.   When the campaign of 1880 came, despite the fact that the Democratic platform declared that issue to precede and dwarf every other, the orators of the party were utterly unable to interest the people in the subject. [1] The cry of "fraud" had lost its effectiveness; and Garfield, one of the members of the Electoral Commission, was triumphantly elected over Hancock.

---

1 Stanwood, History of Presidential Elections, p. 372.

CHAPTER XIV

Well-nigh thirty years have passed since the beginning of the electoral controversy which it has been the purpose of this volume to describe. All the chief candidates, most of the party managers, all but two of the members of the Commission, are dead. The vast majority of living Americans have no personal remembrance of the great dispute. The rights and wrongs of the controversy no longer play a part in politics. It would seem, therefore, that the time has come when the investigator may hope to frame a judgment on the whole matter that will be free from prejudice.

As regards the election proper, it is manifest to any candid mind that many regrettable things were done by both parties. In the states of South Carolina and Louisiana, for example, the white people had by a long period of terrible misgovernment been brought to such a pitch of desperation that they felt inclined to use any means which would put their governments once more into the hands of the intelligent and the reputable. Having been forced to accept negro suffrage sorely against their will, they naturally had little compunction in attempting to eliminate as much of the black vote as possible. In general this work was accomplished by methods which, considering the exasperation of the whites, were comparatively mild, but which in exceptional instances resulted in outrages horrible almost beyond belief. In Florida, also, while the amount of corruption in the government had not been great, the whites were almost equally eager to carry the election. In Louisiana, and perhaps in Florida, by methods which have been described in detail in previous chapters, the Democrats succeeded in their attempts to get a majority of votes into the ballot-boxes. In South Carolina they failed so far as the national ticket was concerned but succeeded on the state ticket. Had there been a free election in these states, there is every reason to believe that all would have returned substantial majorities for Hayes. Here, then, not to speak too euphemistically, was what may be denominated "the first steal."

But in these states there were laws intended to meet such emergencies as those just described. If these laws had been properly applied, but little could justly have been said against such a procedure; for assuredly there is nothing sacred about returns of votes when the election in which such votes were cast has been affected by violence and fraud. But, in Louisiana at least, the law was so imperfect that if it had been followed to the letter by the returning board the majority rolled up by the Democrats would probably not have been overcome. The returning officers, however, were no sticklers for the letter of the law.

By and with the counsel of Republican "visiting statesmen" they proceeded in the most irregular manner
not only to throw out enough votes to secure the
election of the state and national tickets, which
would have been elected with a fair and free vote, but
also to manufacture majorities for congressional, legislative, and other candidates, who would have been
defeated under any circumstances. Reputable men in
the Republican party no doubt condoned such action
because their opponents were guilty of wrong practices and because they deemed it necessary to fight the
devil with fire. [1]   Herein they are to be condemned;
for wrong should not be met by wrong but by
recourse to law, and free institutions are in grave
danger when citizens, however good their intentions, endeavor to correct one wrong by another.
From the mere selfish point of view it may safely be
said that had the Republican party acquiesced in the
result, upon discovering that the law strictly applied
would not correct the wrongs committed by their opponents in the disputed states, they would not have
suffered in the end. But the temptation was too great
to be resisted. The situation was such that the leaders saw an opportunity to obtain, by violating the law,
a result that would be in a certain sense legal; hence
ensued in Louisiana and perhaps in Florida what may
be designated as "the second steal," as a result of which

---

1 Conversely the Democrats condoned bulldozing and kindred
practices because of Republican misgovernment and because of
previous frauds by returning officers.

the electoral votes of the two states remained in the hands of the Republicans.

The situation after the electoral colleges had met then amounted to this: In Louisiana and perhaps in Florida there had been a "double steal," as a result of which the regularly declared electors of those states had cast their votes for Hayes. To render matters yet more complicated there had been attempted "steals" in two other states. In South Carolina the attempt had failed so far as the national ticket was concerned, but the attempt had been productive of much disorder and many irregularities, so that a claim could be made that the vote of the state should not be received at all. In Oregon also a most bare-faced attempt had been made to override the law with such a result as greatly to complicate the situation.

The controversy now entered the halls of Congress. Had the outcome not hinged upon every one of the points in dispute, Congress would doubtless have evaded the difficulties of the situation as they had evaded like difficulties in the past, either by throwing out the votes of the states or perhaps by counting them in the alternative. But if all the votes were not counted and counted for the Republicans, then the choice of a President would be thrown into the Democratic House. Had the Republicans been the original offenders in the states in dispute then unquestionably it would have been equitable to throw out some or all of the votes and secure this result. But with some justice the Republicans could say: With a fair election these states would have cast their votes for Hayes, and it is not right that Tilden should reap the reward, even indirectly, of Democratic wrong-doing. To have thrown out the votes of states under such circumstances would have established a precedent which might have led to dangerous temptation in the future.

The whole controversy therefore resolved itself into the question of who should count the electoral votes. Extreme Republicans said that the president of the Senate should do the counting; extreme Democrats said that the House must participate, and that no vote should be counted against its consent; moderates on both sides said that the votes must be counted by both houses. Clearly the moderates were right. It was not reasonable that a partisan president of the Senate should decide the dispute; nor was it reasonable that a partisan House should be allowed to reject votes when by so doing it would be able to elect the candidate of its choice. Granted, however, that to both houses belonged the coveted power, the way was still beset with difficulties. *How* should they count? What should be done in case of a deadlock between the two? Evidently some arrangement must be made which would obviate the difficulties. The result was the Electoral Commission.

Without a shadow of doubt the act creating that Commission was one of the wisest pieces of statecraft ever evolved by an American Congress. To be sure, the result of the Commission's work was a disappointment to one party; but any settlement of the dispute

would have been productive of equal disappointment
and might have been attended with far more lamentable consequences. The situation was, in fact, eminently one for compromise. Unlike the slavery issue,
it was comparatively unimportant, save to a hundred
thousand office-holders and to five hundred thousand
office-seekers, which party was victorious; compromise
evaded no all-important questions which the future
would have to solve. To have resorted to anything
else than compromise would have been wicked and
criminal to the last degree. To the men therefore who
worked for compromise, to President Grant, to Mr.
McCrary, to Senators Edmunds, Thurman, and Bayard, to Mr. Hewitt and Mr. Hoar, is due the highest
praise. In this praise neither Mr. Hayes nor Mr.
Tilden has any right to share; for Mr. Hayes favored
the declaration of the result by the president of the
Senate, while Mr. Tilden was wedded to the theory
that the House could throw out votes, and was always
resentful towards Senators Thurman and Bayard and
the other Democratic leaders who were instrumental in
helping create the Commission. So far as the two
parties as a whole are concerned, the plan adopted was
favored by more Democrats than Republicans. This
in part was due to the fact that the Democrats realized that tactically they were at a disadvantage; while
the Republicans, confident of the strength of their
position, were unwilling, in the words of Morton, to
give to their "political opponents advantages and
chances which they now have not."

The question whether the Electoral Commission Act was warranted by the Constitution is interesting but not important. Most of the best constitutional lawyers in both houses of Congress defended the bill; it was passed by Congress by large majorities; it was signed by the President; and a majority of the judges of the supreme court consented to sit on the Commission created by it. To all practical intents and purposes, therefore, it was constitutional. And, without going further into the question, it may be remarked in passing that the Constitution has suffered many severer wrenches than it did when the forty-fourth Congress decided that under the "general clause" the expression "and the votes shall then be counted" conferred power to create an Electoral Commission.

The chief criticisms that have been made of the Commission and its work are: 1. That the Commission behaved in a thoroughly partisan manner. 2. That some of the members allowed their partisanship to betray them into taking positions inconsistent with their formerly declared opinions. 3. That the Commission did wrong in refusing to go behind the counts of the returning boards for the purpose of taking evidence and overthrowing fraud. 4. That the decisions of the Commission in the various cases were inconsistent with each other.[1]

As regards the first and second charges there can

---

[1] E. g., John Goode in *American Law Review*, **XXXVIII**, pp. 174-76, and Gibson, pp. 39-48. The ignorance of constitutional law displayed by Gibson is something lamentable.

be no difference of opinion. The Commission did divide upon party lines; upon every important question the vote was invariably eight to seven. Some of the members did assume positions at variance with their previous records. Senators Thurman and Bayard and Mr. Abbott had in the past advocated the theory that Congress has no power to go behind the decisions of state authorities, but now took the stand that Congress has that power. On the Republican side, Senator Morton and Mr. Garfield had attacked the Commission bill on the ground that it might be interpreted as conferring power to go behind the returns;[1] while Mr. Edmunds and Mr. Hoar by previous utterances regarding the Louisiana returning board had placed themselves in a position somewhat at variance with the deference now paid by them to that body's decisions.[2] Lastly, the stand of some of the Republicans in advocating the rejection of doubtful votes at previous counts is rather difficult to reconcile with their insistence in this case that all doubtful votes should be counted.[3]

The charge that the Commission did wrong in refusing to take evidence to show that returning officers had fraudulently declared the result, is by no means so well sustained. The taking of such evidence would have been open to at least two serious objections. In the first place, the taking of evidence on these points

---

[1] But they did not say that the Commission would have such power.

[2] Technically they were perhaps not inconsistent. In his criticism of Edmunds, Gibson fails to state that Edmunds was referring to a returning board created by a former law.

[3] The chief Republican inconsistency in the course of the struggle was in Congress, not in the Commission.

would have entailed an amount of labor so great that months of time would necessarily have been consumed; for, as the Republicans correctly urged, such an investigation must have extended not only to the acts of the returning officers but also to the election itself and to the intimidation and outrages which had preceded it. In the second place, the Republicans unquestionably stood upon a sound constitutional principle when they contended that Congress does not possess the power to go behind the action of state canvassing officers. That they took this stand was, however, due rather to accident than to any anxiety on their part to safeguard the rights of the states.[1]

The charges that the Commission was inconsistent in its rulings are in part an outgrowth of a misapprehension of the principle upon which the rulings were based. For this misapprehension the reports of the Commission to Congress are in part responsible; they are so roughly drawn as to make rulings appear inconsistent which really are not at all so. Had the reports been drawn in such a way as to reveal all the grounds of the decisions, some of the criticisms of the Commission could not have been made with any show of reason. As it was, those who read the decisions were likely to get the idea that the Commission claimed to take the stand that evidence *aliunde* the papers opened by the president of the Senate could not be received,

---

[1] It is open to question, however, whether the Commission might not properly have received some of the evidence tendered to prove that the returning boards had not correctly represented the states.

whereas the Commission really followed the line of cleavage between state and Federal powers.

Starting with the erroneous premise just mentioned, Democratic writers have asserted that the Commission was guilty of a glaring inconsistency in its rulings in the Florida case. They point triumphantly to the fact that the Commission refused "to go into evidence *aliunde* the papers opened by the president of the Senate in the presence of the two houses" to prove that other than the Republican claimants were appointed electors, and then did go into evidence *aliunde* to prove that one of the electors was not ineligible. [1] These critics fail to see that the Commission did not lay down the principle that it was not competent to take "evidence *aliunde* the papers opened by the president of the Senate" upon any and all points; that, on the contrary, it merely held that it was not competent to take such evidence upon one single point, namely, "to prove that other persons than those regularly certified to by the governor of the state of Florida, *in and according to the determination and declaration of their appointment by the board of state canvassers of said state prior to the time required for the performance of their duties, had been appointed electors.*" [2] This decision was a sound one, for it was based on the theory that the Commission had no right to trench upon the sphere of state powers. But the examination

---

1 According to Senator Hoar, four of the Democratic members of the Commission believed that the Republicans stood on solid constitutional ground.—*McClure's*, XXIII, p. 84.

2 The italics are mine.

into the eligibility of the elector was an entirely different matter; this examination could be entered into because the question of his ineligibility was one which lay within the sphere of Federal powers. Hence the two rulings were not at all inconsistent.

Again it has been said that because the Commission received evidence regarding the eligibility of the Florida elector, refused it in the case of electors in Louisiana, and received it in the case of Watts in Oregon, here was another inconsistency. But the seeming inconsistency is easily explained. Humphreys in Florida was alleged to be ineligible under a Federal statute. Four of the Louisiana electors were alleged to be ineligible under a state statute; while the objections against the eligibility of the other two related to the time of the election in November, not to the time of their re-appointment on the 6th day of December. Watts was alleged to be ineligible under the Federal statute. Clearly, therefore, the Commission was competent to investigate the case of Humphreys and the case of Watts but was not competent to investigate the cases of the four Louisiana electors who were alleged to be ineligible under a state statute; while as for Brewster and Levissee, since the objections did not relate to the time of the appointment under which they acted, the Commission did not need to make an investigation.

Yet again it has been claimed that the Commission refused to go behind the governor's certificate in Louisiana and Florida but went behind it in Oregon.

This claim completely misrepresents the truth of the matter. In no case did the Commission hold that the governor's certificate was conclusive; on the contrary, the Republican counsel and the Republican Commissioners held throughout that while the governor's certificate was *prima facie* evidence, his action, having been performed under a Federal statute, was subject to review.

At the same time it must be said that in their action in some phases of the Oregon case the Republican eight probably sailed closer to the wind than on any other occasion. If, however, we accept their interpretation of the nature of the Oregon canvass and their interpretation of the nature of an appointment — interpretations as capable of defense as any — we can reconcile their rulings even in this case.

But even though the Commission's decisions were based upon sound law, were they, it will be asked, in accordance with the equities of the case? The answer to this question must always remain more or less a matter of opinion, yet it is probable that as time goes on the consensus of opinion will more and more incline one way. It is entirely clear that in only two of the four disputed states — namely, Florida and Louisiana — did the Democrats have the shadow of an equitable claim to a single electoral vote. Had there been a fair and free election in those states, there can be little if any doubt that the result in both would have been favorable to Hayes. If there had been a fair and free election throughout the South, there can

be little question that Mississippi, with its great preponderance of blacks, and perhaps Alabama and North Carolina, would have ranged themselves in the Republican column, and that the much vaunted Democratic majority of the popular vote — which, after all, stood for absolutely nothing — would have been overcome.

Something can be said in behalf of the ingenious theory that it was not unjust that the Republicans should retain control of the national government, whereas the Democrats should get control of the contested Southern states. The arguments in behalf of intimidation rested on the evils of negro rule. It could therefore be urged that while there was some justification for preventing a negro from voting for a Republican candidate for state office, there was no such justification for suppressing his vote for Republican electors.

All things considered, it appears that both legally [1] and ethically the decision was the proper one. That a majority of the American people thought so is shown pretty conclusively by the result of the next Presidential election. Had they believed otherwise, they would doubtless have resented the "Great Fraud" in a manner not to be mistaken. But they realized that the cries of the Democrats were but another illus-

---

[1] Against the argument that the negroes ought not to have voted nothing further need be said than that their right to do so was guaranteed by "the law of the land." Furthermore, it should not be forgotten that the negro population of the South gave that section an added representation of about thirty-three in the Electoral colleges.

tration of the pot calling the kettle black. They knew that while Hayes was undoubtedly the beneficiary of fraud, Tilden would just as truly have been the beneficiary of violence and murder. They decided that the situation was one of those rare ones in which two wrongs go to make a right; and, therefore, in 1880 they elected to the Presidency a member of the Electoral Commission.

But, while the outcome of the great controversy was in the main a just one, the contest was unquestionably attended by many deplorable incidents. No true patriot can contemplate without regret the terrible outrages upon the blacks, the frauds committed by election officers, the violence of party feeling, the questionable conduct of leaders on both sides, the attempts to purchase returning boards and electors, the bargain between the friends of Hayes and certain Southern leaders, the prostitution of the civil service in rewarding some of the most disreputable of the Southern Republicans, the partisanship displayed by the members of the Commission, and many other phases of the struggle. In fact, it seemed as if the whole cesspool of political filth had been suddenly and vigorously stirred and that it had given off its most noxious vapors. Unfortunately, however, it may well be doubted whether, after all, the election of 1876 was much more productive of corrupt actions than some other elections both before and since. More of such actions came to light, but probably because the searchlight was turned on as in no other contest.

Yet there were other aspects which revealed in the American people characteristics that are beyond praise. A bitter contest which might have resulted in a conflict that would have leveled the foundations of the Republic had been settled without a resort to arms. A great party had gone down to what most of its members believed was a foul defeat. But the result had been acquiesced in for the good of the country; and though the enmities engendered by the controversy were to linger long in American public life, they were finally to disappear without leaving any appreciable scar upon the body-politic.

APPENDIX

THE ELECTORAL COMMISSION ACT

An act to provide for and regulate the counting of votes for President and Vice-President, and the decision of questions arising thereon, for the term commencing March 4, A. D. 1877.

Be it enacted, etc., That the Senate and House of Representatives shall meet in the Hall of the House of Representatives at the hour of one o'clock, post meridian, on the first Thursday in February, A. D. 1877, and the President of the Senate shall be their presiding officer. Two tellers shall be previously appointed on the part of the Senate, and two on the part of the House of Representatives, to whom shall be handed, as they are opened by the President of the Senate, all the certificates and papers purporting to be certificates of the electoral votes, which certificates and papers shall be opened, presented, and acted upon in the alphabetical order of the States, beginning with the letter A; and said tellers having then read the same in the presence and hearing of the two houses, shall make a list of the votes as they shall appear from the said certificates; and the votes having been ascertained and counted as in this act provided, the result of the same shall be delivered to the President of the Senate, who shall thereupon announce the state of the vote and the names of the persons, if any, elected, which announcement shall be deemed a sufficient declaration of the persons elected President and Vice-President of the United States, and, together with a list of the votes, shall be entered upon the journals of the two houses. Upon such reading of any such certificate, or paper, when there shall be only one return from a State, the President of the Senate shall call for objections, if any. Every objection shall be made in writing, and shall state clearly and concisely, and without argument, the ground thereof, and shall be signed by at least one Senator and one member of the House of Representatives, before the same shall be received. When all objections so made to any vote or paper from a State shall have been received and read, the Senate shall thereupon withdraw, and such objections shall be submitted to the Senate for its decision, and the Speaker of the House of Representatives shall in like manner submit such objections to the House of Representatives for its decision, and no electoral vote or votes from any State from which but one return has been received shall be rejected except by the affirmative vote of the two houses. When the two houses have voted they shall immediately again meet, and the presiding officer shall then announce the decision of the question submitted.

Sec. 2. That if more than one return or paper, purporting to be a return from a State, shall have been received by the President of the Senate, purporting to be the certificates of the electoral votes given at the last preceding election for President and Vice-President in such State, unless they shall be duplicates of the same return, all such returns and papers shall be opened by him in the presence of the two houses when met as aforesaid, and read by the tellers; and all such returns and papers shall thereupon be submitted to the judgment and decision, as to which is the true and lawful electoral vote of such State, of a commission constituted as follows, namely:

During the session of each house on the Tuesday next preceding the first Thursday in February, A. D. 1877, each house shall by *viva voce* vote appoint five of its members, who, with the five associate justices of the Supreme Court of the United States, to be ascertained as hereinafter provided, shall constitute a commission for the decision of all questions upon or in respect of such double returns named in this section. On the Tuesday next preceding the first Thursday in February, A. D. 1877, or as soon thereafter as may be, the associate justices of the Supreme Court of the United States, now assigned to the first, third, eighth, and ninth circuits. shall select, in such manner as a majority of them shall deem fit, another of the associate justices of said court, which five persons shall be members of said commission; and the person longest in commission of said five justices shall be the president of said commission. Members of said commission shall respectively take and subscribe the following oath:—

"I, ..., do solemnly swear (or affirm, as the case may be) that I will impartially examine and consider all questions submitted to the commission of which I am a member, and a true judgment give thereon, agreeably to the Constitution and the laws, so help me God."

Which oath shall be filed with the secretary of the Senate. When the commission shall have been thus organized it shall not be in the power of either house to dissolve the same, or to withdraw any of its members; but if any such Senator or member shall die, or become physically unable to perform the duties required by this act, the fact of such death or physical inability shall be by said commission, before it shall proceed further, communicated to the Senate or House of Representatives, as the case may be, which body shall immediately and without debate proceed by *viva voce* vote to fill the place so vacated, and the person so appointed shall take and subscribe the oath hereinbefore prescribed, and become a member of said commission; and, in like manner, if any of said justices of the Supreme Court shall die or become physically incapable of performing the duties required by this act, the other of said justices, members of the said commission, shall immediately appoint another justice of said court a member of said commission (and in such appointments regard shall be had to the impartiality and freedom from bias sought by the original appointments to said commission), who shall thereupon immediately take and subscribe to the oath hereinbefore prescribed, and become a member of said commission to fill the vacancy so occasioned.

All the certificates and papers purporting to be certificates of the electoral votes of each State shall be opened in the alphabetical order of the States as provided in section 1 of this act; and when there shall be more than one such certificate or paper, as the certificate and papers from such States shall so be opened (excepting duplicates of the same return), they shall be read by the tellers, and thereupon the president of the Senate shall call for objections if any. Every objection shall be made in writing, and shall state clearly and concisely, and without argument, the ground thereof, and shall be signed by at least one Senator and one member of the House of Representatives before the same shall be received. When all such objections so made to any certificate, vote, or paper from a State shall have been received and read, all such certificates, votes, and papers so objected to, and all papers accompanying the same, together with such objections, shall be forthwith submitted to said commission, which shall proceed to consider the same, with the same powers, if any, now possessed for that purpose by the two houses, acting separately or together, and, by a majority of votes, decide whether any and what votes from such State are the votes provided for by the Constitution of the United States, and how many and what persons were duly appointed electors in such State; and may therein take into view such petitions, depositions, and other papers, if any, as shall, by the Constitution and now existing law, be competent and pertinent in such consideration, which decision shall be made in writing, stating briefly the ground thereof, and signed by the members of said commission agreeing therein; whereupon the two houses shall again meet, and such decision shall be read and entered in the journal of each house, and the counting of the votes shall proceed in conformity therewith, unless, upon objection made thereto in writing by at least five Senators and five members of the House of Representatives, the two houses shall separately concur in ordering otherwise, in which case such concurrent order shall govern. No votes or papers from any other State shall be acted upon until the objections previously made to the votes or papers from any State shall have been finally disposed of.

SEC. 3. That while the two houses shall be in meeting, as provided in this act, no debate shall be allowed, and no question shall be put by the presiding officer, except to either house on a motion to withdraw, and he shall have power to preserve order.

SEC. 4. That when the two houses separate to decide upon an objection that may have been made to the counting of any electoral vote or votes from any State, or upon objection to a report of said commission, or other question arising under this act, each Senator and Representative may speak to such objection or question ten minutes, and not oftener than once; but, after such debate shall have lasted two hours, it shall be the duty of each house to put the main question without further debate.

SEC. 5. That at such joint meeting of the two houses seats shall be provided as follows: For the President of the Senate, the Speaker's chair; for the Speaker, immediately upon his left; for the Senators in the body of the hall, upon the right of the presiding officer; for the Representatives, in the body of the hall not provided for the Senators; for the tellers, Secretary of the Senate, and clerk of the House of Representatives, at the Clerk's desk; for the other officers of the two houses, in front of the Clerk's desk, and upon each side of the Speaker's platform. Such joint meeting shall not be dissolved until the count of the electoral votes shall be completed and the result declared; and no recess shall be taken unless a question shall have arisen in regard to counting any such votes or otherwise under this act, in which case it shall be competent for either house, acting separately in the manner hereinbefore provided, to direct a recess of such house, not beyond the next day, Sunday excepted, at the hour of ten o'clock in the forenoon; and while any question is being considered by said commission, either house may proceed with its legislative or other business.

SEC. 6. That nothing in this act shall be held to impair or affect any right now existing under the Constitution and laws to question by proceeding in the judicial courts of the United States the right or title of the person who shall be declared elected, or who shall claim to be President or Vice-President of the United States, if any such right exists.

SEC. 7. That said commission shall make its own rules, keep a record of its proceedings, and shall have power to employ such persons as may be necessary for the transaction of its business and the execution of its powers.

INDEX

356 INDEX

GARFIELD, James A., a "visiting statesman" in Louisiana, 95; speaks against Electoral Commission bill, 206; a member of the Commission, 220; at Wormley Conference, 269; elected President, 328; mentioned, 336.

Georgia, Senate orders investigation of election in, 174; electoral votes of counted in the alternative in 1869, 181.

Georgians, vote in South Carolina, 146.

Gibson, A. M., absurd view of the Pinkston case, 108.

Gibson, Randall, presents an objection against counting the votes of Louisiana, 244.

Gleaves, R. H., presides over South Carolina Senate, 288; declared re-elected, 291.

Godwin, Parke, attends Fifth Avenue Conference, 16; supports Tilden, 38.

Gordon, John B., thinks Tilden is certain of victory, 209; at a secret conference, 269.

Grant, Gen. U. S., re-elected President, 2; government expenditures under, 4; misgovernment under, 5-6; praised in Republican platform, 21; writes to Gen. Harry White concerning third term, 11; order to General Sherman, 55; mentioned, 171, 208; reported that he would declare himself dictator, 172; Democrats wish to impeach, 175; rumor that he intended to imprison Democrats, 187; anxious for a compromise, 191; approves Electoral Commission bill, 220; promises to preserve the *status quo* in Louisiana, 271, 278; course of during the crisis, 284; causes Hayes to be secretly sworn in, 286-287; credit due to, 334.

Grant parish, vote of thrown out, 113.

Greeley, Horace, candidate for President, 2.

Greenbackers, *see* Independent Nationals.

Grosvenor, William M., deciphers cipher dispatches, 316.

Grover, L. F., governor of Oregon, 158; receives a telegram from Hewitt, 159; issues a certificate to Cronin, 163; burned in effigy, 166; mentioned, 254; denounced, 256.

Gwin, William M., works for Tilden's nomination, 31.

HALE, Eugene, a "visiting statesman" in Louisiana, 95.

Hamburg Massacre, 131.

Hamilton county, action of returning board on, 70.

Hampton, Wade, nominated for governor of South Carolina, 133; declared elected, 291; attempts to pardon a prisoner, 292; payment of taxes to, 293; goes to Washington, 296; receives the executive office, 297; mentioned, 304.

Hancock, Gen. Winfield S., talked of for Presidential nomination, 26; supporters of, 27; name presented to convention, 33; vote for, 34-35; rumor that he was to be transferred to the west, 187.

Harlan, Gen. John M., nominates Bristow, 21; member of the MacVeagh Commission, 298.

Hartranft, John F., candidate for Presidential nomination, 12; supporters of, 15; name presented in convention, 21; votes received by, 22-25.

Hassard, John R. G., deciphers cipher dispatches, 316.

Hawley, Joseph R., name presented for Vice-Presidential nomination, 25; member of MacVeagh Commission, 298.

Hayes, Rutherford B., candidate for Presidential nomination, 15; name presented in convention, 21; votes received by, 23-25; nominated, 25; how nomination of was received, 36; his letter of acceptance, 37; Florida electors cast their votes for, 76; entitled to votes of Florida, 76; vote for electors supporting in Louisiana, 94; Louisiana electors vote for, 114; has a majority in South Carolina, 151, 152; elec-

25

Missouri, objections made to receiving electoral votes of in 1821, 179.

Moncure *vs.* Dubuclet, in case of Louisiana supreme court holds that decisions of returning board are not subject to review, 117.

Monroe, negroes gather in to vote, 110.

Morehouse, a "selected" parish, 90; vote of, 118; mentioned, 120.

Morrisey, John, works for Tilden's nomination, 30.

Morrison, William R., spoken of for Vice-Presidential nomination, 35.

Morton, Oliver P., a dispenser of patronage, 5, 7; candidate for Presidential nomination, 11; supporters of, 13; attacked by New York *World,* 14; following at Cincinnati, 18; name presented to convention, 21; votes received by, 22-25; brings in report upon Louisiana election of 1872, 182; attempts to change method of electing the President, 184-185; moves that Twenty-Second Joint Rule shall not be readopted, 186; appointed a member of a committee, 192; refuses to sign report accompanying Electoral Commission bill, 204; opposes the bill in the Senate, 211-214; accused by Conkling of trying to provoke a deadlock, 212; a member of the Commission, 220; mentioned, 225; moves that votes contained in No. 1 of the Louisiana certificates be counted, 242; would have been made President if count had not been completed, 273; mentioned, 336.

Moses, F. J., elected governor of South Carolina, 126; elected circuit judge, 128; chief justice of South Carolina, 149; illness of, 292.

NATION, The, comments on Bristow's supporters, 17; comments of. on Republican platform, 37; opinion of South Carolina Democratic platform, 134; suggests that a Republican elector vote for Tilden, 173.

Nevada, objection to vote of an elector of, 250.

New England Society, dinner of on Forefather's Day, 193.

New, Jeptha D., speech on Louisiana decision, 246.

New Orleans, society of, 81; riots of 1855 in, 82; massacre of 1866, 84; registration in, 93; a goal of "visiting statesmen," 95; assistant supervisors throw out polls in, 113.

News and Courier, the Charleston, commends Chamberlain, 128; endeavors to induce Democrats to support Chamberlain; says Democrats can carry the state only by armed force, 130; resolution in concerning employment of Republicans, 139.

Nicholls, F. T., nominated for governor of Louisiana, 87; promises fair treatment for negroes, 271; declared elected, 294; transmits resolutions to MacVeagh Commission, 299; mentioned, 304.

Norris, Tilda, pardoned, 292.

North Carolina, goes from Hayes to Blaine, 24.

North Carolinians, vote in South Carolina, 146.

Northrup, Milton H., quoted, 200.

Noyes, E. F., a "visiting statesman" in Florida, 64; alleged promises made by him, 309-310.

O'BRIEN, William J., an irreconcilable, 257, 274.

"October States," results of election in, 42.

Odell, W. H., receives a majority of votes for elector in Oregon, 162; election certified by Grover, 163; helps to organize the electoral college, 164; votes for Hayes, 165.

Ohio, Republican majority in at October election, 42.

Oregon, chapter on contest in, 157; mentioned, 171; Senate committee instructed to investigate election in, 174; mentioned, 175; case of before Congress and the Commission, 250-261; mentioned, 332, 339, 340.

Ottendorfer, Oswald, a "visiting statesman" in Louisiana, 95.

Ouachita, a "selected" parish, 90; outrages in, 104-110; vote in, 118; mentioned, 120.

PACKARD, S. B., receives telegram from W. E. Chandler, 51; nominated for governor of Louisiana, 87; returning board gives him a majority, 114; declared elected, 294; gives up the contest, 300; title of, 301-302.

Palmer, John M., spoken of for Vice-Presidential nomination, 35; a "visiting statesman" in Louisiana, 95.

Panic of 1873, 3.

Parker, Joel, name presented to Democratic convention, 33; vote for, 34-35.

Patrick, J. N. H., takes a dictionary to Oregon, 160; sends cipher telegram to Pelton, 161; money furnished him, 162.

Patterson, John J., a dispenser of patronage, 5, 7; defeated by Chamberlain in contest for position as delegate to Cincinnati, 129.

Payne, Henry B., appointed a member of a House Committee, 193; announces that House Committee will not agree to six-justices plan, 200; refuses to accept Davis as a Democrat, 202; a member of the Commission, 220.

Pelton, W. T., sends telegrams to Oregon, 159; receives telegram from Patrick, 161; mentioned, 191; connection with the cipher dispatches, 317-323.

Pendleton, George H., defeated by Hayes, 15.

Piatt, Don., counsels assassination of Hayes, 284.

Pickett, John T., offers vote of Louisiana returning board to Democrats, 111.

Pierce, Edward L., moves amendment to Republican platform, 20.

Pierce, Henry L., wishes to throw out the Louisiana return, 248.

Pinkston, Eliza, testimony of, 105.

Pinkston, Henry, murdered, 106; was a Radical, 107.

Plaquemine, frauds in, 82.

Platt vs. Goode, 67.

Poppleton, Early F., inquires whether any other returns have been received from Vermont, 274; resolution introduced by, 276.

Post Trader frauds, mentioned, 39.

Potter, Clarkson N., calls for a Congressional inquiry, 307; chairman of the investigating committee, 308.

Potter Committee, chapter on, 305.

Presidential Counts, compiled and published, 199.

Prohibition Reform Party, convention of, 38.

QUAY, Matthew S., rooms with R. S. Mackay, 22.

RANDALL, Samuel J., a "visiting statesman" in Louisiana, 95; elected Speaker, 173; mentioned, 191; announces members of a House committee, 193; stand against the Force Bill, 258; firmness of, 276, 277; mentioned, 281.

Ransom, M. W., appointed a member of a Senate committee, 193.

Redfield, H. V., explains the purposes of the South Carolina Democrats, 139.

Reed, Thomas B., a member of the Potter Committee, 308; mentioned, 324; cross-examines Tilden, 325.

Reid, John C., erroneous statement concerning, 46; at Fifth Avenue Hotel, 49-51.

Reid, Whitelaw, testimony of regarding cipher dispatches, 316.

Resumption Act, passed, 6; attitude of Republican convention toward, 20; opposition of certain Democrats to, 33.

Richardson's School House Precinct, alleged frauds at, 73.
Richmond, Democratic convention at, 195.
Rhodes, Merrimon, killed by a rifle club, 109.
Rifle clubs, activity of in Louisiana, 90; outrages by in Ouachita, 105, 107; picket approaches to Monroe, 110; active in South Carolina, 136; ordered to disperse, 143.
Rivers, Prince, complaint made before against members of a militia company, 131; maltreated by mob, 132.
Robbins Precinct, Republican frauds at, 147; thrown out by returning board, 150.
Robinson, Governor Lucius, inaugural address of contains an argument written by Tilden, 194.
Ruger, General T. H., commander of troops in South Carolina, 289.

SABRE CLUBS, formed by South Carolina Democrats, 136.
St. Patrick's Hall, Democratic legislature of Louisiana meet in, 294.
Salary Grab, 3; harped on by the Democrats, 39.
Sanborn Contract, 3.
Sargent, Aaron A., introduces resolution to elect a new president of the Senate, 272.
Schell, Augustus, chairman Democratic national committee, calls convention to order, 31.
Schurz, Carl, signs call for a conference of independents, 15; writes the Address of the Conference, 16.
Scott, R. K., elected governor of South Carolina, 126; Chamberlain refuses to commission as judge, 128.
Scott, William L., supports Tilden, 30.
Seelye, Prof. Julius H., attends Fifth Avenue Conference, 16; opposes counting the votes of Louisiana, 248.
"Sewing machine circulars" sent out in New Orleans in effort to detect illegal registration, 93.

Sheridan, General Philip, characterizes Wells as a dishonest man, 98; rumor that he would be used to bulldoze New York, 187.
Sherman, John, a "visiting statesman" in Louisiana, 95; moves an investigation into election of 1872 in Louisiana and Arkansas, 181; rumor that he would supplant Ferry, 187; defends the Louisiana decision, 245; at Wormley Conference, 269; alleged to have given a written promise of reward, 312.
Sherman, Gen. W. T., is directed to hold troops in readiness to quell disturbances, 43.
Simpson, William D., declared elected, 291.
Smith, Avery, supports Tilden, 30.
Smith, Green Clay, nominated for president by the Prohibitionists, 38.
Smith, John, burlesque certificate from Florida signed by, 238.
Solomon, Hardy, alleged agent of South Carolina returning board, 320, 324.
Sons of Liberty, see Knights of the Golden Circle.
South Carolina, Republican delegates from vote for Blaine, 24; troops sent to, 44; chapter on contest in, 122; investigating committees sent to, 173-174; mentioned, 175; dual government in, 196; case of before Congress and the Commission, 261-274; settlement in, 287-293, 295-297, 301; mentioned, 329.
Spofford, Henry Martyn, pleads for publicity of returning board's proceedings, 100.
Springer, William M., appointed a member of a House committee, 193; mentioned, 198; considers Davis an Independent, 201; an irreconcilable, 257; attempts to delay the count, 258, 274; wild behavior of, 275.
Stearns, Marcellus L., telegraphs that a train has been "ku-kluxed," 54; issues a proclamation to prevent Georgians